103 HIKES

IN SOUTHWESTERN BRITISH COLUMBIA

JACK BRYCELAND
and Mary & David Macaree

GREYSTONE BOOKS
DOUGLAS & MCINTYRE PUBLISHING GROUP
VANCOUVER/TORONTO/BERKELEY

Greystone Books
A division of Douglas & McIntyre Ltd.
2323 Quebec Street, Suite 201
Vancouver, British Columbia
Canada V5T 4S7
www.greystonebooks.com

Library and Archives Canada Cataloguing in Publication
Bryceland, Jack
    103 hikes in southwestern British Columbia

    Previous eds. by: Mary and David Macaree
    Includes bibliographic references and index.
    ISBN 1-55054-775-5

    1. Hiking—British Columbia—Guidebooks. 2. British Columbia—Guidebooks. I. Macaree,
Mary. II. Macaree, David. III. Title. IV. Title: One hundred and three hikes in southwestern
British Columbia.
GV199.44C22 B746 2001   917.11'3044   C2001-910282-8

Library of Congress information is available upon request.

Photographs not by the author are by:

CM Carol MacMillan   DH David Hughes
DM Dan McAuliffe   IM Ian McArthur
JNS John Scott   JS John Sapac
LB Lisa Baile   MM Michelle Martineau
TH Tracey Heron   TP Todd Ponzini

Editing by Lucy Kenward (fifth edition)
Cover and text design by Val Speidel
Cover photograph by Randall Cosco
Typeset by Tanya Lloyd/Spotlight Designs and Val Speidel
Maps by Mary Macaree and Gray Mouse Graphics
Printed and bound in Canada by Friesens
Printed on acid-free paper ∞
Distributed in the U.S. by Publishers Group West

We gratefully acknowledge the financial support of the Canada Council for the Arts, the British
Columbia Arts Council, and the Government of Canada through the Book Publishing Industry
Development Program (BPIDP) for our publishing activities.

CONTENTS

KEY TO MAP SYMBOLS

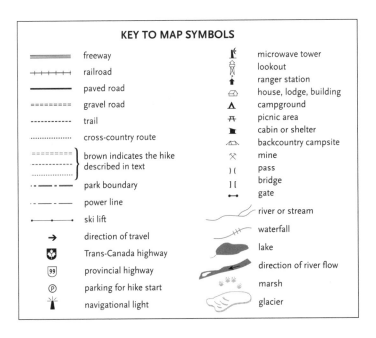

═══════	freeway	microwave tower
++++++	railroad	lookout
▬▬▬▬	paved road	ranger station
=========	gravel road	house, lodge, building
------------	trail	▲ campground
....	cross-country route	picnic area
========= ------------	brown indicates the hike described in text	cabin or shelter
		backcountry campsite
·—·—·—	park boundary	mine
·—·—·—	power line	) (pass
•—•—•	ski lift	] [bridge
→	direction of travel	gate
	Trans-Canada highway	river or stream
99	provincial highway	waterfall
P	parking for hike start	lake
	navigational light	direction of river flow
		marsh
		glacier

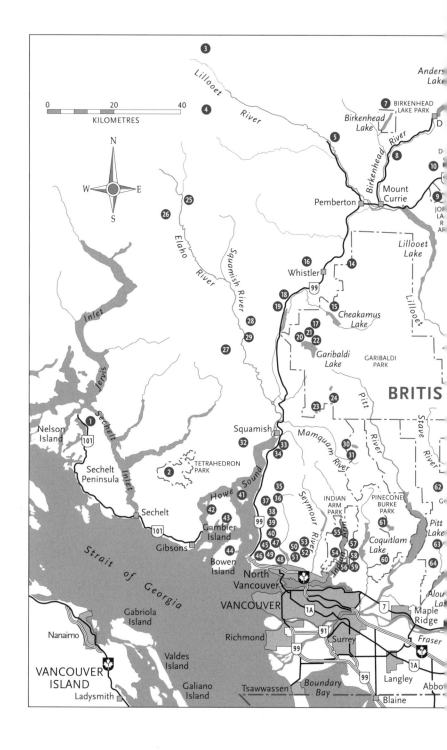

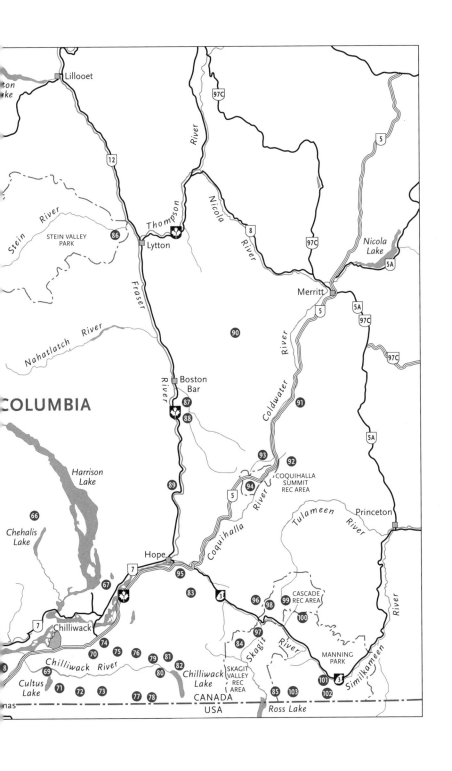

INTRODUCTION

This fifth edition of *103 Hikes in Southwestern British Columbia* is a major change in a thirty-year tradition. Mary and David Macaree have authored this publication through four editions and set a standard that is hard to meet. However due to David's illness (subsequent death in 1998) they had decided, in 1997, to pass the torch. They approached the British Columbia Mountaineering Club (BCMC) of which they were long-term members, as am I, and told the club of their intentions. Being at one of life's junctions, and looking for a project on which to concentrate my energies, I jumped at the opportunity to produce this fifth edition. Little did I realize the magnitude of the commitment in time and energy that such a project requires. My admiration for the Macarees has always been high: I now hold them and their accomplishment in absolute awe! It has been a struggle attempting to meet the quality and accuracy of their output; the decision on how close this edition has come to meeting the standard will be decided by you, the hikers who use this book.

103 Hikes in Southwestern British Columbia was the first commercially published hiking guide for this area, and it evolved from earlier data accumulated and distributed by the Mountain Access Committee, an ad hoc group representing the major hiking and climbing clubs of the day: the Varsity Outdoor Club, North Shore Hikers, BCMC, and the Alpine Club of Canada (Vancouver Section). This committee later evolved into the Federation of Mountain Clubs of British Columbia (FMCBC). However, it is with the BCMC that these books have had their closest association. It was a group of club members who, in 1967, decided to pool their collective knowledge, organize their information and produce a "real" guidebook. This book was to be an information source for hikers, a complement to the earlier climbers' information source by Dick Culbert, *A Climber's Guide to the Coastal Ranges of British Columbia*. By 1973 the Macarees had become the prime movers of this group and, as is said, the rest is history.

The area covered by this edition has not changed from earlier ones. In the west the boundary is the Sunshine Coast, in the north the

Pemberton–Duffey–Lytton line, in the east Manning Provincial Park, and the International Boundary is obviously the southern limit. However, the order in which the trips are listed has changed and this might make it look, at first glance, that the area is not the same. This edition starts in the west and north, and lists the hikes moving south and east. Like all human-created categorizations, some hikes do not fit neatly into this system; however, they have been slotted in as logically as possible. Although there are exceptions to all rules, the criteria for a hike's inclusion are:

- A hike longer than 3 hours but less than 12; i.e., a one-day hike. A few longer hikes that are accessible in a weekend are included.
- A well-marked or obvious trailbed. The exceptions are topographically defined routes.
- A peak or geographical feature in alpine terrain as the objective.
- A trail or route that is typical of the flora and fauna in the region.

Together the hikes present a true representation of the topography and current ecological condition of southwestern British Columbia.

Hikes that are easier than the above are published in Mary and David Macaree's *109 Walks in British Columbia's Lower Mainland*. Mary is currently working on a fifth edition of that book.

Trips have been removed and trips have been added. Some have been dropped just to make room for newer trips, but usually a hike is removed because of deterioration in the travel conditions: deadfall lying across the trail, avalanche debris covering the route, mud or rock slides blocking access to the hike, running water changing the trail to a creek bed, etc. In particular, the winter of 1998–99 brought a large snowpack and several windstorms that severely damaged a significant number of trails. Some trails are still not hikeable.

Most of these trails depend on hikers and other volunteers to help maintain the routes. The FMCBC (604 878-7007) runs the Adopt-a-Trail Program, and you do not have to be a club to look after a hiking route, so why don't you and your hiking buddies adopt a trail? If you cannot do that, make sure that as you hike, you do some simple trail maintenance: move fallen branches aside, roll large rocks off the footbed, snip intruding brush with a pair of hand pruners. Do your bit! Every trail should be in better shape after you hike it than it was before you started. Some trips have been added to expand the number away from the urban core. Others have been added to take advantage of new provincial parks.

All hikers should heartily thank the provincial government for the number of new parks created in the last ten years. Now if only there was some more money to work with and some more parks personnel to spend it. Which brings us back to maintenance. Again, do your bit! Just because a trail is in a park, do not assume that someone else is going to look after it. Be especially wary of fixed ropes on the steep sections of some trails. Do not trust your weight on a rope unless you have inspected its whole length and the anchor to which it is attached. Yellow polypropylene rope is often used because it is easily obtained and cheap. It deteriorates dramatically in sunshine and can break without warning. Remember, the law of gravity will be strictly enforced!

The trip description format in this book is very similar to previous editions. Some statistics regarding the hike are stated, then some descriptive paragraphs of text outline the trip. With regard to the statistics, keep in mind Disraeli's observation: "There are three kinds of lies: lies, damned lies and statistics." The statistics given here are for your general guidance; they are not exact numbers. A distance of 14.5 km is approximately fourteen-and-a-half kilometres; it is not precisely between 14.4 km and 14.6 km. The numbers are decimalized for convenience, not to imply scientific accuracy. The driving distances from Vancouver, which are new in this edition, are rounded to the nearest 5 km since odometer readings vary from vehicle to vehicle. Distances are quoted to a tenth of a kilometre, e.g., 4.7 km, when they are short and the variations will be small. Longer distances are usually rounded down so that you will reach the objective before the next kilometre rolls around, e.g., 35.6 km is quoted as 35 km. Elevations are usually rounded off to the nearest 5 m or the nearest 20 ft, unless specific information was known to indicate a more accurate figure. The time required for a trip, e.g., allow 8 hours, will only be of value to you when you have completed a number of the hikes and compared your time to the suggested ones. The intention is to have all quoted times as a generous time, i.e., the average party should complete the hike easily within that time allotment. However if you are feeling unwell, carrying a large pack, having difficulty with the route, etc., you may need more time. At the back of the guide are sorted tables of the hikes to allow better comparison. If you find any glaring errors in the numbers, please let me know (604 858-6601, jackb@imag.net).

With regard to personal preparedness, the usual provisos apply. Carry the ten essentials: sunglasses, pocket knife, matches, fire starter, flashlight, compass and map, first-aid kit, extra clothing, food and liquid.

Wear strong, comfortable footwear and suitable socks, and carry adequate rain gear. Leave, with someone you trust, a note explaining in detail where you are going and when you will be back. If an accident happens, the volunteer search-and-rescue teams will come and get you: if they know where to look. If you are prepared, careful and alert, your emergency equipment will never need to be used—but take it anyway! Learn how to use your map and compass; they're useless otherwise. If a bearing is quoted in this guide, it is a grid bearing. If you do not know how to read a six-figure grid reference, consult the right-hand side of any topographic map; an example is given there. When directions are given for streams and rivers, they are given looking downstream. Therefore river-right is the true right bank as you look downriver. If you want help in gaining experience and learning outdoor skills, join a club.

If I listed all the people who have provided advice, information and assistance with this guide, there would be no hikes in the book; it would just be a list of names. Therefore, to you all, my heartfelt thanks. I thought, a number of times, about giving up on this project; and then I thought about all the people who had given of their time and energy to assist. I hope that no one is disappointed with the final product.

MOUNT HALLOWELL

from start of 4WD	Round trip 17 km (10.6 mi)	Allow 7.5 hours
	Elevation gain 1010 m (3300 ft)	High point 1250 m (4100 ft)
	Average grade 11.9%	
from washout	Round trip 13 km (8.1 mi)	Allow 6 hours
	Elevation gain 760 m (2500 ft)	High point 1250 m (4100 ft)
	Average grade 11.7%	
	Best May to October	Map 92G/12 Sechelt Inlet
	Driving distance from Vancouver 100 km (62 mi), excluding ferry	

Sakinaw Lake and Texada Island, seen southwest from the summit.

Mount Hallowell is an old B.C. Forest Service (BCFS) lookout with the lookout tower intact. It should be in better condition considering the heritage significance of such structures. As can be expected with all BCFS lookouts, the views are panoramic and spectacular. This area is now part of the new 3000-ha (7400-acre) Spipiyus Provincial Park, which contains some of the oldest yellow cedar left uncut in Canada. A tree cut just south of here was more than 1800 years old.

Take the ferry from Horseshoe Bay to Langdale. Drive approximately 73 km (45 mi) towards Earls Cove, and turn right onto Malaspina Substation Road. About 1 km (0.6 mi) up the road, and 100 m (325 ft) before the B.C. Hydro substation, turn right onto a narrow, overgrowing dirt road. Follow this, underneath the power lines, for less than 2 km

(1.2 mi) to a junction where a road switchbacks left. Take this left road, which deteriorates rapidly. With a tough 4WD, you can go about 3 km (1.9 mi) to a washout. With a less rugged vehicle, park before 1 km (0.6 mi).

From wherever you park, follow the road uphill. About 25 minutes past the washout the road switchbacks south, and 15 minutes after that is a view to the southwest over the tops of small second-growth trees. Less than 10 minutes later the road starts a long S-bend, switchbacking north then south then north again. Ten minutes past the last northerly switchback and after another less dramatic washout, you arrive at a junction, elevation 930 m (2920 ft). Take the right, uphill fork (left goes past an old mine). In a distance of little more than 200 m (650 ft), go left at a T-junction onto a more travelled road. Follow this road, gaining height gradually, and watch for a trail on the left. At the start of the trail, against the butt of a tree, are the decaying remains of an old red-painted cable spool. There is also a small cairn on the roadside. The elevation here is 970 m (3180 ft), which leaves you only 280 m (920 ft) to the summit.

Initially, the trail rolls up and down through some big timber. You follow a good footbed marked with flagging tape, old and new, then enter an old clear-cut and follow the skid road. About 700 m (2300 ft) beyond the red spool, go left at a fork with a painted blue arrow on a boulder. From here to the top of the clear-cut you gain height, eating huckleberries as you go, and enter the old growth. It is now only half an hour to the lookout on the summit, which provides you with amazing views: from Vancouver Island in the west to the Stoltmann Wilderness in the northeast.

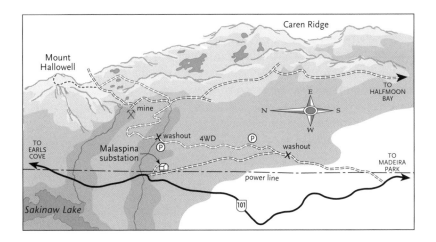

2 MOUNT STEELE

to Mount Steele Cabin	Round trip 17 km (10.6 mi)	Allow 7 hours
	Elevation gain 545 m (1780 ft)	High point 1500 m (4920 ft)
	Average grade 6.0%	
to the summit	Round trip 18 km (11.2 mi)	Allow 8 hours
	Elevation gain 690 m (2260 ft)	High point 1645 m (5400 ft)
	Average grade 7.3%	
	Best July to October	Map 92G/12 Sechelt Inlet
	Driving distance from Vancouver 85 km (50 mi), excluding ferry	

View northwest from the summit to Mount Steele Cabin.

This trip takes you into the heart of the new 6000-ha (14,830-acre) Tetrahedron Provincial Park. The summit of Mount Steele gives views of more isolated peaks such as Tetrahedron and Panther, the latter also visible northwest from Point Grey in Vancouver as a steep summit on the far side of Howe Sound. The park also has four well-maintained cabins, and trails around five lakes. Since Gray Creek is a water source for Sechelt, there is great concern about hiker behaviour. Logging activities are apparently exempt from such concern.

From the Langdale ferry terminal, drive 27 km (17 mi) to the traffic light in Sechelt. Turn right onto Wharf Road and right at the stop sign onto Porpoise Bay Road, which becomes Sechelt Inlet Road. After 9 km (5.6 mi), cross Gray Creek and 400 m (1300 ft) after that turn right and uphill onto a gravel road. At a fork 1 km (0.6 mi) later, go left onto West Road. Just before you reach the 7 km sign, stay right at a fork, and 50 m

(160 ft) after the sign you cross Gray Creek to river-left. In another 4 km (2.5 mi) you reach the park signs and the lower parking area. If the yellow gate on Branch 500, to the right, is open, a 4WD vehicle could drive another 1 km (0.6 mi) to the upper parking area.

Hike on an old logging road for 15 minutes, then a short section of parklike trail, then another 15 minutes of road. About 1 hour from the lower parking area, you arrive at a junction where the hiker symbol on the post directs you left, contouring the north slope of the hillside. After about 20 minutes on this open road, you reach a real trail and drop into the trees, which are marked high up with orange metal markers. Edwards Lake is ahead, shining through the big timber. Just before the lake is a signed junction, at which you go left for Mount Steele Cabin, still 4.7 km (2.9 mi) away. In another 30 minutes, after rising past the lake with ponds and occasional boardwalk, you arrive at Edwards Lake Cabin. The trail to Mount Steele is behind the cabin and shortly crosses Steele Creek. Across the creek is a junction: left for Mount Steele, right for McNair Lake. From here the trail wends upward on the true left side of the creek. About 1 hour above the cabin is an open rocky bowl with heather, lupines and daisies. The trail traverses left around the bowl towards the obvious col, from which you turn right up the ridge, the route being well defined. It is only 15 minutes to the cabin situated on the north side of a rocky bowl and, from the cabin, only 145 m (480 ft) higher up the pleasant northeast ridge to the summit of Mount Steele.

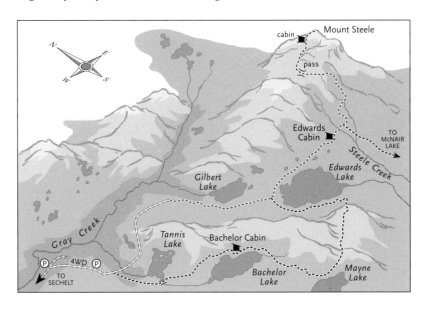

SALAL CREEK

to the west fork	Round trip 10 km (6.2 mi)	Allow 4 hours
	Elevation gain 150 m (500 ft)	High point 1180 m (3880 ft)
	Average grade 3.0%	
to Athelney Pass	Round trip 30 km (18 mi)	Allow 12 hours
	Elevation gain 800 m (2620 ft)	High point 1830 m (6000 ft)
	Average grade 5.3%	
	Best May to October	Maps 92J/11 North Creek;
		92J/14 Dickson Range
	Driving distance from Vancouver 235 km (145 mi)	

View north up Salal Creek to Peak 7031.

This recently created trail takes you to the northwest edge of the area covered by this guide. Even the short trip to the west fork will allow you to experience, in the trail makers' opinion, "the most spectacular valley in the Squamish/Lillooet watershed." The caveat: as you read this, the logging roads are being pushed farther up this unlogged valley, permanently changing its character.

Zero your odometer at the Pemberton PetroCanada junction, 90 km (60 mi) north of Squamish. Turn left into Pemberton. At 1 km (0.6 mi) go right at the T-junction. At 3 km (1.9 mi) turn left for Pemberton Meadows. At 25 km (15 mi), with a public telephone on your left, turn right onto Lillooet River Forest Service Road (Upper Lillooet Road). Cross the river on two bridges and follow the gravel road upstream on river-left. Opposite the 9 km sign, at 34 km (21 mi), stay left as Hurley River Forest Service Road goes right. Just past the 41 km sign, at 66 km (41 mi), you start to gain elevation to pass Lillooet Canyon. The road cranks up the hill in a series of switchbacks, and you drive through a creek flowing across the road. At the crest of the hill, odometer 73 km (45 mi), take the spur road to the right signed BRS25. Drive as high and as far on the east slope of Salal Creek as the current logging roads allow.

The road makers are following the trail makers. Wherever you park, the trail should be straight ahead through the slash. Watch for flagging tape, mostly orange. Do not be confused by the tapes that say "Road Location"; a footbed is visible much of the time. Where the trail turns towards the creek, some confusion is possible. However, on the south edge of a large slide-alder patch/gravel flat, with the west fork visible some way ahead, turn towards Salal Creek and find an alder-choked stream crossing that has 2x4s on the first fork and logs on the second. The trail breaks into the open on the true left bank of Salal Creek at GR666188, 1.5 hours from your start. From here, you are mostly in the open on the gravel bars beside the creek. About 1 km (0.6 mi) farther, after you rise onto a higher gravel bar on your right, are the remains of an old campsite. The confluence with the west fork is to your left. From here upstream you can stay on the gravel flats unless the water is high, whereupon you may have to detour into the woods for short sections. If you are intent upon Athelney Pass, there is a longer section in the woods around the north fork of Salal Creek. From the north fork, it is still 7 km (4.3 mi) to the pass. It may be open country but it is rarely travelled. A decrepit old cabin lies in the pass.

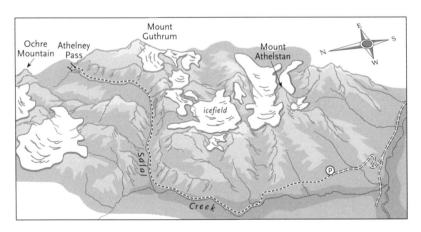

4HUNDRED LAKES PLATEAU

Round trip 10 km (6.2 mi)	Allow 7 hours
Elevation gain 745 m (2440 ft)	High point 1690 m (5540 ft)
Average grade 14.9%	

Best July to September	Maps 92J/05 Clendenning Creek; 92J/12 Mount Dalgleish; WCWC Elaho–Meager Trail

Driving distance from Vancouver 245 km (150 mi)

Pylon Peak, seen north from the trail.

This is the northern section of Western Canada Wilderness Committee's (WCWC) 22 km (14 mi) Elaho to Meager Hiking Trail in the proposed Stoltmann National Park. The southern section is described in Hike 25. The drive crosses the wild volcanic landscape of Meager Creek and the trail takes you into a gorgeous subalpine area. Your eastern skyline is the Pemberton Icefield. Make sure, however, that your navigation skills are up to par. The trail is marked, but this plateau is a natural maze of ponds, hillocks, creeks, timber patches, heather meadows and granite outcrops.

Zero your odometer at the Pemberton PetroCanada junction, 90 km (60 mi) north of Squamish. Turn left into Pemberton. At 1 km (0.6 mi) go right at the T-junction. At 3 km (1.9 mi) turn left for Pemberton Meadows. At 25 km (15 mi), with a public telephone on your left, turn right onto Lillooet River Forest Service Road (Upper Lillooet Road). Cross the river on two bridges and follow the gravel road upstream on river-left. Opposite the 9 km sign, at 34 km (21 mi), stay left as Hurley

River Forest Service Road goes right. At the 37 km sign, at 63 km (39 mi), turn left onto the Meager Creek Branch. Immediately, there is the gated bridge over the Lillooet River. The road is currently closed due to road and bridge washouts from this point on. If the road reopens stay left at forks for the next 7 km (4.3 mi) until you reach Meager Creek Hot Springs. At 75 km (47 mi), just after the 11 km sign, go right at a major fork. The bridge over Meager Creek's south fork is 1 km (0.6 mi) later. The water bars start here but the trailhead is only 2 km (1.2 mi) down this west side of the creek, so choose your parking spot. The trailhead (GR647972) is at a fork in the road shown by orange flagging tape.

Take the left fork for 50 m (160 ft) to its end, then drop through the clear-cut to cross the creek, which flows east from Meager (Fish) Lake. There are orange diamond markers. One hour from your start, a knoll gives views north up Meager Creek and northwest to Meager (Fish) Lake. Shortly you switchback up through a boulder field. On a couple of wet heather sections higher, there are rope handlines. As you enter the subalpine, elevation 1650 m (5400 ft), pay attention to the markers as sightlines are not necessarily the route. Where the angle eases and rocky knolls appear is Chain Lakes Camp. Memorize this point for your return. The high point of the trail is only a half hour ahead and gives views south to Mist Lake and the Elaho Valley. Depending on the time, follow the trail south or ascend the rocks to the west, for views of the true Elaho–Meager Divide.

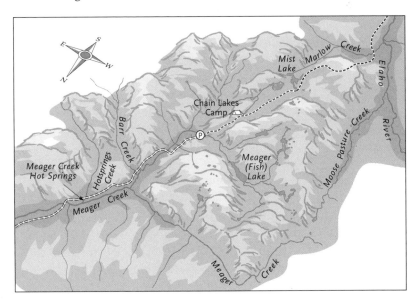

5 TENQUILLE LAKE

Round trip 26 km (16 mi)   Allow 10 hours
Elevation gain 1460 m (4800 ft)   High point 1710 m (5600 ft)
Average grade 11.2%

Best July to October   Map 92J/10 Birkenhead Lake
Driving distance from Vancouver 185 km (115 mi)

Alpine Club group at the lake, with Sun God Mountain in the distance. (CM)

Three trails lead to Tenquille Lake: from Hurley River Forest Service Road, from Owl Lakes on the D'Arcy road and this one straight from the Pemberton Valley. The route described here was built as a mining access trail more than eighty years ago. It is a scenic trip that culminates in splendid alpine meadows around the lake. The waters are crystal clear and there is a log cabin, albeit old and decrepit. There are many pleasant summits to hike above the lake, although they would probably require an overnight trip.

Zero your odometer at the Pemberton PetroCanada junction, 90 km (60 mi) north of Squamish. Turn left into Pemberton. At 1 km (0.6 mi) go right at the T-junction. At 3 km (1.9 mi) turn left for Pemberton Meadows. At 25 km (15 mi), with a public telephone on your left, turn right onto Lillooet River Forest Service Road (Upper Lillooet Road).

Cross the river on two bridges. Park just off the road to the right of the second bridge, beside a British Columbia Forest Service trail sign.

As you start up this trail on foot, be aware that it is a descent route for mountain bikers who have pedalled, pushed and carried their machines in from Hurley River Forest Service Road. However, it is a gnarly descent that is not seeing major use. At first the marked route zigzags uphill to the east, merges with the original trail coming up from the right, then turns back north. Your way lies through open forest, giving you tantalizing glimpses of the rich Pemberton Valley below and Mount Ipsoot opposite. En route you cross several small streams (possibly dry in late summer), then work into the valley of the Wolverine, finally crossing the creek at about 1500 m (5000 ft), at which height the trees are sparser and you have already traversed some small meadows. Shortly thereafter, the alternative trail from Hurley River Forest Service Road joins from the left. Beyond this point you pass through lush flower meadows, which give way to smaller, more modest plants and heather as you approach the high point in Tenquille Pass. The trail drops down 60 m (200 ft) to the lake, where the cabin and many tent sites testify to its popularity. There is alleged to be good fishing or you may inspect old mining claims. Various hikes are possible: Copper Mound and Mount McLeod to the south, Goat Peak and Tenquille Mountain to the north, and a crossover for fit and experienced backpackers southeast via Ogre Lake and the Mount Ronayne Trail to the Owl Lake trailhead and thence to the D'Arcy road.

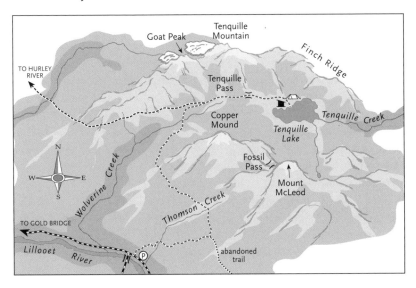

6 HAYLMORE–MELVIN DIVIDE

Round trip 20 km (12.4 mi)   Allow 8 hours
Elevation gain 1040 m (3400 ft)   High point 2260 m (7400 ft)
Average grade 10.4%

Best July to September   Maps 92J/08 Duffey Lake;
                                      92J/09 Shalalth
Driving distance from Vancouver 215 km (130 mi)

View east down Melvin Creek from the divide.

Although much of this hike is on an all-terrain vehicle (ATV) track, it leads through the Barkley Valley, a unique area with an interesting and varied history. The final kilometre is foot-access only and leads up the well-named Crystal Creek to two beautiful alpine lakes. The trail gives easy access to the high open ridges on the divide between Haylmore and Melvin Creeks. Melvin is an unlogged watershed: experience this virgin area now before it becomes a destination resort!

Zero your odometer at the Pemberton PetroCanada junction, 90 km (60 mi) north of Squamish. Drive east 7 km (4.3 mi) to Mount Currie, then straight ahead onto the D'Arcy road. At 41 km (25 mi) turn right into the community of Devine. Less than 2 km (1.2 mi) later turn right onto Haylmore Creek Forest Service Road. After the 16 km sign, at about

59 km (37 mi), watch for a steep narrow ATV track on your left. Park on the roadside here, elevation 1220 m (4000 ft).

A sign just above the road explains some of the area's history. The track initially parallels the road through a recent clear-cut, but soon turns east into Common Johnny Creek, then into the Elliott Creek drainage. The survey tapes here probably indicate imminent logging activity. After about an hour you encounter the first of the avalanche zones, as the timber begins to thin out and the subalpine meadows become more numerous. As you come out of the trees, the big wide Barkley Valley of Elliott Creek beckons you on. Five kilometres (3.1 mi) from the start, elevation 1615 m (5300 ft), you arrive at the remains of a settlement from the 1960s. There is also a camping area, with a toilet and a bear cache, and a small A-frame cabin maintained by snowmobilers. Twenty minutes past the camp, you cross Crystal Creek flowing down from your objective: Twin Lakes. Just beyond, the trail forks: right goes to the head of Elliott Creek; left heads up the numerous switchbacks towards the lakes and the divide. If you time it right, these meadows are a riot of colourful flowers. After ten switchbacks you reach the end of the track at 2100 m (6900 ft) and the start of the trail proper. The first lake is only 10 minutes away, although you may be distracted by the quartzite intrusions that give the creek its name. The lake has a gorgeous green hue and is strangely shallower in the middle than at the edges. A sketchy trail around the west side of the lake leads, in 30 minutes, to the upper lake right on the divide. Depending on the time available, you could investigate the open ridges or just savour the views down into Melvin Creek.

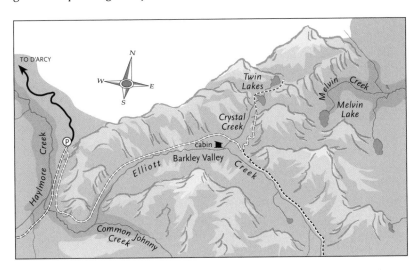

7 PHELIX CREEK

from start of 4WD	Round trip 20 km (12.4 mi)	Allow 9 hours
	Elevation gain 1010 m (3300 ft)	High point 1710 m (5600 ft)
	Average grade 10.1%	
from road end	Round trip 10 km (6.2 mi)	Allow 6 hours
	Elevation gain 430 m (1400 ft)	High point 1710 m (5600 ft)
	Average grade 8.6%	
	Best July (see note)	Map 92J/10 Birkenhead Lake
	Driving distance from Vancouver 215 km (130 mi)	

Northwestern summit view from Mount Gandalf, above Phelix Creek. (JS)

The access to this area improved recently when the University of British Columbia (UBC) Varsity Outdoor Club put in a new trail to their Brian Waddington Memorial Hut on the shore of Long Lake, in the drainage of Phelix Creek's west fork. If you do not find creek crossings exhilarating, pass on this hike! Although the area around the lake is still treed, access to the alpine ridges of the southern Cadwallader Range and the peaks of

Mounts Gandalf, Aragorn and Shadowfax is straightforward. There have been no confirmed sightings of hobbits in the area.

Zero your odometer at the Pemberton PetroCanada junction, 90 km (60 mi) north of Squamish. Drive east 7 km (4.3 mi) to Mount Currie, then straight ahead onto the D'Arcy road. At 41 km (25 mi), following the signs for Birkenhead Provincial Park, turn left onto Blackwater Road. About 13 km (8.1 mi) up this road, just before the park boundary, elevation 700 m (2300 ft), turn right onto Phelix Creek Forest Service Road. With a rugged 4WD vehicle you may be able to drive 5 km (3.1 mi) farther. Otherwise park where convenient!

Follow the road for a couple of kilometres to a bridge crossing to the east side (river-right to river-left). Another couple of kilometres takes you to a left fork where the road crosses back to the west side. After an uphill switchback, stay right at the next fork. The road end is not far past here. Look for an enormous boulder at the far side of the clear-cut. Do not be distracted by flagging tape partway across! At the boulder, drop to the creek. Cross to the east side, on the logs over the creek, and pick up the trail at an avalanche swath, GR246071, elevation 1280 m (4200 ft). Traverse the creek to the west side again after 1.5 km (0.9 mi), around elevation 1460 m (4800 ft). The ascent is steady from here up to Long Lake. The hut, a project of the Workers' Compensation Board and probably the most solid building in the western mountains, is at the west end of the lake, at GR229086.

Note: The creek crossings are difficult or impossible in high water. Therefore late spring is out! The Ministry of the Environment requests that humans avoid this area from August 15 to October 15 as this is the mating period for the local grizzly bear population. So, choose your time carefully.

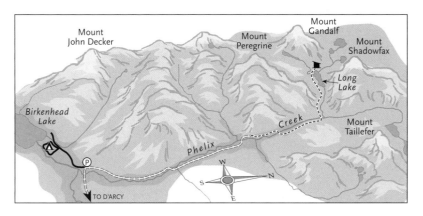

8 PLACE GLACIER

Round trip 21 km (13 mi) Allow 9 hours
Elevation gain 1310 m (4300 ft) High point 1830 m (6000 ft)
Average grade 12.5%

Best July to October Map 92J/07 Pemberton
Driving distance from Vancouver 190 km (120 mi)

View southeast, over the toe, up the Place Glacier. (MM)

This trail has paved road access, a fantastic waterfall and a scenic glacier; you can even get onto the ice if you are equipped and experienced. The Place Creek waterfall is truly spectacular, although you'd need a helicopter to see it all. The Place Glacier is not large but it is the scene of much glaciological research. The scientists' hut at the glacier snout is usable by the public, if you care to overnight there.

Zero your odometer at the Pemberton PetroCanada junction, 90 km (60 mi) north of Squamish. Drive east 7 km (4.3 mi) to Mount Currie, then straight ahead onto the D'Arcy road. Count the B.C. Rail crossings. At 600 m (0.4 mi) after the third crossing, odometer 21 km (13 mi), there is a track on your right. It may have a "Private Property" sign. Either park on the highway here or drive in 200 m (650 ft) to the railroad tracks. Park before the tracks. It used to be acceptable to drive farther, but problems with illegal tree cutting and garbage dumping have reduced access. The property owners are still generously allowing hikers to cross their land on foot. Take care, so that access is not further restricted!

Across the railroad is a locked gate. Climb the gate and follow the track for 100 m (325 ft), which takes you under the first power line.

Across the opening, enter the trees; and 30 m (100 ft) in, fork left; then immediately swing right following the widest, clearest track through the trees. It is 200 m (650 ft) to the second power line. Straight across this is a trail into the trees which begins to ramp up the hill. Shortly, you become aware of water rushing, and with dramatic suddenness you emerge on the edge of a chasm. The fine spray makes the track slippery. Now go straight uphill, with the falls on your right, for the next 400 m (1300 ft) to a rock slide. Thereafter the grade eases with a few short switchbacks. The relief is short-lived; the trail steepens as you go left around a rock spur, the creek for the time being below you. Soon you arrive atop Vodka Rock, a possible destination for a short day, with a view to the Birkenhead Valley and Sun God Mountain in the northwest. Ascend another 300 m (1000 ft) to a spot where several logs have been jammed against a tiny islet in midstream to provide a precarious route across. Here you are at about 1420 m (4660 ft), but now the grade eases as the trail swings away from, and then back to, the creek. Recross here to ascend on river-right, following cairns and orange flagging tape. Finally, you are faced with a scramble up the polished rocks of the head-wall, daunting when wet and slippery, to end by the A-frames once used by glaciologists of the Geological Survey of Canada.

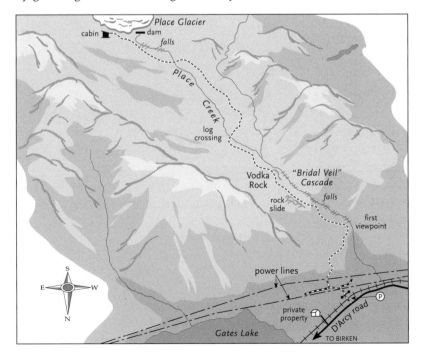

9 JOFFRE LAKES

Round trip 11 km (6.8 mi)   Allow 6 hours
Elevation gain 365 m (1200 ft)   High point 1585 m (5200 ft)
Average grade 6.7%

Best July to October   Map 92J/08 Duffey Lake
Driving distance from Vancouver 190 km (120 mi)

View southeast of Upper Joffre Lake and the Matier Glacier. (MM)

With three beautiful lakes en route, each lovelier than the last, and with a spectacular glacier for your destination, this hike has something for almost everyone. It is not surprising that this area has been protected as a provincial park. There is paved road access to the trailhead. This, and the easy altitude gain on the road, make the Duffey Lake area especially attractive to hikers in summer and backcountry skiers in winter. It is also why developers would love to make this area into a winter Disneyland. Experience it for yourself and decide what you think is right!

Zero your odometer at the Pemberton PetroCanada junction, 90 km (60 mi) north of Squamish. Drive east 7 km (4.3 mi) to Mount Currie, then turn right onto Highway 99 for Lillooet. Cross the Lillooet River then start to ascend towards Cayoosh Pass and Duffey Lake. At 30 km (20 mi), on your right, is the parking area for Joffre Lakes Provincial Park, elevation 1220 m (4000 ft).

A large-scale map at the trailhead provides information about the trail, which heads off into the trees, forking right just before the first lake on the Joffre Alpine Trail. Almost right away you have a spectacular view of the glacier from across the beautiful lake as you follow the trail over the marshy ground. Next comes the crossing of the outlet, Joffre Creek, after which you start to rise, following the west side of the lake and then the creek, the sound of rushing water in your ears. Next you drop a little to a rock slide, followed by a steep stretch before you cross the creek once more just before the second lovely body of water, Middle Joffre Lake, at elevation 1540 m (5050 ft). Work around this lake to the left and over the stream again, then drop briefly to its shore before continuing uphill. Finally comes the jewel of the three lakes, at 1590 m (5220 ft), nestling beneath the towering icefalls of Matier Glacier. The trail itself heads to the right above the shoreline, then rises over talus, finally becoming a cairned route as it veers east across the creek and ends just below the snout of the glacier. In addition to the superb views of the lake and the surrounding country with its stark evidence of recent glaciation, there is the special thrill of crashing ice blocks on a warm afternoon.

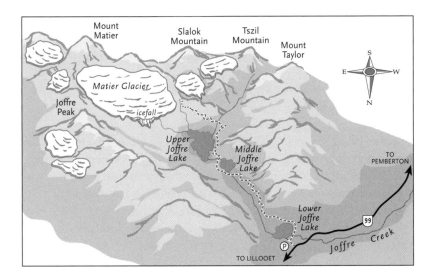

10 MARRIOTT MEADOWS

from start of 4WD	Round trip 14 km (8.7 mi)	Allow 7 hours
	Elevation gain 400 m (1300 ft)	High point 1740 m (5700 ft)
	Average grade 5.7%	
from trailhead	Round trip 10 km (6.2 mi)	Allow 6 hours
	Elevation gain 310 m (1000 ft)	High point 1740 m (5700 ft)
	Average grade 6.2%	

Best June to October	Map 92J/08 Duffey Lake
Driving distance from Vancouver 195 km (120 mi)	

Mount Rohr, seen southeast from the meadows. (CM)

One of the attractions of the Duffey Lake area is the ability to drive a paved road to 1300 m (4300 ft), making alpine terrain a feasible day hike. This trip leads to a readily accessible mountain basin with pleasant meadows and subalpine lakes. The Whistler Section of the Alpine Club of Canada is currently building the Wendy Thompson Memorial Hut at the west end of the lower lake, as well as improving the access road and trail. It is also possible to hike to more lakes another 400 m (1300 ft) above the basin. Many of the adjacent peaks are steep and to reach their tops requires some scrambling ability, but there is good ridge walking to be had.

Zero your odometer at the Pemberton PetroCanada junction, 90 km (60 mi) north of Squamish. Drive east 7 km (4.3 mi) to Mount Currie, then turn right onto Highway 99 for Lillooet. Cross the Lillooet River then start to ascend towards Cayoosh Pass and Duffey Lake. After 33 km (20 mi), 400 m (1300 ft) past the Cayoosh Creek bridge, turn left onto Cayoosh Creek Forest Service Road. You may need a 4WD vehicle to cover the next 2 km (1.2 mi), staying left at two forks, to the trailhead.

Shortly after you start hiking, and just after you enter the trees, drop down to cross Rohr Creek. The trail then climbs steeply to a junction. The right fork leads to the Rohr Lake Trail, which ascends to the east into another attractive basin 365 m (1200 ft) higher. Save this trail and the straightforward ascent of Mount Rohr for another day. Instead, follow the left fork at the junction. The route is signed "Aspen" since the area to which you are hiking has often been referred to as Aspen–Marriott Meadows. In a couple of hundred metres, the angle eases. The trade-off is a wet footbed with a number of boggy sections. At an elevation of 1650 m (5400 ft), you cross to the west side of Cayoosh Creek. There are actually two crossings, both on logs. Both require a great deal of care, particularly the second of the two. Beyond the creek lie open areas that have been cleared by avalanches from the steep walls of the basin into which you are travelling. The trail traverses some talus slopes before reaching the lake. It then follows around above the shoreline, circling towards the location of the cabin at GR379861. There is lots of terrain to investigate, for example, the next lake which is only 100 m (325 ft) higher than your present location.

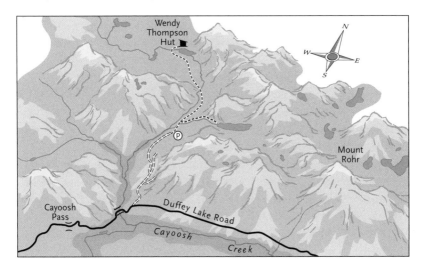

11 CERISE CREEK

Round trip 9 km (5.6 mi)	Allow 4.5 hours
Elevation gain 275 m (900 ft)	High point 1680 m (5500 ft)
Average grade 6.1%	

Best July to October	Map 92J/08 Duffey Lake
Driving distance from Vancouver 210 km (130 mi)	

View southeast to Anniversary Glacier and Mount Matier.

This short hike takes you up moraines to the little lake at the toe of Anniversary Glacier. It is a spectacular location, with the ridges and faces of Mounts Joffre and Matier soaring more than 1000 m (3280 ft) above. A well-maintained hut stands nearby; it was built in memory of Keith Flavelle who died on the east ridge of Mount Logan in 1986. Unless you intend to overnight in the hut, which is open to the public, the glacier is a good objective. This trail is one of the most well used in the area, summer and winter. However, do not be deluded by the short distance and mimimal elevation gain: the trail is full of rooty sections and mud holes, which do not make for fast travel.

Zero your odometer at the Pemberton PetroCanada junction, 90 km (60 mi) north of Squamish. Drive east 7 km (4.3 mi) to Mount Currie, then turn right onto Highway 99 for Lillooet. Cross the Lillooet River then ascend towards Cayoosh Pass and Duffey Lake. At 43 km (27 mi), just before the bridge over Van Horlick Creek, turn right onto Cerise Creek East Main, which curves back towards the west. Zero your odometer again here. At 2.3 km (1.4 mi) cross Caspar Creek. Ignore an old right fork and a new right fork and, 200 m (650 ft) past the bridge, switchback right. The road is in good 2WD condition although alders are intruding from the sides. At 5.9 km (3.7 mi) is the head of the Alpine Area Trail, the winter route that follows up the east side of the creek (river-right). Drive another 150 m (490 ft) over the Cerise Creek bridge and park in the large landing. Drive another 500 m (0.3 mi) along a rough little road to the left, if your vehicle allows. The elevation here is 1340 m (4400 ft).

From the landing by the bridge, walk south on the rough little road, staying straight ahead at a fork and making for the far side of another landing. The trail starts into the clear-cut here, following the bottom of the cut for 5 minutes to the trees. There are no markers, just sporadic flagging tape, but the footbed is obvious and well worn. After 45 minutes you will encounter a major mud hole, with a drier route uphill; although that too will become part of the hole with enough traffic. One hour from your start are short switchbacks to gain elevation. At the top of these switchbacks is a junction. Take the left trail for the glacier. Another 20 minutes takes you to the boulder field below the moraines. Follow the cairns through the boulders then rejoin the trail as it makes for the low point between the two lateral moraines. There are a couple of campsites at the lake. Be cautious about going too far towards the glacier toe as debris can fall from the peaks above at any time.

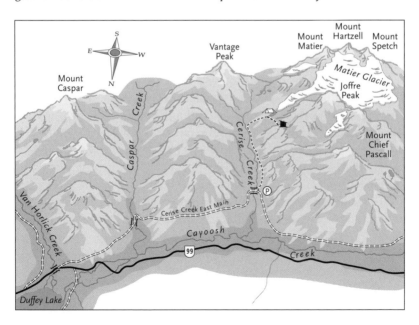

12 BLOWDOWN PASS

to Blowdown Pass	Round trip 7.5 km (4.7 mi)	Allow 5 hours
	Elevation gain 580 m (1900 ft)	High point 2195 m (7200 ft)
	Average grade 15.5%	
to Gott Peak	Round trip 10.5 km (6.5 mi)	Allow 7 hours
	Elevation gain 915 m (3000 ft)	High point 2530 m (8300 ft)
	Average grade 17.4%	
	Best July to September	Map 92J/08 Duffey Lake
	Driving distance from Vancouver 220 km (135 mi)	

Blowdown Pass and Gotcha Peak, seen east from the meadows below Gott Peak.

Blowdown Pass is on the divide between Cayoosh Creek and Cottonwood Creek, a tributary of the Stein River. It is therefore one of the access routes, albeit a long one, to the Stein Valley Heritage Provincial Park. There is a beautiful lake with campsites before the pass, and the meadows on the slopes above are spectacularly colourful if you time it right. A mine road leads from the Duffey Lake Road through the pass and another 10 km (6.2 mi) down Cottonwood Creek to the closed Silver Queen Mine. Gott Peak is an easy hike up the open ridge from the pass.

Zero your odometer at the Pemberton PetroCanada junction, 90 km (60 mi) north of Squamish. Drive east 7 km (4.3 mi) to Mount Currie, then turn right onto Highway 99 for Lillooet. Cross the Lillooet River then ascend towards Cayoosh Pass and Duffey Lake. At 53 km (33 mi) turn right onto Blowdown Creek Road. It is 15 km (9.3 mi) to the pass; how far you drive depends on the ruggedness of your vehicle and the condition of the deteriorating road. Two-wheel drive vehicles can certainly drive 9 km (5.6 mi) to a fork and, going left, perhaps another 1.5 km (0.9 mi) to a parking space on the left.

From wherever you decide to walk, follow the road up the valley to a point where the present road doubles back on an S-bend and an older version, now disused and trail-like, goes straight on. For hikers, the old route is more attractive, especially as it provides an approach to the lake just below the pass. To make the lake your destination, drop to the right off the old road, heading for the meadow near the lake's outlet. Otherwise, stay with the road until you come to the pass, which overlooks the beautiful U-shaped South Cottonwood Valley, plentifully bedecked with heather and alpine flowers in the short summer season. The road itself descends the valley towards the turnoff to the Silver Queen Mine. Beyond the turnoff a reconstructed trail continues downstream, following an old pack route along the south fork to its confluence with the north fork of Cottonwood Creek and eventually linking with the main trail down the Stein River to its mouth. If you decide to spend a day or so in the area, you will find no lack of camping spots on either side of the pass. From here you may explore ridges north and south, head over to the valley of the North Cottonwood or ascend Gott Peak, which stands like a sentinel to the north of the divide. The country is all open and the views seem to go on forever. Gott Peak, incidentally, commemorates a noted Indian fugitive who eluded the Mounties for several years. Another comment: the area supports a number of grizzly bears—be careful, therefore, when hiking or camping, especially with food supplies.

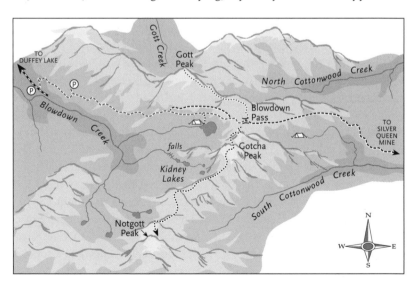

13 LIZZIE–STEIN DIVIDE

to the cabin	Round trip 6 km (3.7 mi)	Allow 3.5 hours
(from parking area)	Elevation gain 320 m (1050 ft)	High point 1600 m (5250 ft)
	Average grade 10.7%	
to Heart Lake	Round trip 12 km (7.5 mi)	Allow 7 hours
(from parking area)	Elevation gain 640 m (2100 ft)	High point 1920 m (6300 ft)
	Average grade 10.7%	

Best July to September   Map 92J/01 Stein Lake
Driving distance from Vancouver 200 km (124 mi)

View east to the entrance to the Gates of Shangri-La.

This is another hike that takes you into an unspoiled region of great natural beauty in the high country. It is on the divide leading to the Stein Valley Heritage Provincial Park, although the trail between Cottonwood Creek and Stein Lake is currently closed due to a 1996 fire. However, this alpine divide has numerous lakes to explore and many fine summits of no technical difficulty. Note that the Lizzie Cabin is 2 hours past Lizzie Lake, in the subalpine. The cabin, which is open to the public, and the trail are maintained by the British Columbia Mountaineering Club.

Zero your odometer at the Pemberton PetroCanada junction, 90 km (60 mi) north of Squamish. Drive east 7 km (4.3 mi) to Mount Currie, then turn right onto Highway 99 for Lillooet. Cross the Lillooet River, then as you start to rise, at 17 km (10.6 mi), watch for a road on your right. It is marked with a large sign for Lillooet Lake Lodge and a smaller Forest Service sign for In-Shuck-Ch Forest Service Road. After 16 km

(9.9 mi) on this bumpy road down the east side of Lillooet Lake, pass the Lizzie Bay Forest Service Recreation Site. Cross Lizzie Creek and turn left onto the Lizzie Creek Branch, Pemberton–Port Douglas Forest Service Road. It is another 11 km (6.8 mi) to the parking area at Lizzie Lake; note that a washout has made this road impassable in a vehicle. Go right at the first two forks and left at the third; they are all signed.

From the parking area at the Lizzie Lake Forest Service Recreation Site, elevation 1340 m (4400 ft), head through the fringe of trees towards the lake. The trail marked with orange diamonds goes left and has many windfalls. The trail to the right, closer to the lake, is unmarked but has been cleared. They rejoin shortly. After 15 minutes along the gorgeous green-blue lake, you turn left and uphill as you leave the lake behind. After rising steeply through forest with glimpses of the waters glinting below, you come into a narrow gorge with the romantic local name, the Gates of Shangri-La. Beyond this, after a scramble over a large rock slide, you arrive at the small mountain cabin. Above here you are in open meadows, and with more than one day at your disposal you may visit as many lakes as you can possibly desire. A long day's round trip from here takes you past pretty little Caltha Lake and brings you to a view over the most beautiful of all, Tundra Lake, just over the Stein Divide, its deep-blue waters catching every trick of the sun's rays. Closer at hand, though, are lakes almost as attractive: Arrowhead, Iceberg, Long and Sapphire, for instance. For the ridge walker, too, there are numerous appealing possibilities—White Lupine Ridge, to name only one.

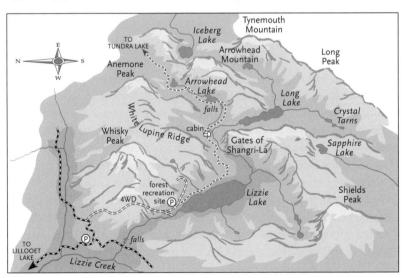

14 WEDGEMOUNT LAKE

Round trip 14 km (8.7 mi)   Allow 7.5 hours
Elevation gain 1160 m (3800 ft)   High point 1920 m (6300 ft)
Average grade 16.6%

Best July to September   Map 92J/02 Whistler
Driving distance from Vancouver 145 km (90 mi)

Wedge Mountain, viewed southeast from across the lake. (MM)

A spectacular lake lying in the shadow of Wedge Mountain and ringed by glaciers serves as the destination of this hike. The beautifully sited lake has the toe of the Wedgemount Glacier at its upper end and the great snowfields of Garibaldi Provincial Park's highest summit, Wedge Mountain, standing above it to the south. To the east are the ribbed slopes of Mount Weart and to the west, the jagged crest of Rethel Mountain. On a small rise above the shore is a British Columbia Mountaineering Club cabin, open to climbers who may have their eyes on some or all of these peaks. There is also a wilderness campsite.

The approach is via Highway 99 with a right turn to cross the B.C. Rail tracks and the Green River 11.5 km (7.1 mi) north of the Whistler Village traffic light as you travel towards Pemberton. At first you are on a broad gravel road that goes left just across the river and passes to the right of a large sandpit. At the next fork go right and shortly thereafter left again on an old logging road that has been reconstructed by B.C. Parks. Continue to road's end at a small parking lot with a toilet and trailhead information nearly 2 km (1.2 mi) from the highway.

On foot you travel upward through the regenerating forest, where deciduous shrubs and trees are interspersed with young conifers and with views of the valley below and mountains beyond. Gradually the sound of Wedgemount Creek on the left becomes louder, and a high cut-bank appears across the rushing stream as you approach the crossing. Once across, you ascend a small spine on the north bank heading into the standing forest; from here continue eastward, remaining parallel to but well above the channel as you rise. This trail is steep; you climb 1100 m (3600 ft) in less than 6 km (3.7 mi). Fortunately, a few easier stretches allow you to take your eyes off the trail to look around. The forest is thick and tall on the lower reaches of the trail, with moss and unobtrusive little plants in the understory; later, however, it is interrupted by rock slides to be crossed, and still later, as the trees thin out, you are tantalized by fugitive glimpses of Wedgemount Creek dropping some 300 m (980 ft) in a cloud of white spray. For the final part of the hike, beyond the last clumps of stunted trees, you are on steep, rocky alpine meadows; remember, though, that snow stays late, often lingering into July, so you should save this trip until later to see it at its summer best. Finally you reach the heathery pass above your objective, its turquoise-coloured glory spread at your feet.

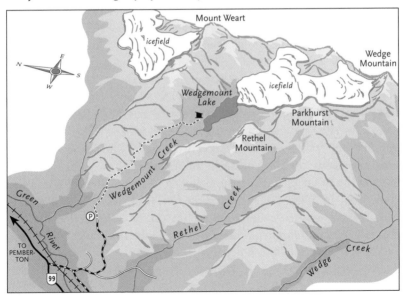

15 RUSSET LAKE

Round trip 27 km (17 mi)	Allow 10 hours
Elevation gain 1250 m (4100 ft)	High point 1950 m (6400 ft)
Average grade 9.3%	

Best July to October	Map 92J/02 Whistler
Driving distance from Vancouver 125 km (75 mi)	

Fissile and Whirlwind Peaks, seen southeast from across the lake. (TP)

Russet Lake is located in alpine country within Garibaldi Provincial Park. It is above Singing Pass, which is at the east end of the ridge running back from Whistler Mountain. The ridge is known as the Musical Bumps (Oboe, Flute and Piccolo summits) and the drainage from the pass is Melody Creek. You'll also cross Harmony Creek on the way. At the pass you view a seemingly endless meadow with a lush growth of the flowering plants common in British Columbia's mountain meadows—those plants described on the information board at Singing Pass as "tough... but delicate," with a plea to respect their fragility and stay on the trail. From the pass to the lake you are in the sublimity of the alpine, with the glaciated summits of the Spearhead and Fitzsimmons Ranges ahead and above you, and with the glistening snowfields of Castle Towers and its neighbours across the valley to the south. At the northwest end of the lake is a British Columbia Mountaineering Club cabin, open to the public. Camping is also allowed here.

In Whistler, turn right off Highway 99 onto Village Gate Boulevard. At a T-intersection 400 m (1300 ft) farther, turn right onto Blackcomb

Way, which you follow for 300 m (1000 ft) to the bus loop. Just beyond that is the trailhead: a gravel road. Park in any convenient day lot. If you intend to park overnight, use the designated area of Lot 4.

On this gravel road you start to rise, doubling back left past a water tower where Whistler Control Road bears right, then heading up into the valley of Fitzsimmons Creek for nearly 5 km (3.1 mi). You reach a parking area at what was, until very recently, the trailhead. Your elevation here is 1040 m (3400 ft). On the trail itself, you soon come to two washouts, the results of clearing the tree cover many years ago, and between them the old mine adit with some rusty rails dangling where once was roadbed. Shortly you reach the park boundary and a fork where you keep left, now travelling southeastward in shady forest high above Fitzsimmons Creek, crossing Harmony, Flute and Oboe Creeks in succession. As you progress, the woodland changes from tall timber and open forest floor to the subalpine with its sparser trees and heavy underbrush. Then as you veer south up Melody Creek the bush gives way to lush meadow. At 1710 m (5600 ft) you are in the middle of the expansive meadows of Singing Pass. The trail forks here: right takes you northwest over the Musical Bumps to the top of the Whistler ski runs; left towards Russet Lake, another 150 m (500 ft) above. First you switchback up eastward to a high, rocky pass at 1950 m (6400 ft) before dropping again to the lake.

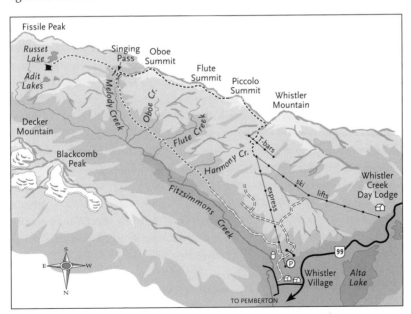

41

16 RAINBOW LAKE

Round trip 16 km (9.9 mi)	Allow 6 hours
Elevation gain 825 m (2700 ft)	High point 1465 m (4800 ft)
Average grade 10.3%	

Best July to October	Maps 92J/02 Whistler;
	92J/03 Brandywine Falls;
	BCFS Rainbow–Madeley Trail

Driving distance from Vancouver 130 km (80 mi)

The campsite at Hanging Lake southwest of Rainbow Lake. (MM)

Twentyone Mile Creek is on the west side of the valley across from Whistler and Blackcomb Mountains. The trail provides several hiking options and is also a popular winter trip for backcountry skiers. The hike described here is an easy day to Rainbow Lake. However, the energetic could ascend Rainbow Mountain. It is an easy ascent if you continue along the length of the lake before striking upward to the ridge south of the peak. Another possibility is the short side trip to Gin and Tonic Lakes, reached by turning left off the main trail before it crosses Twentyone Mile Creek and heading up the valley to the west. And from Tonic Lake, if you are really enthusiastic, you may make for Sproatt Ridge with its panoramic views. There is also a route westward over the divide to Madeley Lake in the Callaghan Creek watershed, so that a crossover is another attractive possibility for a two-car party. Because this is the watershed supply area for Whistler Township, camping is not allowed; nevertheless there is pleasant camping just over the divide towards the Callaghan Valley, at Hanging Lake.

Zero your odometer at the Cleveland Avenue traffic lights in Squamish. Drive north on Highway 99 towards Whistler for 53 km (33 mi) then turn left onto Alta Lake Road. Cross the B.C. Rail tracks and follow the west side of the valley for 7 km (4.3 mi). Just after the Whistler Cemetery, where the road crosses Twentyone Mile Creek, parking space has been provided on both sides of the road.

The trail starts on the west side of the road following the creek upstream on river-right. After 10 minutes you reach a road and a pumphouse. Follow the road, gaining height along the southwest side of the valley, for 20 minutes to the real trailhead and the end of the mountain bike access. Very soon you enter the fine old forest, a noticeable contrast to the small trees of the regenerating area you have just left. The trail markers are reasonably regular and obvious. Some improvements, in the form of bridges and boardwalks, have been made to the next section of the trail but more would eliminate the widening mud holes. An hour and a half from your start are two stream crossings: the second with a good bridge, the first needing one. Another 45 minutes along, there is a viewpoint back to Blackcomb Mountain, and just after that a suspension bridge over the creek draining Gin and Tonic Lakes. At 1370 m (4500 ft) elevation you cross Twentyone Mile Creek (river-right to river-left) on a footbridge. The bridge is currently badly bent in the centre and can be exciting in high water. It is a short steep ascent from here to the open slopes of the basin that contains Rainbow Lake.

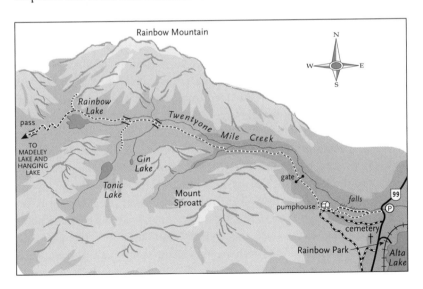

17 HELM LAKE

Round trip 20 km (12.4 mi)   Allow 8.5 hours
Elevation gain 915 m (3000 ft)   High point 1740 m (5700 ft)
Average grade 9.2%

Best July to October   Maps 92G/14 Cheakamus
River; 92J/02 Whistler;
92J/03 Brandywine Falls
Driving distance from Vancouver 125 km (75 mi)

View southwest across the Helm Creek meadows to Black Tusk. (JS)

A bridge over the swift-flowing Cheakamus River makes possible this interesting alternative approach to the high country of Garibaldi Provincial Park around Helm Lake and Black Tusk. It is an access much less frequented than Garibaldi Lake. Here you will not experience the crowd scenes of the trail from Rubble Creek. A campsite along Helm Creek puts numerous points of interest within easy reach: Cinder Cone and Helm Peak, both reminders of the park's volcanic origins, as well as Empetrum Ridge if Helm Creek is fordable. Also, if you have been able to arrange transport at the Rubble Creek parking lot and have lots of staying power, you may continue southward to ford the glacial streams feeding Helm Lake. From there you rise to the Panorama Ridge Trail junction at a point with sweeping views over the country you have just travelled and towards Whistler and the northern mountains of the park. You can then follow the routes described in Hikes 22 and 20 to reach your second vehicle some 24 km (15 mi) by trail from where you left the first.

Zero your odometer at the Cleveland Avenue traffic lights in Squamish. Drive north on Highway 99 towards Whistler for 51 km (32 mi); cross the B.C. Rail tracks, then turn right onto Cheakamus Lake Road. There is a B.C. Parks sign on the highway. After a little over 400 m (1300 ft), stay left at a fork (right is Black Tusk Microwave Road). Remain with the forest road you are now on as it traverses a logged-off area that has been established as a forestry demonstration area. Finally, 8.5 km (5.3 mi) from the highway, the road ends at a parking lot with trail information. Your elevation here is 820 m (2700 ft).

Soon after you start walking, you enter the park and the shade of its fine, tall trees and proceed eastward for about 30 minutes to a fork going right towards the river. Drop down to the river bank and the bridge. On the other side the trail traverses a worn, muddy section but soon improves as it zigzags steadily uphill through the forest and eventually comes within earshot of Helm Creek, with glimpses of it from time to time. At last the grade eases as the track enters the wide upper valley, and the trees thin out to reveal some spectacular views, Black Tusk being particularly striking as it beckons from across the meadows. Soon now you reach a wilderness campsite at around 1555 m (5100 ft) and 8 km (5 mi) from the start. If, however, you plan a day trip, you should push on, gaining another 190 m (620 ft) to crest the next rise. From here, Helm Lake spreads out before you; it is a fine spot to pause and admire the view before you turn your back on the Tusk and wend your way northward again.

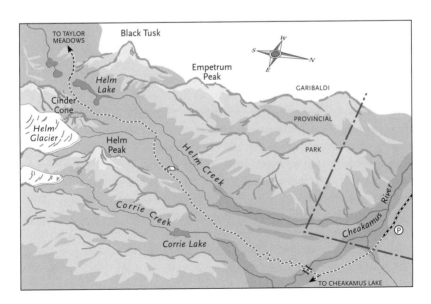

18 BRANDYWINE MEADOWS

Round trip 6 km (3.7 mi)   Allow 3 hours
Elevation gain 550 m (1800 ft)   High point 1500 m (4920 ft)
Average grade 18.3%

Best July to October   Map 92J/03 Brandywine Falls
Driving distance from Vancouver 120 km (75 mi)

The meadows and Brandywine Mountain (top left) blanketed under an early snowfall. (DH)

This very short trip takes you into the alpine area on the divide between the Squamish and Cheakamus Rivers. This open country stretches north-south for more than 30 km (19 mi). Hikes 19 and 28 also access this divide, although Hike 28 begins from the Squamish River side. If your timing is right, the wildflowers in these alpine meadows will be spectacular. From the end of July through September the meadows bloom, but, as in every Eden, there are drawbacks: damp spots early in the season and insects to contend with later. If, of course, your eyes are set on

46

higher things, an intermittent trail continues towards Brandywine Mountain, the approach to which is relatively clear. Remember, though, that you are letting yourself in for another 720 m (2360 ft) of climbing, with an extra 3 hours or so on the trail. This approach road is also an important mountaineering access to Mounts Brew, Fee and Metal Dome. In the winter it is a snowmobile zoo.

Zero your odometer at the Cleveland Avenue traffic lights in Squamish. Drive north on Highway 99 towards Whistler for 44 km (27 mi). Less than 3 km (1.9 mi) past Brandywine Falls Provincial Park, turn left onto Brandywine Forest Service Road. Shortly after leaving the highway the road branches; stay left. Follow this road up the valley for 4.6 km (2.9 mi) to a three-way fork, where you may pause to enjoy the striking view of the jagged peaks of Mount Fee directly ahead. From here you take the middle road, BR10, for another 2.1 km (1.3 mi), continuing to ascend. If your vehicle can handle the road condition, you may drive as far as the trailhead, a distance of 6.7 km (4.2 mi) from the highway. Otherwise park wherever you can. Immediately before a creek is a brown British Columbia Forest Service sign for the Brandywine Meadows Trail.

You immediately start rising steeply in the forest along the east side of the creek until, after some 45 minutes, you approach a logged-over patch with its debris. However, you stay within the margin of the trees as the grade eases briefly, and then negotiate a few damp spots before starting to rise again towards the meadows lying at and above the tree-line. To the east, and lower at 1310 m (4300 ft), is a snowmobile cabin.

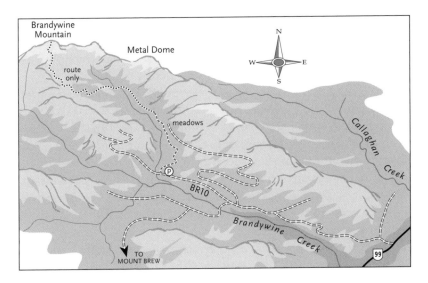

BREW LAKE

Round trip 13 km (8.1 mi)   Allow 7 hours
Elevation gain 1020 m (3350 ft)   High point 1420 m (4650 ft)
Average grade 15.7%

Best July to October   Map 92J/03 Brandywine Falls
Driving distance from Vancouver 110 km (65 mi)

View north across the lake. (CM)

This trip takes you into the alpine terrain that stretches north-south for more than 30 km (19 mi) on the divide between the Squamish and Cheakamus Rivers. Hikes 18 and 28 also access this divide, although Hike 28 starts from the Squamish River side. Your approach to this trail differs from the usual: it follows the B.C. Rail track before turning up the hillside on its way to a series of alpine ridges. There is one large lake, Brew, and several smaller ones. The trail is maintained by University of British Columbia's Varsity Outdoor Club since it gives access to a cabin built on the open ridges, where the depredations of heavy snowfall make maintenance difficult. Although probably overlong for a day trip, an ascent of Mount Brew is straightforward from the lake. Apart from an ascent, the ridges are beautiful rambling country. To the south can be seen Howe Sound, the Stawamus Chief and even Shannon Falls. To the west are Tricouni Peak, Cypress Peak and the spectacular Mount Fee. Brew Lake itself is a very worthwhile objective, although you may well wonder as you struggle up this steep trail.

Zero your odometer at the Cleveland Avenue traffic lights in Squamish. Drive north on Highway 99 towards Whistler for 41 km

(25 mi). Just after crossing the B.C. Rail tracks, turn right into the parking lot of Brandywine Falls Provincial Park.

Walk back down the highway to the tracks. The right-of-way is wide, but watch for trains, especially silent Dayliners. Turn right (south) and walk back along the line for approximately 25 minutes to where it makes a right-angled bend to the west, goes under the B.C. Hydro power line, then turns back sharp south. A short distance beyond this last direction change, on the south side of a small creek, the trail heads off to the west. A small stone pile beside the tracks and a large strip of red cloth in the trees above mark the spot. There is also a post, up the bank, with a Federation of Mountain Clubs of British Columbia Adopt-a-Trail Program sign. This trail has a confusing variety of markers: you will follow small and large orange diamonds, aluminum squares and ovals, and a veritable rainbow of flagging tape. At first you rise through open forest, the understory being predominantly huckleberries! Later come rocky slopes and talus slides. If you have difficulty route-finding in the talus, the trail is usually up the fall-line. As you climb, the route crosses various rocky knolls or works around them. Watch for small cairns at these places and some great views across the valley to Black Tusk. On the higher, gentler stretches, there are blueberries; indeed the upper part of the trail tends to be bushy. The last section traverses a subalpine meadow before rising to the lake in its open bowl.

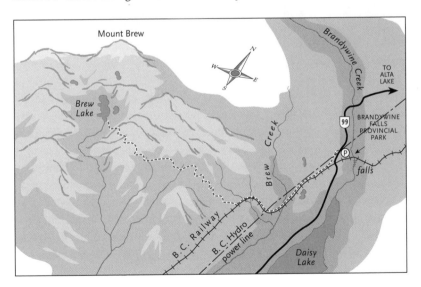

GARIBALDI LAKE

Round trip 18.5 km (11.5 mi)	Allow 6.5 hours
Elevation gain 920 m (3020 ft)	High point 1500 m (4910 ft)
Average grade 9.9%	
Best July to October	Map 92G/14 Cheakamus River
Driving distance from Vancouver 110 km (65 mi)	

Garibaldi Meadows with the Cheakamus and Squamish Valleys and the Tantalus Range beyond. (CM)

The area around Garibaldi Lake is the jewel in the crown that is Garibaldi Provincial Park. There is a large turquoise lake with glaciers flowing into it, wild mountain scenery, volcanic landscapes and colourful flower meadows. No matter how often you experience this place, it is breathtaking every time. The hike described here is a one-day trip that loops up through the meadows below Black Tusk and descends past Garibaldi Lake. On the way you pass through the Taylor Meadows campground, which is the starting point for Hikes 21 and 22. This area is deservedly one of the most popular hiking destinations in southwestern British Columbia. There will be crowds unless you go late in the season, but then you'd miss the flowers.

Zero your odometer at the Cleveland Avenue traffic lights in Squamish. Drive north on Highway 99 towards Whistler for 33 km

(20 mi). There is a B.C. Parks sign on the highway before you branch right on a paved road that, in less than 3 km (1.9 mi), takes you to the Rubble Creek parking lot. The elevation here is 580 m (1900 ft).

From here the well-graded trail zigzags upward through an impressive forest of large Douglas-fir and red cedar. Just above the 6 km sign, you come to an intersection with a map and trail directions and distances. The right branch leads directly to Garibaldi Lake and its satellites. To make a circuit, however, go left, ascending some 150 m (500 ft) until the trees begin to open out as you approach Taylor Meadows. The camp-ground and shelter are all connected by boardwalks, now so necessary to protect the fragile terrain from multitudes of feet. Continuing eastward you descend to cross Taylor Creek and soon come to the old ranger cabin. Take the left fork and travel eastward across the meadows to the next fork, Outhouse Junction, with signs indicating distances to various des-tinations. Turn right and descend gently in long, easy sweeps with the turquoise blue of Garibaldi Lake shining up through the trees. Just above the outlet of Garibaldi Lake you go right at the trail junction. Going left across the creek would take you to the campground beside the lake, the ranger station and the Battleship Islands; but that's another trip. To complete your circuit, follow this right fork, passing two other junctions that return to the Taylor Meadows campground. After circling around Lesser Garibaldi and Barrier Lakes you will arrive at the intersection with map and trail directions; from here it is only 6 km (3.7 mi) back to the parking lot.

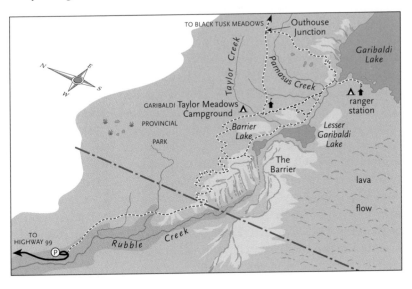

21 BLACK TUSK

from Taylor Meadows campground	Round trip 11 km (6.8 km)	Allow 5 hours
	Elevation gain 820 m (2690 ft)	High point 2315 m (7600 ft)
	Average grade 14.9%	
from parking lot	Round trip 29 km (18 mi)	Allow 10 hours
	Elevation gain 1740 m (5700 ft)	High point 2315 m (7600 ft)
	Average grade 13.4%	
	Best July to October	Map 92G/14 Cheakamus River
	Driving distance from Vancouver 110 km (65 mi)	

The Tusk, seen from the talus slopes below. (CM)

Black Tusk is such a visible and identifiable summit from so many locations in southwestern British Columbia that it is on the tick list of a large percentage of the area's hikers. The view from the top spreads the park before you: with Helm Lake and the Cinder Flats almost at your feet and the glistening summits of the Fitzsimmons Range farther off beyond Cheakamus Lake, with the matchless Garibaldi Lake and its ring of peaks and glaciers to the south, and with the mountains of the Tantalus Range away beyond the Squamish Valley in the southwest. To access the area, see the directions in Hike 20. This is a trip that may be done in one long day from the Rubble Creek parking lot but is much more enjoyable if undertaken from the campgrounds at Taylor Meadows or Garibaldi Lake. The description here is from Taylor Meadows. The main test of the outing comes at the end, since the only way up the last stretch to the crown of the Tusk is by a narrow chimney involving a climb of about 100 m (330 ft). Thus, only properly equipped and experienced parties should attempt it. One other warning: the volcanic rock of the Tusk is loose and friable so beware of falling debris if other climbers are ahead of you, particularly if they are descending.

From the Taylor Meadows campground the route crosses Taylor Creek and goes left at the old ranger cabin and the fork to Garibaldi Lake. Stay with the trail as it makes its way across meadows and alongside small valleys resplendent with flowers of all the colours of the spectrum. Then after some 2 km (1.2 mi) you come to Outhouse Junction and trail directions. The trail from Garibaldi Lake joins you from the right. From this junction, continue eastward a short distance to another fork, and go left on the branch signed "Black Tusk 2.5 km." This new park trail, replacing the old boot-beaten tracks across the meadows, ascends in an ordered fashion, gradually leaving the lush growth of the lower slopes for the unforgiving talus that so plentifully surrounds the great pillar towering above. Just east of the Tusk is a saddle that may serve as a destination for the inexperienced or weary hiker; if you are going all the way, however, continue westward under the almost vertical south wall, passing several chimneys as you go. The last of these provides the only ascent that is relatively safe, and it is here that the trail ends. The chimney should be negotiated with care, although handholds are numerous and the rock formation gives some protection from exposure. Be careful, too, to note the route once you reach the top to ensure that you return by the same one after you have enjoyed the sublime view from the summit.

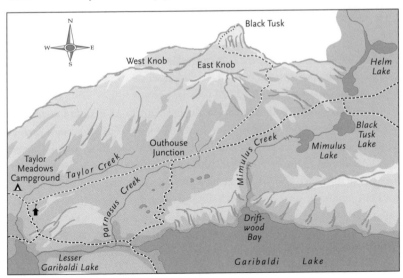

22 PANORAMA RIDGE

from Taylor Meadows campground	Round trip 15 km (9.3 mi)	Allow 5 hours
	Elevation gain 610 m (1990 ft)	High point 2105 m (6900 ft)
	Average grade 8.1%	
from parking lot	Round trip 30 km (19 mi)	Allow 10 hours
	Elevation gain 1520 m (5000 ft)	High point 2105 m (6900 ft)
	Average grade 10.1%	
	Best July to October	Map 92G/14 Cheakamus River
	Driving distance from Vancouver 110 km (65 mi)	

View south from the ridge across Garibaldi Lake to Mount Garibaldi.

Garibaldi Provincial Park's Panorama Ridge is aptly named. On every side your views are superb: the opaque blue-green water of the main lake at your feet contrasts with the gleaming white of Mount Garibaldi's glaciers and snowfields and those in turn with the dark shadow of Table Mountain. You also have the whole variety of volcanic features: Castle Towers and the quaintly named Phyllis's Engine amongst the remnants on the one hand, and the several cones that form Mount Price and Clinker Peak on the other. Behind to the northwest looms the dramatic presence of Black Tusk itself. On the descent from the ridge you look northward along Empetrum Ridge, which is accessible in about 2 hours from the

54

Panorama Ridge junction but which has no official trail. You also look across Cinder Cone and down the Helm Creek Valley, the ascent of which is Hike 17. To access the area, see the directions in Hike 20. Like Hike 21, this trip may be done in one long day from the Rubble Creek parking lot but is much more enjoyable if undertaken from the campgrounds at Taylor Meadows or Garibaldi Lake. From either one you may enjoy it as a gentle hike, giving yourself time to take in the magnificent scenery and appreciate the variety and colour of the flowers.

From the Taylor Meadows campground the route crosses Taylor Creek and goes left at the old ranger cabin and the fork to Garibaldi Lake. Stay with the trail as it meanders across meadows and alongside small valleys full of brightly coloured wildflowers. After 2 km (1.2 mi) you come to Outhouse Junction where the trail from Garibaldi Lake joins you from the right. There are trail directions and, appropriately enough, an outhouse at this intersection. From this junction you continue eastward passing the Black Tusk fork and rising gently as the vegetation becomes ever more lush, enjoying occasional glimpses of Mimulus Lake below and, farther off, Garibaldi Lake and its mountain beyond. Then you come out at the top of a rise overlooking Helm Lake and the wide valley with the dormant Cinder Cone in its midst. Again the trail forks and you go right for Panorama Ridge, dropping to pass east of Black Tusk Lake before zigzagging up through patches of trees and heather to the spine that runs south towards the high point. Very soon you are above the trees, following cairns that guide you over the shattered rocks of this open, windy ridge. Finally you circle a little to the west and join the old route to the top from that side. With time to spare you may wander east and west along the crest, admiring the many small plants that cling to life in the crevices and sheltered places.

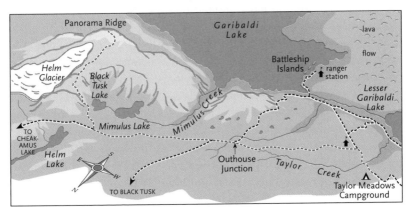

ELFIN LAKES

Round trip 22 km (14 mi)

Allow 6.5 hours

Elevation gain 620 m (2030 ft)

High point 1565 m (5130 ft)

Average grade 5.6%

Best July to October

Maps 92G/14 Cheakamus River; 92G/15 Mamquam Mountain

Driving distance from Vancouver 85 km (50 mi)

Atwell Peak and Mount Garibaldi, with Opal Cone behind the lakes. (JS)

The trip to Elfin Lakes and Diamond Head Lodge is probably Garibaldi Provincial Park's second most popular hike, after Garibaldi Lake. There are beautiful summer meadows with flowers galore, contrasting with the wild glaciers spilling off the east side of Mount Garibaldi. The volcanic landscape flowing east leads to Mamquam Mountain, another riotously glaciated peak. Although the lodge has not provided accommodation for many years, you may still stay overnight in the Elfin Lakes Shelter ($10 per night) erected by B.C. Parks or in the campground ($3 per night) if you wish to spend more than one day in this scenic area. There are then easy trips for those who wish to explore farther: a track continues to The Saddle, lying between The Gargoyles and Columnar Peak, or still farther to Little Diamond Head at the end of Alice Ridge. There is also Hike 24 to Mamquam Lake.

From the Cleveland Avenue traffic lights in Squamish, drive north on Highway 99 for 4 km (2.5 mi). Turn right onto the road signed for Garibaldi Park (Diamond Head); it is also signed Mamquam Road. Follow this route 16 km (9.9 mi) to the parking lot at the trailhead. The road first parallels the river, rising steadily, then after passing a small cabin development, makes a sharp left turn and enters the park. After this point the going may be rough in spots but is generally quite passable for a 2WD.

Beyond the gate and the information boards a rough road switchbacks up high on the south side of Mashiter Creek, first through forest, then over the subalpine Red Heather Meadows where there is a day shelter and campground, 5 km (3.1 mi) from your start. Just past the campground, the hiking trail diverges left from the bike trail, which stays on the old 4WD road. They rejoin 1 km (0.6 mi) later to rise steadily to the trail's high point on Paul Ridge, along whose west side you have been working so far. The best views have been behind to the pointed summits of Mount Habrich and the Sky Pilot group in the south and to the snowy peaks of the Tantalus Range in the southwest. Now the spectacle ahead opens up with Mount Garibaldi standing proudly above its glaciers on the one hand and Mamquam Mountain and its icefields on the other. From the ridge, a gentle descent of 150 m (500 ft) leads to the lakes, the shelter and the old lodge. The campground is situated in the meadow below, only 1 km (0.6 mi) farther.

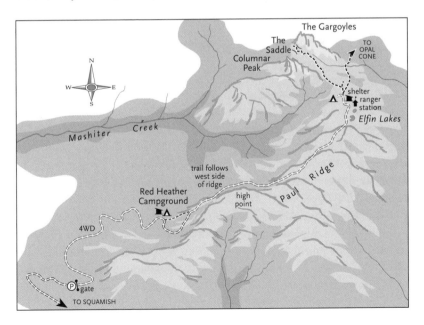

24 MAMQUAM LAKE

to Opal Cone	Round trip 13 km (8.1 mi)	Allow 6 hours
	Elevation gain 365 m (1200 ft)	High point 1740 m (5700 ft)
	Average grade 5.6%	
to Mamquam Lake	Round trip 22 km (14 mi)	Allow 9 hours
	Elevation gain 610 m (2000 ft)	High point 1525 m (5000 ft)
	Average grade 5.5%	
	Best July to September	Map 92G/15 Mamquam Mountain
	Driving distance from Vancouver 85 km (50 mi)	

Bridge over Ring Creek.

If you have followed the directions for Hike 23, you will now be in position to travel this route. It is one of the most rewarding trips from Elfin Lakes and takes you across Ring Creek and past Opal Cone. You also cross Zig Zag Creek to reach this lake, beautifully situated at the foot of Pyramid Mountain. Alas the lake is 150 m (500 ft) lower than your start at Elfin Lakes. This is a longish one-day trip with most of the climbing on the return journey. However, you do have a shorter alternative in Opal Cone itself, a round trip that gives splendid views of Mount Garibaldi and the Bishop Glacier as well as of the glaciated sprawl of the Mamquam Massif. Of course, if you are feeling energetic, you can traverse over the top of Opal Cone on your way to Mamquam Lake. Another warning: before setting out on the trail you should check with B.C. Parks to find out whether the creeks to be negotiated en route are passable; in hot weather they may run high with glacial meltwater, and the bridge is subject to misadventure.

A short distance beyond the Elfin Lakes Shelter, above the campground, a sign points right for Mamquam Lake. Going left is the Saddle Trail and a route to Little Diamond Head. This is the limit of access for mountain bikes. At first you descend on an easy grade into the valley of Ring Creek with its steep lateral moraine sides. Cross the creek, possibly on a bridge, and once on the east bank continue north for a short distance before your route swings back and ascends the valley sidewall. This brings you to the edge of Opal Cone's meadows. To climb to the rim of this extinct volcano, you may go left here and follow the moraine crest to a steep grassy slope, thence along the rim to the top. If you are going directly to Mamquam Lake, continue on the main trail to the next lateral moraine. Here is where the route that traversed over the Cone rejoins. The main trail continues eastward, crossing the kind of lunar landscape associated with areas recently glaciated. Then it descends to the valley of Zig Zag Creek, the west branch of Skookum Creek, before rising again on the other side to the small glacial lakes called Rampart Ponds. Finally you reach the view of Mamquam Lake, 250 m (800 ft) below you, with the trail switchbacking down to it. There is a campsite by the lake for those who have chosen to stay overnight.

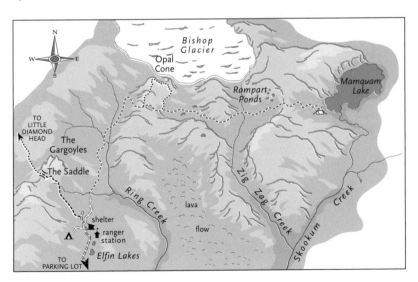

25 ELAHO CANYON

Round trip 13 km (8.1 mi)	Allow 5 hours
Elevation gain 90 m (300 ft)	High point 640 m (2100 ft)
Average grade 1.4%	

Best May to November	Maps 92J/05 Clendenning Creek; wcwc Elaho–Meager Trail

Driving distance from Vancouver 170 km (105 mi)

Blueberry Falls dropping into the Elaho River.

This is the southern section of Western Canada Wilderness Committee's 22 km (14 mi) Elaho to Meager Hiking Trail in the proposed Stoltmann National Park. The northern section is described in Hike 4. It is an area of controversy. Interfor has cutting rights and wishes to exercise them. Environmentalists wish to preserve the largest remaining valley-bottom temperate rainforest in southwestern British Columbia. Described here is the trail past Blueberry Falls to Canyon Camp, including the Douglas-fir Loop Trail. The loop takes you through a stand of more than fifty huge old growth trees; if they have not been felled before you get there! You could just hike the loop, but the canyon of the Elaho River is a wild place and its tributary streams are no more tame.

Zero your odometer at the Cleveland Avenue traffic lights in Squamish. Drive north on

Highway 99 for 10 km (6.2 mi) and turn left onto Squamish Valley Road. Keep left at the fork at 13 km (8.1 mi). At 33 km (20 mi) the gravel surface starts and you will see that the distance signs on this road, which is called S-Main, are in miles from Squamish. At the 37 mile sign, turn left and cross the bridge over the Squamish River. The road is now called E-Main and you follow the Elaho River upstream, staying on river-left. At 96 km (60 mi) take the left fork onto E-1000. Stay on E-1000 and, after crossing Lava Creek at about 102 km (63 mi), look for trailhead signs.

From the trailhead, drop down to the main hiking trail along the canyon rim. The roaring water is 120 m (390 ft) below. As you travel farther up the valley the trees are not of impressive size, although there are numerous yellow cedars and western white pines. Less than an hour into the hike you arrive at the impressive canyon of Cesna Creek. It requires you to travel up the creek to where a splendid bridge has been constructed. There are plenty of orange markers to keep you on the trail. Rocky Camp is situated on an open knoll a couple of hours from your start. Back down on the canyon rim, another hour or so will get you to 70-m (230-ft) Blueberry Falls. Not far past the falls is Canyon Camp, a small opening with a great view up the river and a fine site for a tent. The trail, of course, continues; but if you have not walked the Douglas-fir Loop Trail, return and do it now!

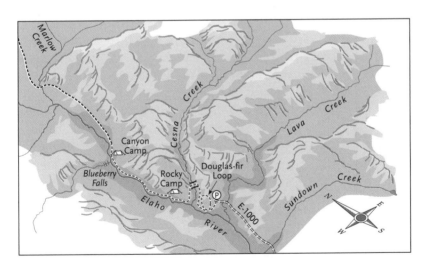

BUG LAKE

Round trip 6 km (3.7 mi)	Allow 5 hours
Elevation gain 850 m (2800 ft)	High point 1250 m (4100 ft)
Average grade 28.3%	
Best July to September	Maps 92J/04 Princess Louisa Inlet; 92J/05 Clendenning Creek
Driving distance from Vancouver 160 km (100 mi)	

This trip to Bug Lake on the slopes below Sun Peak is the east end of the JCWild Trail, which starts in Sims Creek and connects to the Loquilts Trail descending into Princess Louisa Inlet. The trail is in the southwest corner of the proposed Stoltmann National Park. With time and energy you can hike above the lake, but Sun Peak is another 820 m (2700 ft) higher and an extra 10 km (6.2 mi) return. Sims Creek has also been the scene of controversy between loggers and environmentalists. The Magic Grove of western red cedars was cut in 1998, including one tree more than 800 years old.

Zero your odometer at the Cleveland Avenue traffic lights in Squamish. Drive north on Highway 99 for 10 km (6.2 mi) and turn left onto Squamish Valley Road. Keep left at the fork at 10 km (8.1 mi). At 33 km (20 mi) the gravel surface starts and you will see that the distance signs on this road, which is called S-Main, are in miles from Squamish. At the 37 mile sign, turn left and cross the bridge over the Squamish River. The road is now called E-Main and you follow the Elaho River

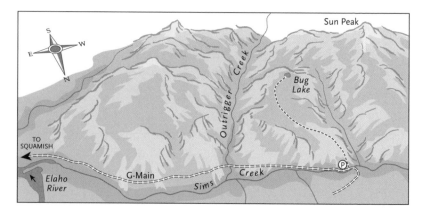

upstream, staying on river-left. After the 43 mile sign, turn left and cross the bridge onto G-Main. At 85 km (53 mi), the road begins to curve into Sims Creek and at 88 km (55 mi) you cross Outrigger Creek. Less than 2 km (1.2 mi) later, before the road begins to dip to cross Sims Creek, there is a large landing on your right. Park here.

Southwestern view across the lake towards Sun Peak.

Less than 100 m (325 ft) back along the road, flagging tape up the steep bank indicates the start of the trail. The lower part of the trail is hiked regularly by participants in the Witness Program, a cross-cultural collaboration designed to promote respect for nature. Above that the trail sees very little use. The trailbed is, however, generally good; and flagging tape is usually visible. The spectacularly large trees in the first hour of the hike will give you some excuse to take a break on this steep ascent. You follow a creek to your east finally crossing it about 1 hour from your start. You also encounter some bluffs with water running over them which you negotiate. After about 2 hours, there are views across the Sims Creek Valley to the rocky bowls of the peaks there. As you start into the subalpine area, several ropes, in wet spots, can be used as handlines on the descent. The views improve steadily as you gain elevation. Finally at Bug Lake, in the heather meadows, the ridge to Princess Louisa Inlet rises above.

27 SIGURD CREEK

to Crooked Falls	Round trip 6 km (3.7 mi)	Allow 3 hours
	Elevation gain 425 m (1400 ft)	High point 490 m (1600 ft)
	Average grade 14.1%	
	Best June to October	
to second viewpoint	Round trip 9 km (5.6 mi)	Allow 5 hours
	Elevation gain 825 m (2700 ft)	High point 885 m (2900 ft)
	Average grade 18.3%	
	Best July to September	

Map 92G/14 Cheakamus River
Driving distance from Vancouver 105 km (65 mi)

The north slopes of Pelion and Ossa Mountains, seen from west of the second viewpoint.

This trip takes you into the rarely hiked Ashlu River Valley. You can take a short hike to Crooked Falls, which is good at any time of year but especially spectacular during spring runoff. Or you can make a longer hike by continuing up the trail past the falls junction to two viewpoints that look out over the confluence of the Ashlu and Squamish Rivers to Garibaldi Lake and its surrounding peaks. Cloudburst Mountain is in the foreground. If you do not mind hiking in the dark, catch these views at sunset. The trail is a work-in-progress past the second viewpoint. If you are not averse to negotiating slide alder, another hour's hike beyond the upper viewpoint will give you an amazing view of the glaciers spilling off Ossa and Pelion Mountains.

Zero your odometer at the Cleveland Avenue traffic lights in Squamish. Drive north on Highway 99 for 10 km (6.2 mi) and turn left onto Squamish Valley Road. Keep left at the fork at 13 km (8.1 mi). At 33 km (20 mi) the gravel surface starts and you will see that the distance signs on this road, which is called S-Main, are in miles from Squamish. Cross the two bridges, over the Squamish River at the 21 mile sign, that access the Ashlu Main. Do not take any possible right turns. Stay on the main road to cross two more bridges, this time over the Ashlu River. Just across the second of these bridges, a bit before 36 km (22 mi), is branch road A-200 on your left. With a rugged 4WD vehicle it is possible to drive a short distance up this road, otherwise park on A-Main. It is less than 15 minutes walk up A-200 to the actual trailhead.

The walking trail takes off to the left at a right-hand bend (the second switchback) in the road, traversing an older, overgrown road for about 15 minutes before turning uphill. There are orange markers on the trail. It is about 300 m (1000 ft) of elevation gain on an open hillside with some fine large Douglas-fir from here to the falls junction. Just before the junction, a large white quartz rock intrudes onto the trail, then you traverse south under a mossy rock wall. The falls are less than 1 km (0.6 mi) from the trail fork but 50 m (160 ft) lower. The first viewpoint is not far above the falls junction. It is marked with a small plaque in memory of Randy Stoltmann, after whom the proposed Stoltmann National Park is named. From the first to the second viewpoints is 380 m (1240 ft) of elevation gain. The trail approaches Sigurd Creek, and some cascades are visible through the trees. A fairly stiff ascent follows through fine open forest before you arrive at a second viewpoint, which is on a knoll just off the trail.

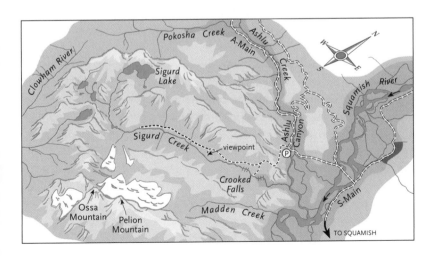

28 TRICOUNI MEADOWS

to Cypress Lake	Round trip 14 km (8.7 mi)	Allow 5 hours
	Elevation gain 305 m (1000 ft)	High point 1495 m (4900 ft)
	Average grade 4.4%	
	Best July to October	
to Tricouni Peak	Round trip 14 km (8.7 mi)	Allow 7 hours
	Elevation gain 915 m (3000 ft)	High point 2100 m (6900 ft)
	Average grade 13.1%	
	Best July to September	

Maps 92G/14 Cheakamus River; 92J/03 Brandywine Falls
Driving distance from Vancouver 120 km (75 mi)

The west and main summits of Tricouni Peak, viewed northeast from the meadows.

This trip takes you into the alpine country on the divide between the Squamish and Cheakamus Rivers. Hikes 18 and 19 also access this divide but from the Cheakamus side. Among the peaks, glaciers, meadows and lakes are many objectives, only two of which are listed here: the large lake below Cypress Peak or the subsidiary summit of Tricouni Peak, which gives panoramic views. The times and elevations quoted are from the landing at the trailhead.

Zero your odometer at the Cleveland Avenue traffic lights in Squamish. Drive north on Highway 99 for 10 km (6.2 mi) and turn left onto Squamish Valley Road. Keep left at the fork at 13 km (8.1 mi). At 33 km (20 mi) the gravel surface starts and you will see that the distance signs on this road, which is called S-Main, are in miles from Squamish. At 38 km (24 mi), about 1.4 km (0.9 mi) after High Falls Creek bridge, Branch 200 starts uphill on your right. Zero your odometer again here. At the 2.3 km (1.4 mi) fork, go right. As you lose elevation at 5.1 km (3.2 mi), the High Falls Creek Trail comes in from the right. At the 6.0 km (3.7 mi) fork, go right. Do not go left at 6.5 km (4.0 mi) or 6.8 km (4.2 mi); but do go left at 6.9 km (4.3 mi). If you go too far you will come to the bridge over High Falls Creek in 200 m (650 ft). Your road has recently been cross-ditched. At 8.0 km (5.0 mi) swing left onto an older road. High-clearance 2WDs should drive 1 km (0.6 mi) to just before a creek crossing. A rugged 4WD may be able to drive to the landing at 10.5 km (6.5 mi).

From the landing the trail drops slightly to follow the creek upstream on river-left. There is occasional flagging tape for marking but the footbed is obvious, especially when you get to the mud holes! You are immediately into subalpine meadows in a narrow valley bottom, therefore it is wet underfoot. This is not a trail to hike in the wet season. It is a scenic walk beside the creek and less than 1.5 hours to the first lake. Here the views open out, with Tricouni Peak to your right. The west summit is the rounded peak on the left; if that is your objective, take the line of least resistance in that direction. No established trail leads to the top. If you are heading for the big lake, follow the trail around the east side of the first two lakes then through a narrow pass. Time and energy can dictate the rest of your day. The meadows stretch on.

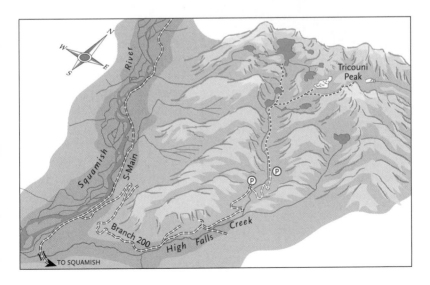

29 HIGH FALLS CREEK

Round trip 12 km (7.5 mi)   Allow 5 hours
Elevation gain 640 m (2100 ft)   High point 715 m (2350 ft)
Average grade 10.7%

Best May to November   Map 92G/14 Cheakamus
    River
Driving distance from Vancouver 105 km (65 mi)

Rainbow below the waterfall.

Do not be misled by the moderate-looking statistics for this outing—in its early stages the trail ascends steeply on bluffs above the falls. Try to choose a clear, sunny day for this hike since its views are superb—of the falls themselves, of the Tantalus Range to the southwest and, on the return trip, of the upper Squamish River and the peaks on the divide between the Squamish and Ashlu Rivers. Clear day or not it is an attractive trail, with some glorious moss gardens to admire: yellow and bronze on the rocks and bright green in the depths of the forest. To make a loop, you can descend by the road rather than reversing your ascent route.

Zero your odometer at the Cleveland Avenue traffic lights in Squamish. Drive north on Highway 99 for 10 km (6.2 mi) and turn left onto Squamish Valley Road. Keep left at the fork at 13 km (8.1 mi). At 33 km (20 mi) the gravel surface starts and you will see that the distance signs on this road, which is called S-Main, are in miles from Squamish. After 36 km

(22 mi) watch up ahead for the bridge over High Falls Creek. Park in the wide pull-off just before the bridge.

Walk north across the bridge, and 100 m (325 ft) farther watch for flagging tape on your right and a sign in the trees. Initially you are on an old skid road, but it quickly becomes a steep trail. After some 30 minutes of steady climbing there is a section of chain for assistance. Then comes your first of three viewpoints of the falls, particularly spectacular in the late spring runoff when a rainbow gives a halo effect to the great torrent of water. Just above is an insulated cable handline. More steady climbing brings you to a bluff with a variety of views of surrounding peaks as well as of the braided Squamish River in its U-shaped valley. Beyond here the trail enters mature forest and veers left, then swings back towards the creek but high above it. Leaving the shade of the tall trees, the trail crosses a cutover area now being reclaimed by young conifers and a variety of shrubs and flowers. A final scramble over a small rock slide brings you up onto the logging road a little beyond its high point, looking northeast towards Tricouni Peak and southeast towards Cloudburst Mountain. Turn back left here to make this Branch 200 road your return route. As an alternative to scrambling down the bluffs, it is 5.1 km (3.2 mi) to S-Main. From the junction of Branch 200 and S-Main, a walk of 1.4 km (0.9 mi) brings you back to your vehicle.

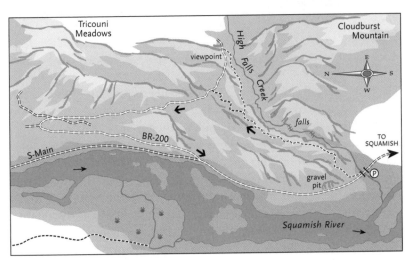

30 PINECONE LAKE

from start of 4WD | Round trip 18 km (12 mi) | Allow 9 hours
Elevation gain 1220 m (4000 ft) | High point 1980 m (6500 ft)
Average grade 13.5%

from road end | Round trip 10 km (6.2 mi) | Allow 6 hours
Elevation gain 670 m (2200 ft) | High point 1980 m (6500 ft)
Average grade 13.4%

Best July to September | Map 92G/10 Pitt River
Driving distance from Vancouver 100 km (60 mi)

View east over the lake to Remote Peak (behind) and Mount Judge Howay (top right). (IM)

The newly established Pinecone Burke Provincial Park stretches through seldom-travelled country from Garibaldi Park to Coquitlam. This trip, a partially flagged route that takes you to the top of a 1980 m (6500 ft) summit looking down on Pinecone Lake, follows a beautiful subalpine ridge that provides obvious direction—as long as you know how to use a map and compass. There are also views north to Mount Garibaldi and Mamquam Mountain, and south to rarely visited Meslilloet Mountain. November Lake nestles in a steep bowl below the ridge.

One kilometre (0.6 mi) south of Squamish, just before Highway 99 crosses the Stawamus River, turn right onto Mamquam River Forest Service Road. Zero your odometer here. At 4 km (2.5 mi) a Mamquam River access road branches off left, so stay right; but 100 m (325 ft) later, when Stawamus–Indian Forest Service Road goes right, you stay left. At 14 km (8.7 mi) cross Nine Mile bridge over the Mamquam River, and

400 m (1300 ft) farther turn right and cross the bridge over Skookum Creek. At 23.2 km (14.4 mi) keep left on M-Line and 300 m (1000 ft) farther, at the 15 Mile sign, stay left. Before 29 km, at the 18 Mile sign, a tracked Madill Spar is parked on the right at the junction of E-Main and S-Main. Go left on E-Main for 300 m (1000 ft), then left again onto E-100. With a 4WD, you drive another 2 km (1.2 mi) to the junction of E-100 and E-110, then left on E-110 for 2 km (1.2 mi) to the road end at GR089986.

It is only 40 m (130 ft) across logging debris into the big trees. Take a bearing of 84°; follow loggers' flagging tape only if it is in this direction. As you ascend, the ridge becomes less rounded and more well defined. You should pick up the orange or pink flagging tape marking the route fairly quickly. If not, check your compass bearing occasionally. As you rise up the ridge, the timber gets smaller and the open patches get larger. After an hour you crest a rise with cairns for route markers. There is also a short steep brushy section where you can haul yourself up on the blueberry bushes. Be cautious about corniced snow on the north side of the ridge. About 2 hours from the road end an open knoll allows panoramic views and a look at your route ahead. From here you have to drop 100 m (330 ft) into a col before rising 365 m (1200 ft) to the top. It is a fairly steep descent; if there is snow on the slope, think twice! Once in the col it is a straightforward hike on a mix of meadow, glacier-polished rock and snow to the summit.

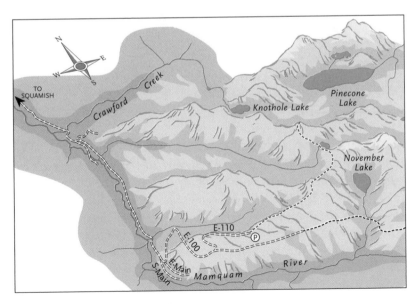

31 BOISE TRAIL

from start of 4WD	Round trip 20 km (12.4 mi)	Allow 8 hours
	Elevation gain 825 m (2700 ft)	High point 1585 m (5200 ft)
	Average grade 8.3%	
from road end	Round trip 12 km (7.5 mi)	Allow 5 hours
	Elevation gain 395 m (1300 ft)	High point 1585 m (5200 ft)
	Average grade 6.6%	
	Best August to October	Maps 92G/10 Pitt River;
		WCWC Boise Valley
	Driving distance from Vancouver 100 km (60 mi)	

Mount Gillespie, viewed north from the trail. (IM)

The Boise Trail was built by the Western Canada Wilderness Committee to demonstrate the value of protecting this area from further resource removal. The result was Pinecone Burke Provincial Park. The 50 km (31 mi) trail takes you from Coquitlam to Squamish. The trip described here is only the first short section of the west end of the trail and leads you into Mamquam Pass, the headwaters of the Mamquam River.

One kilometre (0.6 mi) south of Squamish, just before Highway 99 crosses the Stawamus River, turn right onto Mamquam River Forest Service Road. Zero your odometer here. At 4 km (2.5 mi) a Mamquam

River access road branches off left, so stay right; but 100 m (325 ft) later, when Stawamus–Indian Forest Service Road goes right, you stay left. At 14 km (8.7 mi) cross Nine Mile bridge over the Mamquam River, and 400 m (1300 ft) farther turn right and cross the bridge over Skookum Creek. At 23.2 km (14.4 mi) keep left on M-Line and 300 m (1000 ft) farther, at the 15 Mile sign, stay left. Before 29 km, at the 18 Mile sign, a tracked Madill Spar is parked on the right at the junction of E-Main and S-Main. Go left on E-Main for 300 m (1000 ft), then left again onto E-100. With a 4WD, you drive another 2 km (1.2 mi) to the junction of E-100 and E-110, then right on E-100 for 2 km (1.2 km) to a washout at GR097979.

Walk 2 km (1.2 mi) along the road to November Creek. The logging bridge has been removed but there are three cedar logs cabled together over which you can walk. Just across this bridge there was a road to the left which has now been intentionally destroyed. From where this road once started, look up the slope through the clear-cut at an angle of 45°. You should see some small rocky bluffs about 5 m (16 ft) high. Just past them is a tongue of mature trees that was spared from the chainsaw. Make for the lowest of these trees: the trail starts there. Orange metal markers indicate the sometimes faint footbed. You gain height fairly steadily, with views to the peaks behind November Lake. As you move into the subalpine terrain, there are fewer trees on which to place markers, so that a minor snowfall would make this trail a challenge to follow. An hour and a half should get you to the high point of the trail, with a view south to Meslilloet Mountain. From here it is 3 km (1.9 mi) return and a drop (and subsequent ascent) of 245 m (800 ft) to Mamquam Pass.

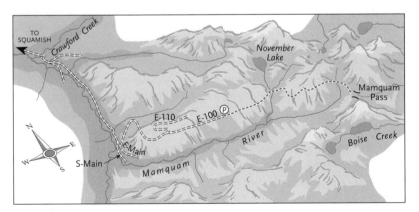

32 MOUNT RODERICK

Round trip 26 km (17.3 mi)   Allow 12 hours
Elevation gain 1475 m (4840 ft)   High point 1475 m (4840 ft)
Average grade 14.7%

Best June to October   Map 92G/11 Squamish
Driving distance from Vancouver 65 km (40 mi)

Henriette Lake and the dam, with Sechelt Ridge in the distance. (CM)

Mount Roderick is on the Sunshine Coast but it has been listed here since the access is from Darrell Bay, just south of Squamish. As you drive Highway 99 north from Horseshoe Bay, your major views are of the peaks on the west side of Howe Sound. Mount Roderick is not one of the more spectacular summits, but it is a pleasant hike, with a free boat ride thrown in. Since Western Pulp, owners of Woodfibre Mill, do not allow private vehicles to use their roads, leave your vehicle on the east side and cross as a foot passenger. Your hike then starts from sea level, and for that reason you may consider making a backpack trip into this magnificent and lonely alpine area, with one of the lakes en route, Henriette or Sylvia, as alternative destinations for a day trip. Phone Western Pulp at (604) 892-6600 prior to your hike.

Drive 39 km (24 mi) north from Horseshoe Bay to the Darrell Bay terminal, just south of Shannon Falls. Park in the public lot. The ferry allows bicycles, and dogs are also accepted. Currently the relevant sailings from Darrell Bay are 7:15 am, 8:30 am and 9:30 am. The relevant return sailings are 5:45 pm, 7:25 pm, and 9:15 pm. When you arrive on the other side, go to the first-aid post and register. You can also ask for directions through the mill site.

Follow the road as it switchbacks uphill, turning first towards Mill Creek then back to the south. In the area cleared for B.C. Hydro power lines, keep right at all junctions as the route rises parallel with, and on the north side of, Woodfibre Creek. Finally, after about 6 km (3.7 mi), the road ends at the creek in a deep gorge spanned by a smart metal footbridge. A short distance beyond, the road dwindles to a trail that zigzags up the ridge, crossing and recrossing the route of the old construction railway from the lake outlet. On the right-hand side stands a cabin and beyond it a helipad on the rock above. To continue, turn right at the helipad and pick up the narrow trail that goes north up the wooded spur of the ridge and finally levels off, more or less, at a little over 1220 m (4000 ft). A shallow basin just west of the ridge contains Sylvia Lake, an attractive centre for ridge walking. Sechelt Ridge stretches south and west from the opposite side of the lake. The trail to Mount Roderick continues along the ridge, mainly on the north side of the crest. From the summit of Mount Roderick, the mass of Mount Sedgwick looms ahead. Only a saddle separates you from Mount Sedgwick's snowfields and rock. One final note: on your descent from Mount Roderick, be sure to take its southwest (right-hand) ridge, not the southeast, which leads you far from the beaten track. And don't forget to sign out on your return to Woodfibre.

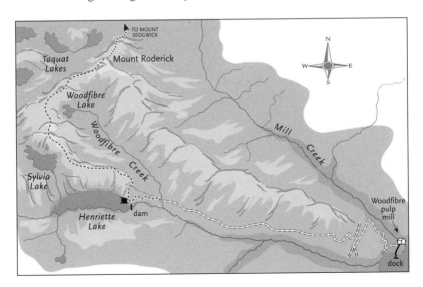

33 STAWAMUS CHIEF

to Centre Peak	Round trip 9 km (5.6 mi)	Allow 3.5 hours
	Elevation gain 590 m (1940 ft)	High point 652 m (2138 ft)
	Average grade 13.1%	
to North Peak	Round trip 11 km (6.8 mi)	Allow 4.5 hours
	Elevation gain 605 m (1980 ft)	High point 665 m (2180 ft)
	Average grade 11.0%	
	Best March to November	Map 92G/11 Squamish
	Driving distance from Vancouver 65 km (40 mi)	

Stawamus Chief is the great rock mass that towers over the highway just south of Squamish. Stawamus Chief Provincial Park, in which it lies, is cooperatively managed by B.C. Parks and the Squamish Rockclimbers Association. Rock climbers scale its face by various routes, but hikers can achieve any one of the three peaks, or all three if they like, if they keep to the rear of the rock. The three summits are South (First), Centre (Second) and North (Third). South Peak is the most visited. Described here is the traverse over the centre and north summits. Once the climbing is past, you can enjoy the summit view of Mount Garibaldi and the Tantalus Range. To return you can descend from the saddle between the summits. However, just reversing your ascent route back over Centre Peak is the most scenic.

Zero your odometer at Horseshoe Bay. Drive north on Highway 99 and, 1 km (0.6 mi) north of Shannon Falls, at 42 km (26 mi) turn right

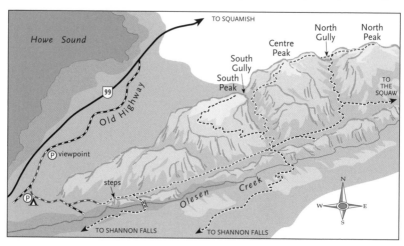

into the Stawamus Chief Viewpoint parking lot. Across the lot, on your right, is access to the campground. If the gate to the campground is open, you can drive a little farther; but it is only a 5-minute difference.

From the campground, the old road ends at a one-time quarry. The trail starts up the rocks at the east end, ascending for the first 50 m (175 ft) or so on a flight of wooden steps, near the top of which a second trail enters from the right. This route crosses the turbulent Olesen Creek from Shannon Falls Provincial Park, an alternative start to the hike. Farther up the main trail, ignore a track to the right that recrosses

View north across the face of the Chief to Squamish and the Smoke Bluffs.

the creek en route to the top of the falls. A couple of minutes later, go left at the next junction. Your major choice is just ahead: left for South Peak, right for Centre and North Peaks. Going right here takes you up a gully, then follows a rocky ledge into the open. Turn right again into a rock cleft crossed by a log bridge, then head steeply up to the rocky slopes of the crest ridge. Walk north along this ridge to the top. To reach North Peak, which is the highest, continue along the crest, descending into the saddle. This saddle, the upper terminal of the North Gully climbing route, is followed by a junction with the alternative trail to North Peak that avoids Centre Peak. Continue into a wooded trench, along a rock face and over a ledge to reach the open. From here turn first left, then right, walking on open rock to the summit.

34 PETGILL LAKE

to the lake	Round trip 11.5 km (7.1 mi)	Allow 6 hours
	Elevation gain 640 m (2100 ft)	High point 760 m (2500 ft)
	Average grade 11.1%	
	Best March to November	
to Goat Ridge	Round trip 19.5 km (12 mi)	Allow 10 hours
	Elevation gain 1630 m (5340 ft)	High point 1750 m (5740 ft)
	Average grade 16.7%	
	Best July to October	

Map 92G/11 Squamish
Driving distance from Vancouver 60 km (35 mi)

Squamish, Mount Garibaldi and the Stawamus Chief, as seen from the trail.

Although it makes a popular hike for a warm day because it winds through shady woods, the trail to Petgill Lake is also suited to winter walking, since its high point is only 760 m (2500 ft) above sea level. This pleasant little lake is in a bowl, so to widen the aspect there is a short trail past the lake to a viewpoint looking out over Howe Sound. If you desire some extra challenge, the trail to Goat Ridge gives you a much more strenuous hike, adding another 990 m (3240 ft) of climbing on a route that is sketchy here and there. On the ridge are attractive meadows and ponds and a close-up view of Sky Pilot Mountain, while Mount Garibaldi and Mamquam Mountain fill in the scene to the north and northeast.

Zero your odometer at Horseshoe Bay. Drive north on Highway 99 and, 3 km (1.9 mi) north of Britannia Beach, at 36 km (22 mi) pass Browning Lake and turn immediately left into the parking lot of Murrin Provincial Park.

The signposted trail begins on the east side of the highway about a 5 minute walk north of the parking area. At first it climbs the bluffs overlooking the highway, heading north along a power line for a short distance before entering the forest. Despite the tree cover, there are nicely spaced viewpoints, west across Howe Sound and north to Squamish and beyond. Next the trail drops slightly to join a logging road, with which you stay until it is blocked at the point where your route turns off left. From here you make your way over several lateral ridges, the first, an attractive little hogsback, providing a view to the southwest. Finally, after descending into yet another dark gully, you come to a fork with a trail signed "Goat Ridge" to the right and almost immediately thereafter another trail going right, this time signed "Lake Circuit." Ignore both right turns for the time being and proceed onto the rock straight ahead for your first sight of the lake below in its pleasant, wooded basin. At the foot of the rock turn left and walk 300 m (1000 ft) to a lookout on a bluff high above Howe Sound with views to Woodfibre Mill and the westerly mountains. On your return, go forward towards the lake and then left to begin the circuit in a clockwise direction. Your circuit nearly ended, you come to a camping spot where a left turn takes you back to your outward route for a speedy return trip; the more exciting choice, however, is to the right via the trailbuilder's cliffhanging whimsy, a narrow ledge to be walked, albeit with a plastic chain for moral support.

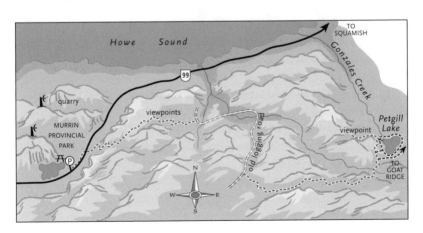

35 DEEKS PEAK

Round trip 16 km (9.9 mi)
Elevation gain 1615 m (5300 ft)
Average grade 20.2%

Allow 10 hours
High point 1675 m (5500 ft)

Best July to October
Driving distance from Vancouver 50 km (30 mi)

Map 92G/11 Squamish

View southwest across Howe Sound, seen from below the peak. (LB)

Much less frequently travelled than the trail to Deeks Lake, the route to Deeks Peak can be overgrown and bushy. Still, it will get you without much difficulty at least as far as attractive little Kallahne Lake beneath the mountain's northwest slopes. En route are fine views across Howe Sound to Mount Sedgwick and the peaks of the Tantalus Range farther north. On top you may enjoy the fruits of your labours, with outstanding views west across Howe Sound and its islands, north to the mountains of Garibaldi Park, northeast to Sky Pilot Mountain and southeast to the North Shore mountains. The trip uses the same parking lot as the Howe Sound Crest Trail (Hike 36), part of which is also called the Deeks Lake Trail.

Zero your odometer at Horseshoe Bay. Drive north on Highway 99 and, at 22 km (14 mi), watch for a brown wooden sign on the right-hand side of the road saying "Deeks Lake Trail 500 m." There is a clearly marked parking area on the left opposite a trailhead signboard.

The trail, designated by orange markers, begins almost opposite and proceeds up the side of a pretty little creek to a power line on an open bluff with a fine view. Back in the trees you join an old logging road on which you go right. In about 5 minutes go left on a washed-out and somewhat overgrown branch (the right fork is signed "Deeks Lake"). You now turn back slightly north, gaining height on a number of switchbacks, in the course of which you approach Kallahne Creek several times. The road is difficult to follow due to intrusive brush but improves at an elevation of 900 m (2950 ft) after you cross the creek, which may be a torrent early in the year or all underground later. Beyond the creek, pick your way across a rockfall, find the ruins of the road again and turn back on it up the creek to the lake at 1160 m (3800 ft), 4.5 km (2.8 mi) from your start. To continue, make your way over the log jam that bridges the outlet and head around the lake, past a cabin near which are views over Howe Sound to the Rainy River peaks. Turn south past the lake, working up the washed-out road to its end at the edge of the standing timber. From here there is no trail, only a taped route starting to the right of a draw full of logs and other debris. After travelling roughly southward, you swing east and scramble up steeply, eventually reaching the main ridge, on which you turn southward again towards the summit, surmounting en route a subsidiary top, itself almost as high as the main peak.

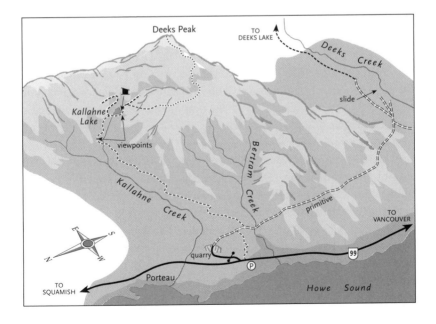

36 HOWE SOUND CREST TRAIL
(North)

to Brunswick Lake

Round trip 20 km (12.4 mi)   Allow 10 hours
Elevation gain 1190 m (3900 ft)   High point 1220 m (4000 ft)
Average grade 11.9%

Best July to October   Map 92G/11 Squamish
Driving distance from Vancouver 50 km (30 mi)

The Lions, Brunswick Mountain and Deeks Peak, viewed from Mount Capilano. (MM)

The Howe Sound Crest Trail is a scenic high-level route that stretches 30 km (20 mi) from Cypress Provincial Park in the south to just before Porteau Cove Provincial Park in the north. Described here is a section of the northern part of this trail, from its northern terminus on Highway 99 south to Brunswick Lake. En route you also pass Deeks and Hanover Lakes. Deeks Lake was enlarged to its present form about 90 years ago, when it was dammed to provide water for a gravel-extracting operation. This trip can also be done as part of a one-day crossover to Lions Bay if you want something shorter than the complete Howe Sound Crest Trail.

Zero your odometer at Horseshoe Bay. Drive north on Highway 99 and, at 22 km (14 mi), watch for a brown wooden sign on the right-hand side of the road saying "Deeks Lake Trail 500 m." There is a clearly marked parking area on the left opposite a trailhead signboard.

The trail, designated by orange markers, begins almost opposite and proceeds up the side of pretty little Kallahne Creek to a power line on an open bluff with a fine view. Back in the trees you soon join an old logging road on which you go right. Despite minor turnoffs, the main track is clear as you gradually turn into the valley of Deeks Creek. After nearly an hour, having passed a small pond on the right, you come to a junction with metal signs and statistics. Here the trail is joined by the alternative and steeper route up Deeks Creek (Hike 37) from its bridge across the highway some 5 km (3.1 mi) south of where you started. Next continue straight ahead for a short distance to a fork where the marked trail swings to the left, rising steeply from the old road to avoid a severe slide area. The trail soon joins the road again, this time higher up the valley. Now in the unheralded northern extension of Cypress Provincial Park, you come within earshot of the creek with Phi Alpha Falls on the right as you switchback up the steepening trail, finally emerging from the forest a little above Deeks Lake. Turn right here along the lakeshore. Cross the outflow on chained logs and follow the scenic trail around the lake's south side before you ascend, first on the west and then the east side of the creek, to the middle lake, sometimes called Hanover Lake, its waters turquoise in the sun. Here you are conscious of the horns of Brunswick Mountain ahead and Hat Mountain's truncated cone to your right. Beyond this lake your rewards are the sight of a fine waterfall and, finally, the irregularly shaped Brunswick Lake with its protruding appendix to the west, which you cross on rocks if you wish. If you are backpacking, this is a beautiful setting for a camping spot.

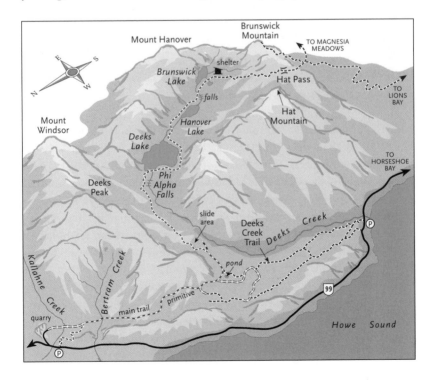

37 DEEKS BLUFFS CIRCUIT

Round trip 10 km (6.2 mi)	Allow 5 hours
Elevation gain 400 m (1300 ft)	High point 480 m (1570 ft)
Average grade 9.6%	

Good most of the year	Map 92G/11 Squamish
Driving distance from Vancouver 40 km (25 mi)	

Anvil Island and Leading Peak, seen from the bluffs.

Here is a low-level hike of modest duration, varied enough and with sufficient small challenges to make a satisfying outing for a short day. As well, for a very little expenditure of energy you are rewarded with superb views over island-dotted Howe Sound from numerous vantage points. The trip is described as a clockwise circuit that lets you enjoy the ocean views on the outward leg.

Zero your odometer at Horseshoe Bay. Drive north on Highway 99 for 17 km (10.6 mi) to cross Deeks Creek. Just across the bridge there is parking space on the left (west) side of the road.

Walk north for about 100 m (325 ft) and ascend at the orange markers. There is a handline at one steep, eroded spot and at bluff-top level you have the first of your views south to Bowen Island. Then, still climbing, you stay left at each of three forks where signs indicate that the right branch connects with the Deeks Lake Trail. Thus you continue, undulating up over dry bluffs, down into moist hollows, visiting a sequence of viewpoints en route and eventually descending to a cat track on which you turn left to resume your trail at its end a few minutes later. Next you rise on an old road to arrive at a sign for a viewpoint to the left. This bump is the high point of the trail, once again with splendid views to the west and south over Howe Sound. Descending, turn left on the old road, curving around the base of the bump, and make your way generally northward past a wet spot to meet the Deeks Lake Trail portion of the Howe Sound Crest Trail (Hike 36). Go right on this trail for about 10 minutes, passing the other end of the cat track that you met earlier, then a small pond and finally coming to a junction with a sign directing you right again for Highway 99. This is the old Deeks Lake Trail, predecessor to the one you just left, and on it you descend quite steeply for a few minutes before, once again, you find your route interrupted by that same cat track. Go left and down on it until your trail, now bearing the sign "Shortcut," reappears on the left. Well marked with orange squares and tapes, it leads through a maze of mossy old logging roads to enter mature forest, cross a small stream on the "Lunden" bridge and rise towards the bluffs before beginning the descent to the highway, drawing closer to the creek as well. As you proceed, the trail becomes steeper with one short, vertical drop that you may wish to avoid, especially if it is wet or icy, by going off uphill a few minutes before the tricky spot, following a taped detour on the right that joins the lowest connector route linking the Deeks Creek and Deeks Bluffs Trails. A left turn then brings you down to rejoin Deeks Creek Trail below the problem area, and you go right to end at the highway by the bridge.

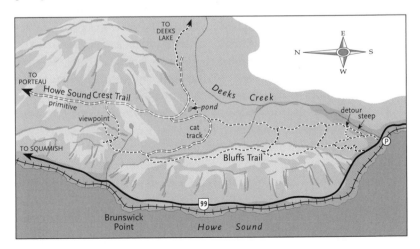

38

BRUNSWICK MOUNTAIN

Round trip 14.5 km (9 mi)   Allow 8 hours

Elevation gain 1550 m (5100 ft)   High point 1785 m (5855 ft)

Average grade 21.4%

Best July to October   Map 92G/06 North
Vancouver

Driving distance from Vancouver 40 km (25 mi)

Summit view to Bowen Island and the mouth of Howe Sound. (MM)

This prominent ridge and its peak are immediately to the north of Mount Harvey. The connection is not just geographical, HMS *Brunswick* was the ship commanded by Capt. John Harvey, a British naval officer of the eighteenth century. It is the highest peak in the area, and therefore has commanding views in all directions. The Howe Sound Crest Trail traverses the slopes west of Brunswick Mountain's summit. You therefore cross it on your ascent. The last 100 m (325 ft) are steep, open and rocky. If there is snow or ice on the ground, be extremely cautious!

Drive north from Horseshoe Bay on Highway 99 to Lions Bay. Turn right onto Oceanview Road, left onto Cross Creek Road over Harvey Creek, then right onto Centre Road. Next go left onto Bayview Road for 1 km (0.6 mi), left again briefly onto Mountain Drive and finally left onto Sunset Drive to the gate that bars farther progress. If the gate is open, do not drive through! Parking may be a problem, especially on weekends, so be careful where you leave your vehicle. Park illegally and you will be towed. Additional parking is available at Lions Bay Elementary School, 1 km (0.6 mi) below on Mountain Drive. Hikes 38, 39 and 40 share this vehicle access.

Take the old logging road beyond the gate. After 15 minutes keep right at the fork. After about 45 minutes, at the next fork, go left. You shortly cross Magnesia Creek, then comes another fork and you go steeply uphill to the right, switchbacking up the deteriorating logging road to where it ends just below the standing timber at 1050 m (3450 ft). From here it is trail. Initially the path switchbacks before going steeply up the fall-line for another 475 m (1560 ft) to its intersection with the Howe Sound Crest Trail. Beyond here the trail continues steeply, with one or two exposed sections, and requires caution, especially in snow, as you approach or leave the summit ridge. The western and central peaks are now readily accessible and afford splendid views of the surrounding mountains and down to Howe Sound and its islands, down also to the little lakes now named Brunswick and Hanover. From the main peak the broken ridge to the eastern horn is a somewhat challenging scramble that requires a sure foot and a steady head; it may well be left to the experienced hiker since the views do little to improve on those already enjoyed. To return, you can retrace your ascent route. If, however, you have attained the peak and feel like turning your hike into a loop trip, head south on the Howe Sound Crest Trail when you get back down to it. Follow the trail past Magnesia Meadows and the shelter to Harvey Pass, up the rough trail west to the summit of Mount Harvey and down the trail described in Hike 39, an additional 215 m (700 ft) of ascent and an additional 2 hours.

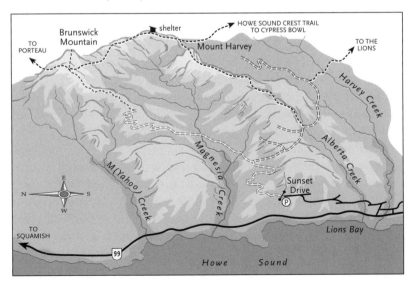

39 MOUNT HARVEY

Round trip 12.5 km (7.8 mi)   Allow 7 hours
Elevation gain 1465 m (4800 ft)   High point 1705 m (5590 ft)
Average grade 23.4%

Best July to October   Map 92G/06 North
                              Vancouver
Driving distance from Vancouver 40 km (25 mi)

Brunswick Mountain, Mount Harvey and The Lions, seen from the ferry.

For long enough the ridge and the peak of this beautifully shaped mountain were accessible only by a bushwhack from a spur that branched left off the Harvey Creek logging road a short distance after it has parted from the Magnesia Creek road. All that changed in the 1980s when Halvor Lunden created a fine route to Harvey's southwest ridge. And the name? Like so many other coastal features it commemorates an eighteenth-century British naval officer, Capt. John Harvey, who served under Admiral Howe. Now the subordinate looks down upon his onetime commander.

Drive north from Horseshoe Bay on Highway 99 to Lions Bay. Turn right onto Oceanview Road, left onto Cross Creek Road over Harvey Creek, then right onto Centre Road. Next go left onto Bayview Road for 1 km (0.6 mi), left again briefly onto Mountain Drive and finally left onto Sunset Drive to the gate that bars farther progress. If the gate is open, do not drive through! Parking may be a problem, especially on weekends, so be careful where you leave your vehicle. Park illegally and you will be towed. Additional parking is available at Lions Bay Elementary School, 1 km (0.6 mi) below on Mountain Drive. Hikes 38, 39 and 40 share this vehicle access.

Take the old logging road beyond the gate. After 15 minutes keep right at the fork. After about 45 minutes, keep right again (left leads to Brunswick Mountain). Follow this road, ignoring two left forks, for a distance of 700 m (2300 ft) to the gully of Alberta Creek. The trail to Mount Harvey starts off uphill immediately before this gully, in which cascades a small waterfall. Soon the trail starts to turn away from the creek, entering a section of young forest before swinging back into the tall timber then zigzagging upward. Soon you skirt the head of a wide basin and strike east to attain the main ridge at a large area accidentally burned many years ago. This spot shows no signs of regeneration but it offers a spectacular view of the neighbouring West Lion. The trail now follows the ridge, beautiful in season with various heaths, flowers, small bushes and trees, until, after one more stretch of silver forest, a final scramble brings you out on the rocky summit. From here the views to the west across Howe Sound match the best, and the Lions dominate to the southeast. Also visible is the Howe Sound Crest Trail (HSCT) swinging north into Harvey Pass thence to the meadows around the head of Magnesia Creek and the shelter located there. Although a trail drops off the east side of Mount Harvey to meet the HSCT in Harvey Pass, it is not a route to be investigated on the descent. It is steep and convoluted. Return, therefore, the way you came.

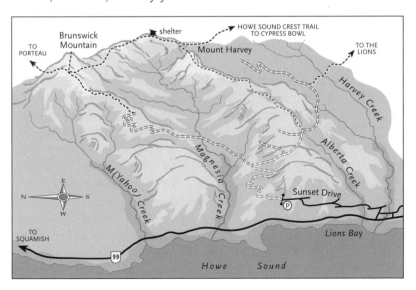

40 BINKERT (LIONS) TRAIL

Round trip 15 km (9.3 mi)   Allow 7 hours
Elevation gain 1280 m (4200 ft)   High point 1525 m (5000 ft)
Average grade 17.1%

Best July to October   Map 92G/06 North
                              Vancouver
Driving distance from Vancouver 40 km (25 mi)

The Lions and Mount Harvey, viewed from Brunswick Mountain.

That this trail, one of the most popular in the Lower Mainland, exists at all is largely the result of efforts by Paul Binkert of the British Columbia Mountaineering Club. As you hike it, therefore, think gratefully of the volunteer work by club members that went into its construction and keeps it maintained. The trail gives access to the ridge on which the West Lion is situated. It does not take you to the top of either Lion. The West Lion itself is a rock climb and, as such, should be attempted only by properly equipped and experienced parties. The same caveat applies to the East Lion, which is also out of bounds, being in the Greater Vancouver watershed. The ridge crest itself is, however, sufficiently spectacular with dramatic close-up views of the twin peaks.

Drive north from Horseshoe Bay on Highway 99 to Lions Bay. Turn right onto Oceanview Road, left onto Cross Creek Road over Harvey Creek, then right onto Centre Road. Next go left onto Bayview Road for 1 km (0.6 mi), left again briefly onto Mountain Drive and finally left onto Sunset Drive to the gate that bars farther progress. If the gate is open, do not drive through! Parking may be a problem, especially on weekends, so be careful where you leave your vehicle. Park illegally and you will be towed. Additional parking is available at Lions Bay Elementary School, 1 km (0.6 mi) below on Mountain Drive. Hikes 38, 39 and 40 share this vehicle access.

Take the old logging road beyond the gate. After 15 minutes keep right at the fork. After about 45 minutes, keep right again (left leads to Brunswick Mountain). Follow this road, ignoring two left forks, for a distance of 700 m (2300 ft) to the gully of Alberta Creek. The trail to Mount Harvey starts off uphill just before the gully. Cross Alberta Creek and then head south and east back into the valley of Harvey Creek. At the next junction, the trail goes off right dropping to cross Harvey Creek on a fine bridge, a memorial to Marcel Andrie of Lions Bay Search & Rescue. The trail then heads up the rocky slope in tall trees to arrive at a vantage point with a splendid view of the West Lion. Beyond here the route lies in the open as it heads southeast towards the main ridge, where the old trail over Unnecessary Mountain (now part of the Howe Sound Crest Trail) joins it from the right. To return you may simply retrace your steps. However, you could also make a crossover to Cypress Bowl by the Howe Sound Crest Trail (Hike 47). Or, if you are familiar with the Unnecessary Mountain Trail (not described in this guide), you could descend by that route.

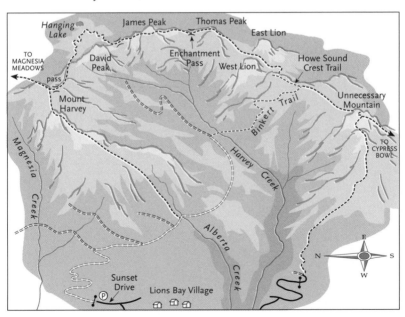

41 LEADING PEAK (Anvil Island)

Round trip 10 km (6.2 mi)   Allow 5 hours
Elevation gain 755 m (2475 ft)   High point 755 m (2475 ft)
Average grade 15.1%

Good most of year   Map 92G/11 Squamish
Driving distance from Vancouver 25 km (15 mi)

From almost anywhere around Howe Sound, Anvil Island is an alluring feature of your viewscape. The rocky horn of Leading Peak is the major contributing factor, although the island's location in the middle of the sound is certainly part of its attraction. Because of the exposed rock, the ascent looks as if it might be technically difficult but that is not the case. This is a straightforward hike with only minor scrambling just before the summit. The views from the top, as might be expected, are panoramic. Why, therefore, does Leading Peak see so few visitors? There is no scheduled boat service to the island, therefore access becomes the main issue for most hikers. The crossing is less than 2 km (1.2 mi) from Brunswick Point if you decide to kayak, although you would need to launch at Lions Bay or Porteau Cove. The simpler, but more expen-

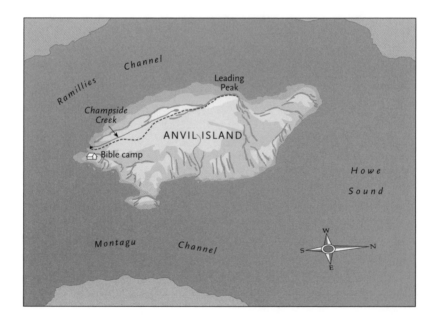

The south slope of the peak, viewed from the trail.

sive option, is to charter a water taxi from Lions Bay Marina. Cormorant Water Taxi (604) 947-2243 will quote you a price. Then again, maybe you have a friend with a boat....

However you plan to reach the island, the usual landing area and the most used trailhead is at the Daybreak Point Bible Camp. Since this is private property, you need approval before landing. The camp's North Vancouver phone number is (604) 987-6109.

From the boat dock, walk along the camp roads to the upper field, at the far end of which is the trail. There are round coloured markers to guide you. You will be following Champside Creek upstream on its east side (river-left). At an elevation of 365 m (1200 ft) there is a viewpoint at the White Spot. The reason for its name will be obvious. The source of Champside Creek is a small lake at 610 m (2000 ft), which you contour on its east side. There is a minor descent into a saddle, with your objective visible ahead. The trail then makes a rising traverse around the west side of Leading Peak into a rocky gulch between the main summit and a lower subsidiary summit to its northeast. Some straightforward, easy scrambling takes you to the top. To return, retrace your ascent route. A sketchy path descends east from the saddle, following a small creek, to a little rocky point on the island's east shore. It is not, however, a route to investigate on your descent because it is rocky and steep. Taking heed of the phrase "The devil you know is better than the devil you don't know," seems particularly appropriate when you are returning to a Bible camp.

42 MOUNT LIDDELL
(Gambier Island)

to Gambier Lake	Round trip 15 km (9.3 mi)	Allow 6 hours
	Elevation gain 520 m (1700 ft)	High point 520 m (1700 ft)
	Average grade 6.9%	
	Good most of year	
to summit	Round trip 22 km (13.7 mi)	Allow 8 hours
	Elevation gain 903 m (2963 ft)	High point 903 m (2963 ft)
	Average grade 12.9%	
	Best May to October	

Maps 92G/06 North Vancouver; 92G/11 Squamish
Driving distance from Vancouver 25 km (15 mi) or Bus 250

Mounts Gardner, Artaban and Liddell seen from Deeks Bluffs.

This is a trip, as is Hike 43, on Gambier Island. However, the boat access here is by B.C. Ferries. Whether that helps or hinders your enterprise is debatable. Start with a foot-passenger ferry ride from Horseshoe Bay to Langdale, followed by a quick change to the *Dogwood Princess II* (which lies in a berth below and to the right as you disembark from the larger ferries) for the shorter voyage to Gambier Island. The landing is at New Brighton on the southwest coast of the island. Check the timetables carefully, especially for your return connections. Two trips, with the same initial approach, are described. The hike to Gambier Lake is a popular destination; however, Mount Liddell, the highest point on the island, is more spectacular scenically.

At New Brighton, walk some 100 m (325 ft) from the pier, taking the second left by the General Store and continuing uphill on a quiet country lane. In about 15 minutes follow the left fork signed "To Lake." Follow this road towards Andys Bay as it drops to traverse north on the island's southwestern flank. Keep left at major forks, reaching Mannion Creek in less than an hour from the ferry. Half a kilometre (0.3 mi) beyond the creek crossing comes a junction where the way to Gambier

Lake forks back sharp right. Look for a white diamond marker at this junction. You rise on this old eroded road to the west (river-right) of Mannion Creek. The next fork is where you decide: right to Gambier Lake, or left to Mount Liddell.

The right fork, with green markers, rises steadily towards the north-south divide at the head of Mannion Creek at an elevation of 520 m (1700 ft). Thereafter, taking first a right then a left fork, you descend some 100 m (330 ft) elevation and 1 km (0.6 mi) distance to the lake. It is tree ringed, and the signs of old campsites indicate its popularity as the destination for an overnight trip.

The left fork, with white markers, ascends on another old road until, after some 20 minutes, you pass the almost grown-over Muskeg Lake. Beyond the lake, ignoring an overgrown spur on the right, follow the road as it rises northward along the west side of the ridge. After one zigzag to gain height, the track resumes its northward direction until at about 590 m (1935 ft) it bends to the east, dropping slightly to cross a ravine on a deteriorating old logging bridge, heading for the divide north of your objective. Thereafter you rise again on the road, now worn to bedrock and rubble, circling around southwest and then south to the final landing. Here you are less than 50 m (160 ft) below the summit. A horizontal bushwhack southward takes you to the top, a rocky knoll that gives views west to Mount Elphinstone and the Rainy River peaks and down to Port Mellon and the log rafts in Thornbrough Channel.

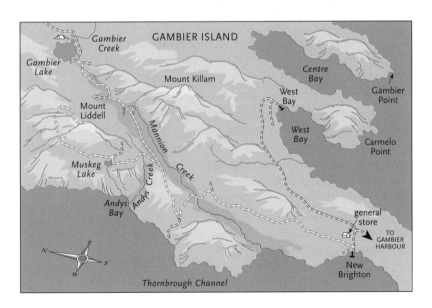

43 MOUNT ARTABAN
(Gambier Island)

Round trip 10 km (6.2 mi)   Allow 6 hours
Elevation gain 609 m (1998 ft)   High point 609 m (1998 ft)
Average grade 12.2%

Good most of year   Map 92G/06 North
   Vancouver
Driving distance from Vancouver 25 km (15 mi)

Mounts Gardner (left) and Artaban (right), viewed from Deeks Bluffs.

The summit of Mount Artaban was once the site of a B.C. Forest Service (BCFS) lookout tower. Since these lookouts were sited to provide all-encompassing views, you can still expect the same—although the tower has been allowed to deteriorate to a pile of boards. Another heritage structure gone! This outing is for the boat owner/hiker, for those with boat-owning friends or for those prepared to use the water taxi from Horseshoe Bay. Mercury Launch & Tug at (604) 921-7451 operates a scheduled water taxi to Gambier Island and makes request stops. The hike begins on the dock in Halkett Bay Provincial Park. The island bears the name of the inevitable British naval officer; however, this little mountain commemorates a character from fiction, the fourth Magus, who sought Christ but was consistently turned aside from his quest by the needs of his fellow humans.

Upon landing, follow the trail past the toilet, turning south parallel to the beach but after about 100 m (325 ft) heading right on an obscure old logging road marked with tapes. This track winds uphill, briefly following a small stream, then veering back southward and levelling off as it approaches and crosses another minor creek. Just beyond, you emerge on a trail coming up from the left and signed "To the Cross and Mount Artaban." This is the trail from a private camp (run by the Camp Fircom Society of the United Church of Canada), itself replacing the original route that previously ascended farther west in the path of a fairly extensive logging operation. Turn right making your way uphill, curving around from the east to the north side of a knoll. On the margin of the clear-cut, you reach a fork with another printed notice pointing left to the cross, which is located some 5 minutes away on a rocky little summit. From this junction continue west for Mount Artaban, going right briefly at another sign in a meadowy stretch, then heading west again through the upper edge of the slash, taking care not to lose sight of the tapes marking the route. Back in the standing forest the trail improves and for a short time, as it meanders westward across the rocky spine of the peninsula, it resembles the trail as it was in the lookout's heyday before age, neglect and logging took their toll. On the west side of the ridge, you next come to a two-way fork: on the left, coming up from the cutover area, is another relatively new connector from Gambier Estates; sharp right your route heads north and uphill, the trail barely discernible in places under the forest litter. Thus you continue, following a gully first, then mounting the rock ridge on the right for the penultimate stretch before the final short scramble left to the summit. Here you find a little pile of boards, silent remains of the one-time BCFS lookout tower.

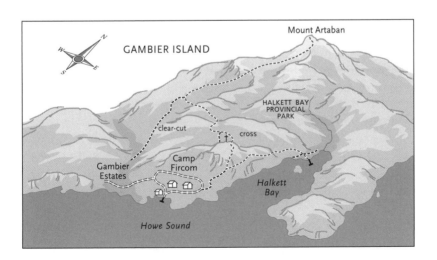

44 MOUNT GARDNER
(Bowen Island)

Round trip 17 km (10.6 mi)   Allow 7 hours
Elevation gain 719 m (2360 ft)   High point 719 m (2360 ft)
Average grade 8.5%

Good most of year   Map 92G/06 North
                                     Vancouver
Driving distance from Vancouver 25 km (15 mi) or Bus 250

Horseshoe Bay and West Vancouver, viewed from the summit. (MM)

Mount Gardner on Bowen Island offers a variety of outings to and around the summits of the little mountain with, for reward, unsurpassed views of Howe Sound and its encircling peaks. The trip described here uses some of the trails available, but is only one of many possibilities. The hike leads you to the north summit with its communication devices and helipads. There are, however, spectacular views on a fine day, which are well worth your effort. By contrast, the south summit, though higher, is treed and viewless; it is not described here. Access is as a foot passenger from Horseshoe Bay to Snug Cove. Check your sailing times, especially for the return.

From Snug Cove, take the more attractive route through Crippen Regional Park. Turn right onto Cardena Road, left onto the Killarney Lake Trail, briefly right onto Miller's Landing Road and left again onto the park trail. Finally, ignoring a wide trail going left into the meadows, go left at the next fork to the lake. There, follow the trail along its southwest shore until, just after a creek crossing, you turn onto a path leading up to Mount Gardner Road. Go right, and at pole 491 head left uphill onto a service road, then right onto Bowen Pit Road to a gate.

Pass the gate and shortly go left onto the Skid Trail, winding uphill and keeping right at a junction before rejoining the road. Go upward around a bend then, leaving the road, go right on Mat Hill Trail, heading around the north side of the hill before working west to a junction. Stay right, descending a little on what is now Handloggers' Trail. Next comes a fine viewpoint overlooking the islands of Howe Sound with, just beyond, a steep trail on the left signed "Alan Garton Memorial Trail." Follow this up to a junction where the road connector arrives from the left. Now on the Mount Gardner North Trail, you turn south along the ridge, rising first to a bluff with magnificent views before re-entering the forest and continuing to a fork. Take the left branch, which is the steeper route to the top of the north peak. Although it is littered with technological debris, the views are spectacular. To return, drop south from the north peak into the hollow where you rejoin Mount Gardner North Trail. Turn left, and about 5 minutes later, ignore the vague trail going left to the south peak. Continuing south you descend gently through forest to yet another fork, where you go left, heading northeast on Mount Gardner South Trail towards the service road, on which you emerge a little above the Mat Hill Trail. All that remains is for you to retrace your steps to Snug Cove and your ferry.

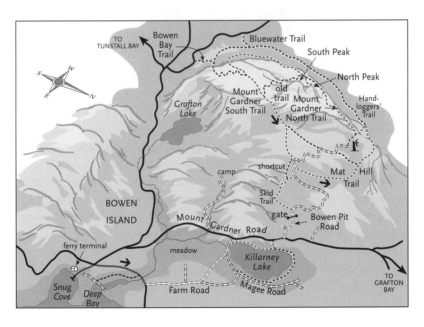

 SUNSET TRAIL

Round trip 9.5 km (6 mi)   Allow 6 hours
Elevation gain 975 m (3200 ft)   High point 1045 m (3425 ft)
Average grade 20.5%

Best May to October   Maps 92G/06 North
Vancouver; B.C. Parks
Cypress Provincial Park
Driving distance from Vancouver 30 km (20 mi)

View across Horseshoe Bay to the south end of Bowen Island.

As an alternative to the road access into Cypress Provincial Park from the south, the trail from the Sea to Sky Highway (Highway 99) to the Howe Sound Crest Trail (HSCT) and the Bowen Island Lookout should appeal to the hiker who prefers cool forests and the peace of the trail to the noise and smell of internal combustion engines. The trail follows Montizambert Creek to the source of its south fork in Yew Lake.

Drive north from Horseshoe Bay on Highway 99 for 5 km (3.1 mi) to Sunset Marina. Just north of Lawrence Way, park on the left (west) side of the highway opposite a paved, private driveway.

Cross the highway to the east side and walk 50 m (160 ft) north of the private driveway. An old road, becoming overgrown, starts up the hill here. A short way up the road you briefly meet the private driveway just before a gate. Pass around the gate and continue uphill. The trail starts between two small water towers. There is an initial steep section of trail before you join an old logging road. Montizambert Creek is audible to your left. About 0.5 hour from your start, you turn sharp right off the road. On a tree is a single orange marker to indicate the turnoff point. Start ascending steeply on a trail that has suffered some ravages of time but can be followed easily as it swings back and forth to gain height. Finally the grade eases, and after crossing a small creek, you traverse an area devastated by winter storms but since made passable by local volunteer trailbuilders. Then, after crossing two more small streams, you reach a bridge over the outlet from Yew Lake. To reduce hiker impact on the meadows, a new section of trail leads straight ahead to a gravel road. Go right onto this road and pass the small pumphouse hut, which is on your left. A few minutes along, the HSCT crosses the road; turn left and follow it uphill. You arrive at another gravel road, which the HSCT follows to the left. Less than 1 km (0.6 mi) along this road, you arrive at a junction and information board. Other than the trail information, there is a tribute to Paul Binkert who was the driving force behind many of the mountain access trails in southwestern British Columbia. At an elevation of 1035 m (3400 ft), this is the high point of this trip. To return, you can retrace your ascent route. Or, for a minor variation, take the trail to the Bowen Island Lookout. As the cutblock below it grows up, it becomes less and less of a lookout. A trail drops from the lookout down through the small plantation. You emerge onto the pumphouse road. There is another viewpoint to your right (west) although your descent trail is to the left. Turn right into the trees before the pumphouse. It's all downhill from here.

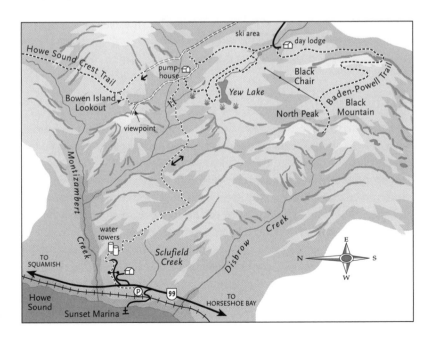

46 BLACK MOUNTAIN

Round trip 16 km (9.9 mi)   Allow 7 hours
Elevation gain 1140 m (3740 ft) High point 1217 m (3992 ft)
Average grade 14.2%

Best May to November   Maps 92G/06 North
Vancouver; B.C. Parks
Cypress Provincial Park
Driving distance from Vancouver 25 km (15 mi) or Bus 250

View from Eagle Bluff to Lighthouse Park and across the harbour to Point Grey.

Like Hike 45, this trip provides an alternative to the road access from the south into Cypress Provincial Park. A steep but rewarding trail with magnificent views over Howe Sound, it leads to the alpine meadows and small lakes of the summit plateau. It is also used as the Baden-Powell Trail. Although close to Vancouver and easily accessible, the two summits of Black Mountain demand considerable expenditure of energy by those who ascend them from the west; the result, however, makes the effort worthwhile. From either peak the view is panoramic, with the great snowfield of the Tantalus Range in the northwest, the dome of Mount Baker in the southeast and Vancouver below. Snow lies late on the plateau around Black Mountain. If summer is late arriving, an ascent to Eagle Bluff is well worthwhile.

Follow Highway 1 towards Horseshoe Bay, stay right (Exit 1) for Squamish where the ferry traffic goes left. Immediately watch for the entry to a small parking space just before a yellow-and-black, diagonally striped road sign on the right retaining wall. Park here, clear of the gate.

Past the gate, this old road rises to a small pond beside which the Baden-Powell Trail enters from the right, after its beginning at Eagleridge Drive. Turn left here and continue upward, passing first a viewpoint on the left under a power line, then some watershed signs on your right. In its upper reaches the road becomes more and more washed out and is finally replaced by a trail that swings from northeast to east in a pleasant old forest. Next you approach Nelson Creek, but before you reach it, a faint trail goes off left. Take this side route to make a loop trip; it leads to Donut Bluff. The trail is steep and rocky, and has some route-finding challenges, with fallen logs near the creek crossing. Do not attempt to descend this route: you should use it only on the ascent! However, the bluff has splendid views of Howe Sound, its islands, the mountains of the Sunshine Coast and the Tantalus Range. From Donut Bluff, follow the vague trail down into the hollow, cross Nelson Creek and rise up the slope to pick up the main trail. Turn left, northeast, on a trail that undulates past little lakes until you reach a fork. Go left (the Baden-Powell Trail goes right), following good orange markers to Black Mountain. The south summit is reached first in a series of switchbacks, while the north summit (Yew Lake Viewpoint) lies beyond, past Cabin Lake, a small lake in the hollow between. To return, retrace your ascent route to the point where the trail from Donut Bluff met the main trail. Now stay left on the main trail to Eagle Bluff, elevation 1070 m (3500 ft), with its breathtaking views. The descent trail drops steeply down the front of the bluff to a large rock slide, some timber, then a talus slope. A short spell in the big trees and a crossing of Nelson Creek get you back to the Donut Bluff junction and familiar terrain.

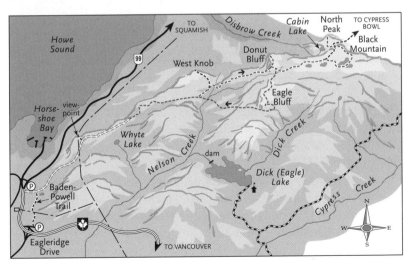

47 HOWE SOUND CREST TRAIL (South)

to St. Marks Summit	Round trip 11 km (6.8 mi)	Allow 5 hours
	Elevation gain 440 m (1450 ft)	High point 1355 m (4450 ft)
	Average grade 8.0%	
to Unnecessary Mountain	Round trip 18 km (11.2 mi)	Allow 7 hours
	Elevation gain 610 m (2000 ft)	High point 1525 m (5000 ft)
	Average grade 6.8%	
	Best July to October	Maps 92G/06 North Vancouver; B.C. Parks, The Howe Sound Crest Trail

Driving distance from Vancouver 30 km (20 mi)

St. Marks Summit, Unnecessary Mountain and the West Lion, seen from Mount Strachan.

The Howe Sound Crest Trail is a scenic high-level route that stretches 30 km (20 mi) from Cypress Provincial Park in the south to just before Porteau Cove Provincial Park in the north. Described here is a section of the southern part of this trail, from Cypress Bowl to the peaks of Unnecessary Mountain, with the possibility of continuing to the base of the West Lion. The trail has something of a history, being the re-creation of the one-time route to the Lions before a road was built along Howe Sound, when access even to Hollyburn Mountain and Mount Strachan was on foot from West Vancouver. Now the trailhead at the parking lot for the Cypress Bowl chairlifts is at 915 m (3000 ft) and some 14 km (8.7 mi) into the valley of the creek that gives the provincial park its name. Some difference!

From Highway 1 westbound towards Horseshoe Bay, take Exit 8 signed for Cypress Bowl. The Cypress Parkway will take you in 14 km (8.7 mi) to the upper parking lot. On your right, as you turn into the lot, is a large signboard, which is the trailhead.

Walk westward along the signposted track that bears right from the one to Yew Lake, then after crossing a roadway, take a path angling uphill among trees. This leads, via a small ravine and a stretch of upper road, to the virtually untouched forest on the west side of Mount Strachan. Along the way you have glimpses of Howe Sound and Sechelt as you gradually veer eastward and, following the line of Montizambert Creek, emerge on a damp meadow which is the descent route from Mount Strachan described in Hike 49. From here, follow the trail along the ridge, negotiating one or two wooded knolls en route, until after nearly 2 hours from the start you reach St. Marks Summit at 1355 m (4450 ft), with viewpoints on either side. Now you are about to start a substantial descent into a col, losing some 150 m (500 ft) in the process. The trail next climbs steeply back to crest level, the route now rocky and open with spectacular views. Either peak of Unnecessary Mountain, South or North, may be your destination, there being only about 600 m (0.4 mi) distance between them, with an altitude loss and gain of 50 m (160 ft). The descent off the north side of South Peak is abrupt and precipitous, so that care should be taken, especially when snow or ice is on the ground. On the ascent to North Peak, just before the summit, the Unnecessary Mountain Trail (not described in this guide) from Lions Bay joins from the left. To return, retrace your ascent route.

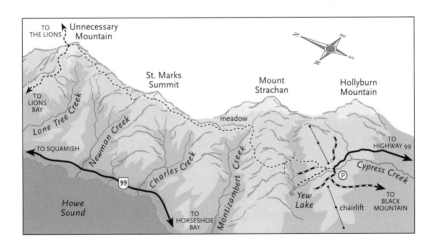

48 HOLLYBURN MOUNTAIN

Round trip 20 km (12.4 mi)   Allow 7 hours
Elevation gain 895 m (2935 ft)   High point 1325 m (4345 ft)
Average grade 9.0%

Best July to November   Maps 92G/06 North
                                    Vancouver; B.C. Parks
                                    Cypress Provincial Park
Driving distance from Vancouver 20 km (10 mi)

View north to The Lions.

The creation of Cypress Provincial Park in 1975, and the accompanying vehicle access, makes the ascent of Hollyburn Mountain today an easy outing for most people. But this was not always so. Old-timers in West Vancouver can remember hikers from the city wending their way up from the ferry to the mountain. Now, although many of these old trails have disappeared, it is still possible to follow the approximate route of a few, a little overgrown and worn in places, but still passable. So savour something of the past in this ascent!

From Highway 1 westbound towards Horseshoe Bay, take Exit 8 signed for Cypress Bowl. The second switchback on the Cypress Parkway is HiView Lookout. Park here.

On the north side, pass through an opening in a fence and take the next two left turns. This, the old Forks Trail, heads up steadily, sometimes on old roads, to arrive at a power line and the Skyline Trail, the site of the long-gone Forks Coffee Shop. Now angle up on a deeply gullied old access road, very soon to go right again on the trail. Next you cross the access road to the one-time Westlake Lodge, pass a CN/CP tower and continue upward on a deeply trenched trail with cabins on either side to meet yet another old road, which is soon joined by the trail that came from the chairlift's upper terminal and HiView Lodge. Proceed to the venerable Hollyburn Lodge beside First Lake, where you go right, then left on the Baden-Powell Trail. This leads you to a power line and a cabin by Fourth Lake, and a fork, where you go right (Baden-Powell goes left). Soon you pass the site of a Water Board cabin, only debris remaining, before the slope steepens and you zigzag upward to a beautiful little meadow and a small pond, preludes to a final scramble to the peak with its panoramic views. To return, retrace your steps to where you joined the Baden-Powell Trail at First Lake. Keep on the Baden-Powell Trail to descend an old ski hill above the site of Westlake Lodge. There is a large cabin and a tiny cabin, between which is a trail signed "Municipal Cabin Area"; follow this. Next cross Marr Creek, and shortly thereafter you take a trail to the left that descends to meet the road connecting Cypress Parkway and the old lodge. On this path you turn right, and, after passing the CN/CP tower, watch for the old Forks Trail on which you ascended.

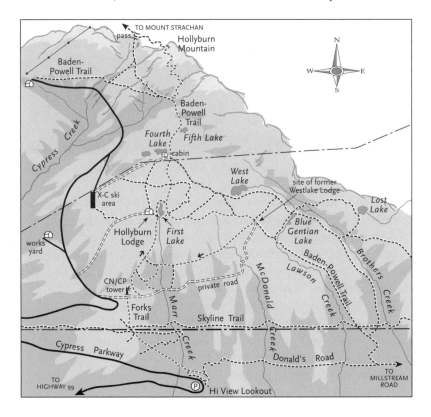

49 MOUNT STRACHAN

Round trip 10 km (6.2 mi)	Allow 5 hours
Elevation gain 538 m (1765 ft)	High point 1454 m (4769 ft)
Average grade 10.8%	

Best July to November	Maps 92G/06 North Vancouver; B.C. Parks Cypress Provincial Park

Driving distance from Vancouver 30 km (20 mi)

View north to The Lions, Sky Pilot Mountain and, on the right horizon, Mount Garibaldi.

More interesting than a simple up-and-back hike to Mount Strachan is a counter-clockwise circuit of the mountain starting at the alpine ski area in Cypress Provincial Park. The trip described here takes the Baden-Powell Trail, then the old Strachan Trail, passes an old airplane wreck thence to the two summits of Mount Strachan. The descent uses the Howe Sound Crest Trail (Hike 47) as a return.

From Highway 1 westbound towards Horseshoe Bay, take Exit 8 signed for Cypress Bowl. The Cypress Parkway will take you in 14 km (8.7 mi) to the upper parking lot. On your right, as you turn into the lot, is a large signboard, which is the trailhead.

Behind the signboard, go right to a trail marker for the Baden-Powell Trail on which you go east, not west! The trail makes a gently ascending traverse across the hillside. Pass the first trail junction but just after the wooden bridge over the north fork of Cypress Creek turn left and uphill at that intersection. The trail swings around the southwest shoulder of Hollyburn Mountain gaining height easily and getting, again, close to Cypress Creek, on the other side of which is a ski area road. The headwaters of the creek is a meadow with an attractive little pond. At an otherwise pleasant little saddle, the road is on your immediate left. Twenty minutes above the pass, you encounter the forty-year-old remains of a light aircraft. The south summit is reached in another 30 minutes of straightforward but steep hiking. It is a long gentle summit marred by the pylons and other impedimenta of the ski resort. To reach the higher north summit, drop north into the saddle between the peaks. Take note here as this is the point from which you descend to the west. From the saddle, follow the markers to the north summit, with its spectacular views in all directions. When sated with the scenery, return to the saddle and drop west down the gully. The route is sometimes in the gully and sometimes in the trees at the side. There is flagging tape and even some fixed rope to guide you. Whether you see any of the markers will depend on how much snow is still on the ground. Where the terrain levels off, 300 m (980 ft) below the saddle, pick up the Howe Sound Crest Trail and turn left (south). It is less than 1 hour at an easy pace from here back to the Cypress Bowl parking lot on a well-marked and well-used trail.

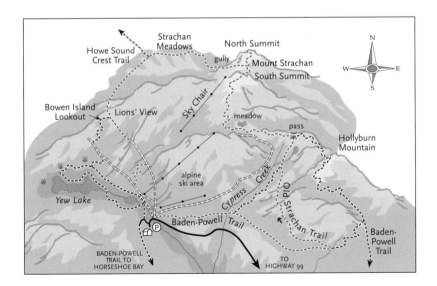

50 GOAT MOUNTAIN

from top of Skyride

Round trip 8 km (5 mi)
Elevation gain 275 m (900 ft)
Average grade 6.9%

Allow 4.5 hours
High point 1401 m (4596 ft)

Best July to October

Map 92G/06 North
Vancouver

Driving distance from Vancouver 15 km (9.3 mi) or Bus 232

Crown Mountain and The Camel, seen from the trail.

A ride on the Grouse Mountain Skyride puts the hike to Goat Mountain within reach of anyone wishing a fairly short outing with splendid views almost every step of the way. The Grouse Mountain–area summits provide superlative views: to the southeast are Mount Baker and the Cascade Mountains, to the west are the Strait of Georgia and Vancouver Island, and to the north and east, the sea of mountain peaks and valleys that is southwestern British Columbia. For even shorter trips, the summit of Dam Mountain or a hike east of Dam on Thunderbird Ridge is a worthwhile objective. For anyone desirous of something more strenuous, the trip up to the Grouse Chalet described in Hike 51 (or any of the other numerous trails on lower Grouse Mountain) may serve as a warm-up.

From the Skyride, you head first towards Grouse Mountain, then follow the service road around its west side. Here the Greater Vancouver Regional District (GVRD) has installed a hiker information and registration board. The GVRD has also placed green and yellow trail markers at various locations. Follow the trail uphill to a pipeline crossing, after which you reach the col between Dam and Grouse Mountains. Keep right to traverse around the east side of Dam, ascending and keeping right at all forks. You again meet the pipeline coming over the shoulder of Dam on its way from Kennedy Lake. Shortly after this, a faint trail goes off right, undulating eastward along Thunderbird Ridge. The next junction allows an abbreviated outing: the fork to the left takes you back south to the 1341 m (4400 ft) summit of Dam Mountain. You would then descend Dam's south slope to rejoin your outward trail just north of the col between Dam and Grouse Mountains. Alternatively, it would add little to your time to traverse over the top of Dam on the return from Goat Mountain. A few minutes north on the main trail is a fine viewpoint towards the steep face of Crown Mountain and the Camel. It also looks down over the route to Hanes Valley via Crown Pass. You next climb sharply up and over Little Goat Mountain, then continue along the ridge towards the final ascent of Goat itself. The most direct but most difficult route to the summit comes just after a fixed chain, when a left fork goes straight up the rocks to the top. However, you may choose to stay with the track as it contours around the southeast slope to the ridge, then turns left and up to your goal. After a pause to refresh yourself and enjoy the views, you can retrace your ascent route or investigate any of the numerous side trails.

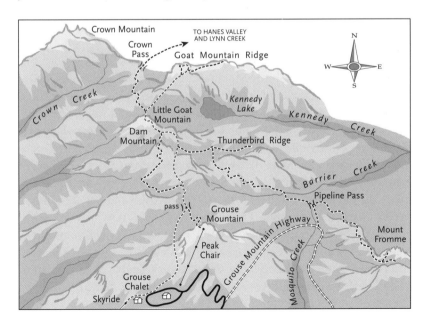

51 LOWER GROUSE MOUNTAIN

Round trip 10 km (6.2 mi)	Allow 5 hours
Elevation gain 685 m (2240 ft)	High point 1125 m (3700 ft)
Average grade 13.7%	

Best April to November	Map 92G/06 North Vancouver

Driving distance from Vancouver 10 km (6.2 mi)

Lions Gate Bridge and Stanley Park, seen from the site of the old BCMC cabin.

As the population of Greater Vancouver has burgeoned, so have the trails on the lower slopes of Grouse Mountain. This area was also an accessible source of trees for the lumber industry in the early years of last century, and it is covered in a multiplicity of old roads and skid trails. There are, therefore, an almost infinite number of permutations of possible trips. The most popular hike is the Grouse Grind, a kind of high-angle social club. Other trails are more difficult to describe because of the number of name changes and switches that have occurred. The trip described here takes the old BCMC Trail to the site of the British Columbia Mountaineering Club's (BCMC) cabin. The start of this trail is now used as part of the Baden-Powell Trail. It then follows the Larsen Trail and some of the new BCMC Trail to the Grouse Chalet. The descent takes the new BCMC Trail down to the Grind, then the Baden-Powell Trail back to your start.

In North Vancouver, drive east from Capilano Road onto Montroyal Boulevard and turn left up Skyline Drive, parking just below the final bend. There is no parking above the bend to where the road ends 100 m (325 ft) later.

Take the Baden-Powell Trail west from the bend in the road. In about 20 minutes you go right, leaving the Baden-Powell Trail, at a junction with the right fork signed "BCMC Trail to Larsen Trail...." Continue upward, crossing two creeks in steep little gullies to arrive at an intersection with signs. Initially, go straight through to the BCMC cabin site and a fine viewpoint. Now retrace your steps to the intersection and go uphill on the Larsen Trail. This route zigzags upward towards the crest of the ridge where it forks again: left for the Grouse Chalet; right for the foot of the Cut ski run, by which you may also reach the chalet. Go left and 10 minutes later you meet the new BCMC Trail, which has orange markers labelled "BCMC." After 30 minutes on this trail you emerge on the rocks below the viewing deck of the Grouse Chalet, 2.5 to 3 hours from your start and 685 m (2240 ft) higher. When sated with the affluent tourist scene descend, initially on your ascent route: the new BCMC Trail. Pass the junction at which you joined this trail on the uphill, and pass the fork that goes left to the BCMC cabin site. Your descent trail then joins the infamous Grind. Twenty minutes down the Grind, go left onto the Baden-Powell Trail, which you follow east. On the way, entering from the left, you will see the steep trail that dropped from the intersection just east of the cabin site. Another kilometre (0.6 mi) gets you to the fork where you left the Baden-Powell Trail on your ascent. It is then familiar ground back to Skyline Drive.

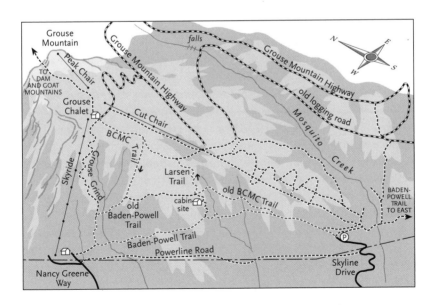

52 HANES VALLEY

Round trip 18 km (11.2 mi)	Allow 8 hours
Elevation gain 1100 m (3610 ft)	High point 1300 m (4260 ft)
Average grade 12.2%	
Best August to October	Map 92G/06 North Vancouver
Driving distance from Vancouver 15 km (9.3 mi) or Buses 228 & 236	

View down Hanes Valley from just below Crown Pass, with Mount Burwell on the horizon. (JS)

Lynn Headwaters Regional Park (LHRP) was, for many years, an off-limits watershed. Now opened to the public, but with the old-growth trees gone, the park offers a number of possibilities for hikers. This trip is a crossover to Grouse Mountain via Hanes Creek and Crown Pass; it should be done late in the season since it requires crossing Lynn Creek on logs and boulders. In high water this is only for the foolhardy. The hike can be done clockwise or counter-clockwise, and you can take the Grouse Mountain Skyride or not. Described here is the minimum-effort method: drive to the Skyride, hike the trail descending, then take the bus back to your vehicle. The start of this hike is the same as for Goat Mountain (Hike 50). Phone (604) 985-1690 for LHRP trail information and parking lot lock-up times.

In North Vancouver, follow Capilano Road to the Grouse Mountain Skyride. Take the first ride of the morning!

Head towards Grouse Mountain but follow the service road around its west side, past the Greater Vancouver Regional District (GVRD) hiker information and registration board. The GVRD has also placed green and yellow trail markers at various locations. Hike north, keeping right at forks, to traverse around the east side of Dam Mountain. On the north side of Dam, go right on the main trail, climb sharply up and over Little

Goat Mountain, and down into the col. Now drop left onto the trail to Crown Pass, rather than ascending to Goat Mountain. In Crown Pass you have a view of your route, a boulder field, down Hanes Valley. The trail stays just left (north) of the fall-line, and 0.5 km (0.3 mi) down you cross a belt of vegetation before traversing another boulder field. After dropping 490 m (1600 ft) from Crown Pass, with your last view of the rocky cirque, you enter the big trees at their closest point. In the timber is a clearing with a signpost and map. It is 2 km (1.2 mi) from here to the Lynn Creek crossing, which is accomplished with boulder jumps and log walks. Another 0.5 hour gets you to the Hanes Valley/Lynn Valley trail junction, and 20 minutes down the Lynn Valley Trail gets you across the Norvan Creek bridge. It is 7 km (4.3 mi) of straightforward trail, descending gently on river-left, from here to the parking lot of the regional park. At the debris chute go right on the Cedar Mill Trail along Lynn Creek, which you cross just before the parking lot and information boards. From there, it is 1.5 km (0.9 mi) along the road to the park gates. On Dempsey Road you can pick up Bus 228 to Lonsdale Quay, where you take Bus 236 back to the Skyride parking area.

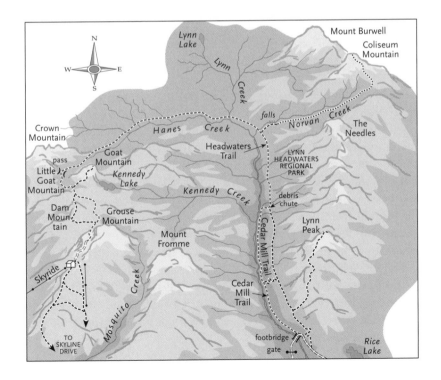

53 COLISEUM MOUNTAIN

Round trip 24.5 km (15.2 mi)	Allow 10.5 hours
Elevation gain 1265 m (4155 ft)	High point 1446 m (4745 ft)
Average grade 10.3%	

Best July to October	Maps 92G/06 North Vancouver; 92G/07 Port Coquitlam

Driving distance from Vancouver 15 km (9.3 mi) or Bus 228

Grouse Mountain, Goat Mountain, Crown Pass and Crown Mountain, west from the summit.

Located in Lynn Headwaters Regional Park (LHRP), this hike is full of contrasts: a well-groomed park trail along a gentle valley bottom; a rugged wilderness route that ranges from steep, forested slopes to wet meadows; and a subalpine, rocky ridge to the open, alpine summit. From the top there are views all around. To the north are nearby Mount Burwell and the distant mountains of Garibaldi Provincial Park, to the southeast are Mounts Seymour, Elsay and Bishop with Mount Baker rising beyond them, across the Strait of Georgia are the Vancouver Island mountains and in the southwest stand nearby Crown and Goat Mountains. Phone (604) 985-1690 for LHRP trail information and parking lot lock-up times.

Take Exit 19 off Highway 1 onto Lynn Valley Road (north) in North Vancouver. Pass Lynn Canyon Park and just after Dempsey Road are the park gates. Another 1.5 km (0.9 mi) brings you to the parking lot and information boards.

Cross Lynn Creek and turn left, following the Cedar Mill Trail upstream on river-left. An hour from your start is a debris chute on which you go right to meet the Loop Trail, which was parallel to you on the hillside above. There is only one upstream trail from here on. Another hour should get you to just beyond the 6.5 km (4.0 mi) marker, with Norvan Creek audible 100 m (325 ft) ahead. Watch for a yellow metal marker felt-penned "Coliseum." Turn uphill to your right at this point. You ascend on a sketchy trail along the little spine above Norvan Creek, heading right again after about 5 minutes to a large round yellow hiker sign. The sign has some estimates of times required: Coliseum Mountain 4.5 hours, Norvan Pass 2.5 hours, Norvan Meadows 1.25 hours. Set off following orange tapes through second-growth forest, with deadfall littering the steep slope. Then the grade eases as you contour above the creek, passing first a left fork to a viewpoint, then a small waterfall and a pool. Next you emerge from the forest at Norvan Meadows, at the foot of an old rock slide covered with vegetation. The avalanche debris here is testament to the depth of the 1998–99 snowfall. At the pass a sign indicates a viewpoint 5 minutes off to the right. Set high on a rock above the Seymour River Valley, this lookout provides a preview of the ridge you must traverse to reach the top, as well as a backward look at The Needles. The summit is still 2 hours away, so go left at the pass and make your way up the ridge in a series of steep steps, interspaced with relatively level subalpine meadows. Finally, after a sharp little descent and the subsequent ascent, you reach alpine terrain and follow paint-splashed rocks to the top. To return, retrace your ascent route.

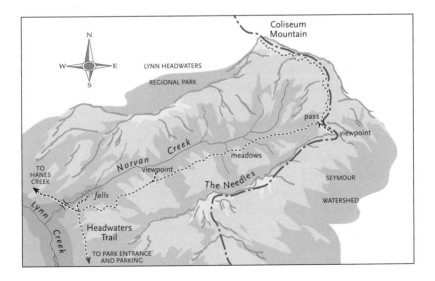

54 MOUNT SEYMOUR

Round trip 9 km (5.6 mi)	Allow 5 hours
Elevation gain 455 m (1495 ft)	High point 1455 m (4774 ft)
Average grade 10.1%	
Best July to October	Maps 92G/07 Port Coquitlam; B.C. Parks Mt. Seymour Provincial Park
Driving distance from Vancouver 25 km (15 mi)	

Mount Seymour, seen west across Indian Arm from the Dilly-Dally Trail.

Visible from Vancouver and with a good trail providing access to all three peaks, Mount Seymour is one of the most popular hikes on the North Shore. The most usual trip is to the second and third peaks, the third and most northerly being the highest. All the tops provide panoramic views: to west, north and east are a seemingly endless sea of mountains, and to the south is the valley of the Fraser River and its delta.

Take the Mount Seymour exit off Highway 1 in North Vancouver. Keep right onto Mount Seymour Parkway and follow it east, watching for the B.C. Parks sign directing you to turn left onto Mount Seymour

Road. Follow this road uphill to its end at the ski area. Park at the far (north) end of the lot near the information boards.

First the trail ascends through pleasant country to the west of the Manning ski run (a road in summer) before joining it briefly just below Mystery Peak. There is a short drop left to pass Sugar Bowl Pond, after which the trail rises to Brockton Point. Ahead looms First Peak (or Pump Peak) of Mount Seymour. Beyond here the trail swings right in an ascending traverse to bypass First Peak. You head down into an attractive meadow and up again until, some 20 minutes past Brockton Point, there is a fork with signs: left to Mount Seymour, right to Elsay Lake. Follow the trail to the left. In summer, lots of paint on the rocks indicates the way. However, with snow cover, this trail can be difficult to find. You arrive on the ridge crest at a point between First and Second Peaks. Heading north, there is a gully to ascend on Second Peak then a rocky scramble to the top. This next section, on the way to Third Peak, can be hazardous because of the steep drop-off. Down the northwest side of Second Peak, you need to descend 100 m (325 ft). If it is snowy or icy, turn around and come back another time. In the saddle between the peaks note the trail dropping off to the left; it is the route to Mount Elsay (Hike 55). From the saddle you have 200 m (655 ft) of steep but straightforward scrambling to the top of Third Peak. So many people have been on this route that, as long as it is not snow-covered, it is easy to follow. Your destination is a fine, open, rocky, rounded summit.

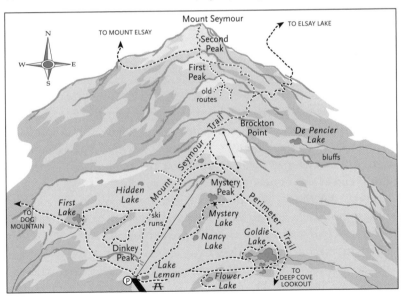

55 MOUNT ELSAY

Round trip 16 km (9.9 mi)	Allow 9 hours
Elevation gain 1050 m (3450 ft)	High point 1422 m (4666 ft)
Average grade 13.1%	

Best July to October	Map 92G/07 Port Coquitlam
Driving distance from Vancouver 25 km (15 mi)	

Elsay Lake, viewed from the summit.

Although it begins and ends on the improved trails of a provincial park, this hike to the peak north of Mount Seymour gives you a taste of true wilderness, with all that implies in terms of necessary equipment and backcountry experience. It is advisable to have done the Mount Seymour trip (Hike 54) before attempting this hike. Described is a clockwise circuit from the Mount Seymour Trail, over Mount Elsay and back by the Elsay Lake Trail.

Take the Mount Seymour exit off Highway 1 in North Vancouver. Keep right onto Mount Seymour Parkway and follow it east, watching for the B.C. Parks sign directing you to turn left onto Mount Seymour Road. Follow this road uphill to its end at the ski area. Park at the far (north) end of the lot near the information boards.

Follow the Mount Seymour Trail past the Manning ski run and Mystery Peak, then drop to Sugar Bowl Pond and rise to Brockton Point. Swing right to bypass First Peak and arrive at the signboard junction: left to Mount Seymour, right to Elsay Lake. This is the point you will return to at the end of the circuit. Go left and ascend to the ridge crest. Traverse over Second Peak. Just beyond the 4 km (2.5 mi) mark, in the saddle between Second and Third Peaks, you go left, descending westward on a faint trail that takes you down a gully before jogging right and down again. Now a mere route marked with tapes, it eventually levels off and contours above a steep slope before rising once more to a rocky summit from which you can see your objective off to the right. Drop down through bush and over one small rock slide to reach a larger one, with two cairns marking the way across. At about 1130 m (3700 ft) this is the low point, and from here the route trends mainly upward. More rocks and blueberries get you to a ridge running north to a pass above an enormous rock slide on your right. The tapes lead you up the slope ahead past a small alpine area, through more blueberries to the west ridge, then up a final rock face to the summit. On top, as well as magnificent scenery to the east, west and north, to the south you may savour the unusual view of Mount Seymour's precipitous north face. To return, hike back to the pass. Descend the huge rock slide noted earlier on the east side of the ridge, staying right to pick up a few cairns marking the way to a relatively flat area at the bottom with two small ponds draining down a valley on the left. Keep right, however, and cross the low ridge ahead, descending on the far side by yet another rock slide to join the Elsay Lake Trail. From here a long, fairly gentle traverse precedes Wes's Staircase, a steep section of trail zigzagging up some 300 m (1000 ft) to meet the main Mount Seymour Trail at the signboard junction.

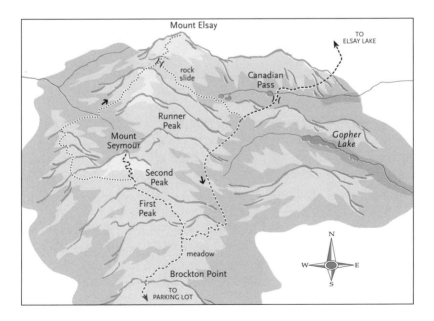

56 DIEZ VISTAS

Round trip 13 km (8.1 mi)   Allow 5.5 hours
Elevation gain 455 m (1490 ft) High point 607 m (1990 ft)
Average grade 7.0%

Best April to November   Map 92G/07 Port Coquitlam;
                                B.C. Hydro Buntzen Lake
                                Reservoir
Driving distance from Vancouver 35 km (20 mi) or Bus 148

View up Indian Arm. (IM)

B.C. Hydro must be given full credit for combining water storage with superlative facilities for hiking, horseback riding and water recreation in the area surrounding Buntzen Lake. And in the case of the trail of the ten viewpoints, the building of a floating bridge over the south arm makes possible a truly delightful circuit up along Buntzen Ridge (the north-south ridge to the west of the lake) and back along the lake. Hikes 56, 57, 58 and 59 all start from the same parking area.

Turn north off Highway 7A (Barnet Highway) onto Ioco Road, at the traffic lights just east of Port Moody. Thereafter, follow the signs for Buntzen Lake. At the gated Powerhouse Road, turn left into the parking lots.

Walk to the southwest end of the lot to pick up your route, a well-maintained trail that takes you across the lake on a floating bridge. Here you meet a road that provides access from Anmore to a pumphouse. The trail sets off into the forest opposite the floating bridge and heads uphill for a few minutes to a fork where the route, marked with orange squares and signed "Diez Vistas," goes off left. Next, Saddle Trail enters from the right, and shortly thereafter you go right to break into the open at a pass that carries an old pipeline and power line. These you cross, passing under the pipe and onto a track that switchbacks upward. Near the top of a steep section, the trail forks, either branch having its own reward: the left provides a viewpoint over Indian Arm, the right a fine outlook across South Beach to Eagle Ridge. The branches reunite at the high point. Now you travel north in open forest with, from time to time, some sensational views over Indian Arm, its waters appearing to be directly below you. After traversing the ridge you drop fairly steeply to an old road, at the end of which you come on B.C. Hydro's service road around the lake. On it you go right, eventually reaching the lake's northern arm and trails going both right and left. Left here is the old, less interesting way around via the lake's north end; so, right it is along the power line for 10 minutes or so to yet another point of decision. This time left leads across a new footbridge to North Beach, up onto Powerhouse Road briefly in order to cross the tunnel from Coquitlam Lake, then down again to the trail that undulates through the forest along the lake's east side back to South Beach.

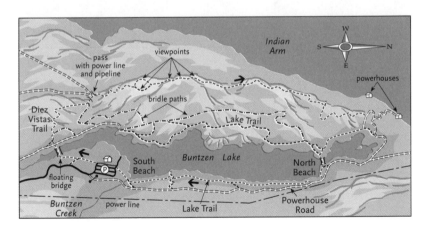

57 DILLY-DALLY PEAK

to Croker Lookout	Round trip 17 km (10.6 mi)	Allow 5 hours
	Elevation gain 315 m (1035 ft)	High point 440 m (1445 ft)
	Average grade 3.7%	
	Best May to November	
to summit	Round trip 23.5 km (14.6 mi)	Allow 10 hours
	Elevation gain 1120 m (3675 ft)	High point 1250 m (4100 ft)
	Average grade 9.5%	
	Best July to October	

Maps 92G/07 Port Coquitlam; B.C. Hydro Buntzen
Lake Reservoir
Driving distance from Vancouver 35 km (20 mi) or Bus 148

Eagle Ridge and the Dilly-Dally Trail (left), seen from Mount Elsay.

You won't find Dilly-Dally Peak on any map. It is the name given to a high point on Eagle Ridge, the long north-south ridge to the east of Buntzen Lake, presumably because to get there and back in one day you can't afford to dilly-dally on the way. Actually this outing gives the choice of two objectives: this one just mentioned and, for a shorter, less strenuous hike, a bluffy knob, informally named Croker Lookout, giving a view north to Croker Island and south down Indian Arm to Vancouver and beyond. Since there are 7 km (4.3 mi) of road along the east side of the lake to the start of the trail proper, you might consider using a bicycle. The times quoted above are for a trip on foot. Hikes 56, 57, 58 and 59 all start from the same parking area.

Turn north off Highway 7A (Barnet Highway) onto Ioco Road, at the traffic lights just east of Port Moody. Thereafter, follow the signs for Buntzen Lake. At the gated Powerhouse Road, turn left into the parking lots.

Walk back to the gate and go north on Powerhouse Road. Continue on this B.C. Hydro service road past the dam and its penstocks. A short distance beyond, the road forks and you stay right, heading for the tiny settlement of Buntzen Bay. Before then, however, you branch off right again on a dead end that leads to a power pylon, beyond which your trail heads off uphill to the trees above the right-of-way. Next turn left, cross two creeks in an area once logged over and join the one-time logging road as it starts its steep ascent. On it—now barely recognizable in spots but for the remains of wooden ties, metal gratings and steel cables—you quickly gain height. A little more than 2 hours from your start you reach a left fork that leads you to Croker Lookout. Beyond the junction the main trail detours twice to the right to avoid windfalls and tangled vegetation; the second diversion leads to another lookout (signed "157 Lookout") with fine views down and across Indian Arm. Soon thereafter you arrive at the end of the old road and the limits of logging. Now a marked trail leads you up through pleasant open forest across the creek to the main ridge, reaching it at Dilly-Dally Pass where your route turns south. For the summit you must still gain some 200 m (650 ft) before your dalliance may begin, with two lakes—one east and one west—below you and mountains all around to admire. If you have previously travelled Hike 58, you could head south along the ridge to the Swan Falls Junction and descend that trail. If not, return by retracing your ascent route.

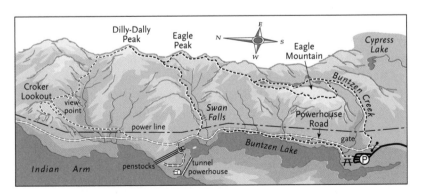

EAGLE PEAK

Round trip 18.5 km (11.5 mi)　　Allow 8 hours
Elevation gain 1150 m (3773 ft)　High point 1280 m (4200 ft)
Average grade 12.4%

Best July to October　　　　　Maps 92G/07 Port Coquitlam;
　　　　　　　　　　　　　　B.C. Hydro Buntzen Lake
　　　　　　　　　　　　　　Reservoir
Driving distance from Vancouver 35 km (20 mi) or Bus 148

View northeast from the summit.

This feature, sometimes called Mount Beautiful, is the true summit of Eagle Ridge, the long north-south ridge to the east of Buntzen Lake. The nearly panoramic outlook encompasses the mountains to the northeast, Mount Baker across the Fraser Valley, the Strait of Georgia beyond Vancouver and down below Coquitlam Lake on one side and on the other, Indian Arm. The trail takes you past Swan Falls, not high, but very scenic. Since there are 4.5 km (2.8 mi) of road along the east side of the lake to the trailhead, you might consider using a bicycle. The times quoted above are for a trip on foot. Hikes 56, 57, 58 and 59 all start from the same parking area.

Turn north off Highway 7A (Barnet Highway) onto Ioco Road, at the traffic lights just east of Port Moody. Thereafter, follow the signs for Buntzen Lake. At the gated Powerhouse Road, turn left into the parking lots.

Walk back to the gate and go north on Powerhouse Road. Continue on this B.C. Hydro service road crossing the intake tunnel that carries water from Coquitlam Lake in the next valley to the east. Pass North Beach and cross the wide bed of Trout Creek, whose unofficially named Swan Falls, high above, you will soon view close-up. Just beyond the creek you turn back sharp right where the road approaches the B.C. Hydro power line, and make for pylon 531.3, where your trail strikes off left, heading for the trees. Now comes the relentless slog up the steep track, the creek on your right. After some 30 minutes, however, comes temporary relief when a short spur to the right gives you a grandstand view over the lake from the top of the lower fall. You have yet one more excuse for a rest a little later, on a bluff high above the creek, from which lofty perch you look across Buntzen Ridge to the mountains of the North Shore and south over the Fraser lowlands. On resuming, you continue to rise before sidehilling into the upper basin, crossing two small tributaries (sometimes dry) en route. Now comes an enormous washout, where the loss of vegetative cover encourages slippage and where you need to keep in view the trail markers on the opposite side. There is a braided cable handline for assistance. Some 20 minutes later you enter a surprisingly extensive meadow, green and lush. It is only 15 minutes from here to the col, Swan Falls Junction. Here you meet the ridge trail, on which you turn right for Eagle Peak, where you have fine but slightly restricted views, the best being at the triangulation marker on a bare bluff a little south of the peak. If you have previously travelled Hike 59, you could head south from here to descend by that trail. If not, return by retracing your ascent route.

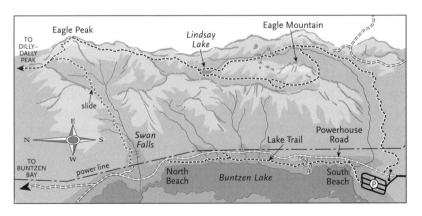

127

LINDSAY LAKE

Round trip 15 km (9.3 mi)	Allow 6 hours
Elevation gain 1020 m (3350 ft)	High point 1160 m (3800 ft)
Average grade 13.6%	

Best July to October	Maps 92G/07 Port Coquitlam;
	B.C. Hydro Buntzen Lake
	Reservoir
Driving distance from Vancouver 35 km (20 mi) or Bus 148	

Not content with creating the Diez Vistas Trail along Buntzen Ridge, the indefatigable Halvor Lunden has produced no fewer than three routes up Eagle Ridge on the opposite (east) side of the valley. These trails could also serve as parts of a ridge traverse from south to north or vice versa. Of these trails, the most southerly has Lindsay Lake as its designated destination, and there are numerous other named lakes to visit. The route passes to the west of Eagle Mountain, which although marked on maps is not the true high point of the ridge. Hike 58 takes you to the highest point. Hikes 56, 57, 58 and 59 all start from the same parking area.

Turn north off Highway 7A (Barnet Highway) onto Ioco Road, at the traffic lights just east of Port Moody. Thereafter, follow the signs for Buntzen Lake. At the gated Powerhouse Road, turn left into the parking lots.

Walk back to the gate on Powerhouse Road. The trailhead, with its map and statistics, is just 20 m (65 ft) north. Starting off in mainly deciduous forest you soon join a bridle trail and go left under a power line. Next you turn right on the marked route and start climbing the ridge's steep west side until, beyond Polytrichum Lookout, you round the head of a gully and emerge onto an area beginning to regenerate after logging. Soon, however, you re-enter the tall trees, walk briefly along an old dyke and arrive at El Paso, a junction with signs. Both branches lead to Lindsay Lake: left via the viewpoints, right via the lower lakes. Taking the viewpoints first, your trail crosses a creek and swings southward to Halvor's lookouts, each one named. You pass in succession Barton Point, Little Valhalla and, as you turn north again by way of a detour left, Spahat Rigg (Bear Ridge). Still heading north, you come on little Jessica Lake, its waters contained within natural dykes and actually above the level of its surroundings. Its drainage is presumably subterranean, for there is no sign of an outflow channel. Thereafter you reach another overlook, West Point, near a rocky outcrop aptly named The Pulpit. Then, fol-

View over Indian Arm to Mount Seymour, Runner Peak and Mount Elsay.

lowing a short, steep rise, you descend gently to Lindsay Lake. There the trail splits, the left branch continuing north along the ridge. Your return route goes right, circling Lindsay Lake and veering south towards a veritable lake district where several choices await you. You may elect to follow the direct route that makes its way through the centre of the area. Or you may go left at Nancycatch Junction and explore the picturesquely named Demelza, Robin and Siskin Lakes. Or staying with the direct trail along Chickadee Lake, you may then go right, passing St. Mary's, Mac and Jay Lakes before regaining the main trail. Now you are only a short walk from El Paso, whence you retrace your ascent route.

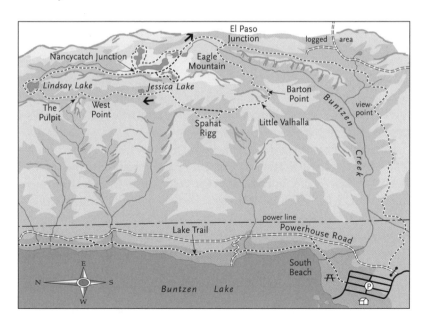

60 DENNETT LAKE

Round trip 10 km (6.2 mi) Allow 6 hours
Elevation gain 860 m (2830 ft) High point 960 m (3150 ft)
Average grade 17.2%

Best May to October Map 92G/07 Port Coquitlam
Driving distance from Vancouver 40 km (25 mi)

The lakeshore. (IM)

This area is included in the recently created Pinecone Burke Provincial Park. Hike 61 and this trip are at the south end of the park. Hikes 30 and 31 are at the north end. The objective of this invigorating hike is an attractive little lake on the lower east side of Burke Ridge, which has its own interesting approach. En route, too, you pass Munro Lake, much shrunken since its dam was removed but revegetating with a variety of marsh plants and certainly worth some attention. The trail can be muddy early in the year.

Turn north off Highway 7 (Lougheed Highway), east of Port Coquitlam, onto Coast Meridian Road and drive for 2.4 km (1.5 mi) to Apel Road. Go right at this junction and right again onto Victoria Drive, staying with its left branch when it splits at the top of a rise. Then follow the signs to Minnekhada Regional Park as your road loses its surface and becomes Quarry Road. From the entrance to Minnekhada drive another 3.1 km (1.9 mi), crossing MacIntyre and Deiner Creeks. Just after the 3.5 km sign on your right, going up a hill your route starts on the left on an old logging road. The Burke Mountain Naturalists have a large sign at the trailhead.

Follow this road uphill for about 5 minutes, then go right onto the trail marked with large red diamonds. Initially the trail traverses close to Deiner Creek before heading northwest. For about 625 m (2000 ft), partway through an old burned-over stretch now being hidden by vigorous second growth, the gradient hardly varies. There are still viewpoints, however, which give a valid excuse for resting while looking over the Pitt River lowlands. They are a striking contrast to the alpine country around Golden Ears and the distant slopes of Mount Baker. Finally, as you reach the shoulder of Burke Ridge, you enter old-growth forest—fine stands of yellow cedar that survived the fire—and from now on the walk is virtually on the level. However, since nothing is perfect in this imperfect world, this part of the trail can be muddy early in the season. Very soon a similar trail marked with yellow joins from the left, coming from the old ski village. In a few minutes more you reach Munro Lake, or what is left of it. To continue, make your way around the lake's west side for about 200 m (650 ft) to where tapes mark the route into the forest. If, traversing around the lake, you arrive at a boulder-filled creek bed, you have passed the trail. Turn left up this (possibly dry) creek bed and pick up the trail where it crosses the watercourse. It is less than 1 km (0.6 mi) distance and 130 m (420 ft) of elevation gain to Dennett Lake, a tiny jewel with a rampart of cliffs behind it. This makes a most satisfactory destination. To return you can retrace your ascent route.

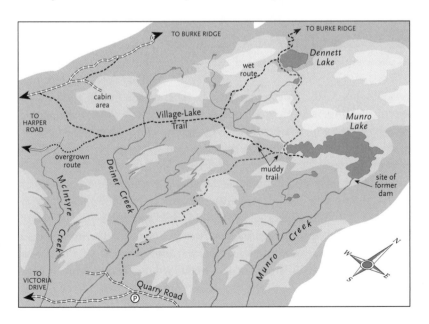

61 WIDGEON LAKE

Round trip 18.5 km (11.5 mi)   Allow 8 hours
Elevation gain 770 m (2530 ft)   High point 770 m (2530 ft)
Average grade 8.3%

Best June to October   Map 92G/07 Port Coquitlam
Driving distance from Vancouver 55 km (35 mi)

The lake, as first glimpsed from the trail. (IM)

This area is included in the recently created Pinecone Burke Provincial Park. Hike 60 and this trip are at the south end of the park. Hikes 30 and 31 are at the north end. The trailhead for this trip is only 6 km (3.7 mi) by road from the start of Hike 60; but, since it is a private road, the approach is by canoe or kayak across Pitt River. This does, though, add over 2 hours to the length of your day. Therefore an early start, or an overnight camp, is essential if you are to enjoy a little time at this scenic body of water, which is hemmed in by granite bluffs except at its outlet to the west fork of Widgeon Creek. Snow lies late on the trail in the bowl beneath the lake.

Travelling east on Highway 7 (Lougheed Highway) turn left, just after crossing the Pitt River, onto Dewdney Trunk Road. Stay on Dewdney Trunk for about 6.2 km (3.9 mi) then turn left onto 208 Street (Neaves Road), which later becomes Rannie Road as it travels north to the public launching ramp at Grant Narrows just before Pitt Lake, nearly 18 km (11.2 mi) from the Pitt River bridge. There is a fee to park overnight here.

Paddle across the river to the north end of Siwash Island, where you enter Widgeon Slough. After 800 m (0.5 mi), keep right and start ascending Widgeon Creek. Stay with the main channel, going left, then right, to reach the landing place about an hour's paddle altogether from the ramp at Grant Narrows. Land at the B.C. Forest Service Recreation Site and take the old logging road that parallels the west (river-right) side of the creek. You may, however, follow a foot trail closer to the creek, past several gorgeous pools and waterfalls. If you take this creek-side trail 3 km (1.9 mi) to the upper falls, you must ascend to an old road and backtrack about 250 m (820 ft) south down this stub road back to the main up-valley road. The one major point of decision comes after about 4 km (2.5 mi) where you go left for the lake instead of crossing Widgeon Creek. Finally, you do cross the creek's wild west fork on a footbridge that is an amazing feat of bush engineering. Then climb quite steeply on river-left to the end of the road and the start of the trail proper, going first through old slash and then continuing in forest. Following that comes a little rock bluff as a final challenge. A few more minutes of ascent and here is your lake just below. If you go right, you finish by its shore; go left and you find yourself at its outlet. Either way your efforts to reach this beautiful destination are well rewarded.

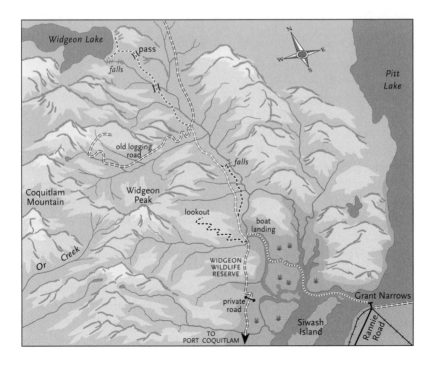

62 HECTOR FERGUSON LAKE

Round trip 28 km (17 mi)   Allow 11 hours
Elevation gain 635 m (2085 ft)   High point 760 m (2495 ft)
Average grade 4.5%

Best July to November   Maps 92G/08 Stave Lake;
                                  B.C. Parks Golden Ears
                                  Provincial Park
Driving distance from Vancouver 60 km (35 mi)

View from the south shore of the lake. (IM)

This is a trip to savour. Gold Creek is a beautiful stream and the trail is close to the water much of the way. The creek crossing is on bleached logs well above the water. On the rise to the lake is a stand of big old trees. The lake itself is deep and clear with rock slides running into it from the cliffs above. However, here's the reality check! To make it to the lake and back in one day, you have to hustle. Bicycles are allowed on the East Canyon Trail, so consider that option! It should be possible to pedal about 6 km (3.7 mi). The park gates are locked overnight, so watch your time on that count also. Although Hikes 62, 63 and 64 are all in the southeast corner of Golden Ears Provincial Park, each trip has a different parking lot and trailhead.

Travelling east on Highway 7 (Lougheed Highway) through Maple Ridge, turn left onto 228 Street at the B.C. Parks sign for Golden Ears Provincial Park. Then go right onto Dewdney Trunk Road. Go left again onto 232 Street, cross the South Alouette River, then travel right onto

Fern Crescent to the entrance of the park. From here, follow the main road 14 km (8.7 mi) to the Gold Creek parking lot.

Do not take the Lower Falls Trail. Go past the horse corrals and take the East Canyon Trail. The trail is actually a sand-covered road, so it is more pleasant walking than the usual logging road. With Gold Creek audible but well off to your left, you gain height easily to 335 m (1100 ft). The road then drops 60 m (200 ft) and runs close to the creek. Just before 4 km (2.5 mi) ignore a trail off left to the creek. From here on you remain close to the water. A half kilometre (0.3 mi) later there are horse corrals and another left branch that you again ignore. As you hike above this point, the creek has beautiful green water with some deep pools. In another kilometre (0.6 mi), for a short distance, the trail goes out onto the sandbars; the fine white sand, the rocks and the water are a sharp contrast with the mountains above. Back in the trees, there are occasional mud holes since this is also a horse trail. A little more than half way to your objective, the creek makes a sweeping right-hand bend which provides good views upstream; and the valley leading to the lake is visible ahead. You cross Gold Creek's multiple channels, at GR406729, on a series of log jams. It's a great place for lunch! You also cross Hector Ferguson Creek right after. The next 3.5 km (2.2 mi) is a gradual ascent through a spectacular stand of old-growth forest. The last 0.5 km (0.3 mi) to the lake is steep with a waterfall and a series of cascades in the creek just below the lake. How far around the lake you can hike will depend on the water level. If high, the outlet may be as far as you go; but that's a fine place!

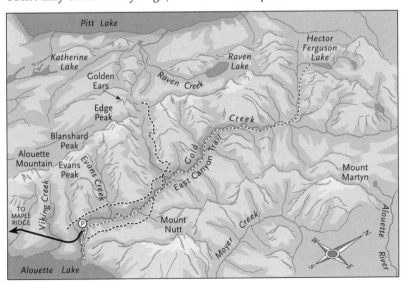

63 GOLDEN EARS

to Panorama Ridge	Round trip 20 km (12.4 mi)	Allow 7.5 hours
	Elevation gain 1040 m (3410 ft)	High point 1200 m (3936 ft)
	Average grade 10.4%	
to summit	Round trip 24 km (15 mi)	Allow 11 hours
	Elevation gain 1500 m (4920 ft)	High point 1706 m (5598 ft)
	Average grade 12.5%	
	Best July to September	Maps 92G/07 Port Coquitlam; 92G/08 Stave Lake; B.C. Parks Golden Ears Provincial Park
	Driving distance from Vancouver 60 km (35 mi)	

This is the peak from which the provincial park takes its name. Remember, though, that the hike to this summit involves a strenuous long day's outing and requires some mountaineering experience. For this trip, come prepared; the weather changes quickly in the mountains. Care and proper equipment are necessary if you aim for the peak. Still, the magnificent views from the top are ample reward, coupled as they are with the sense of well-being that comes from accomplishment. However, if you think the scramble to the peak is beyond you, you may enjoy a leisurely ridge walk if you set your sights on Panorama Ridge, which easily lives up to its name and makes a rewarding destination. Although Hikes 62, 63 and 64 are all in the southeast corner of Golden Ears Provincial Park, each trip has a different parking lot and trailhead.

Travelling east on Highway 7 (Lougheed Highway) through Maple Ridge, turn left onto 228 Street at the B.C. Parks sign for Golden Ears Provincial Park. Then go right onto Dewdney Trunk Road. Go left again onto 232 Street, cross the South Alouette River, then travel right onto Fern Crescent to the entrance of the park. Follow the main access road past the Alouette Lake day-use area; then, just beyond the sani-station and the information board, fork left and left again for the West Canyon parking lot.

Follow the signs for West Canyon Trail, which takes you north with Gold Creek on your right. En route you cross Evans Creek and enjoy a variety of valley scenes, culminating in the prospect from Gold Creek Lookout before the trail bears left up the next valley. Then you pass several creeks and cross the camping spot at Alder Flats to the trail on the right above the outhouse. Just after that, you meet the remains of an old

The descent from the summit. (IM)

logging road coming up from Gold Creek, parallel to an east-flowing tributary. On this path you go left, switchbacking upward for a short distance before climbing dramatically to the ridge crest at its lower end and resuming your northwesterly direction until you reach a little shelter, where you change course again onto the appropriately named Panorama Ridge heading southwest to the summit. Your route is now adorned with a number of bumps to negotiate, but with superb views of Pitt Lake and the mountains to the west as compensation. All the time you are gaining height steadily, and eventually you leave all vegetation behind as you approach and cross a permanent snowfield and turn back westward for the final stretch; it is steep enough for hands to be called into service frequently as you make for the peak of the North Ear. Here you have a true panorama from your elevated perch.

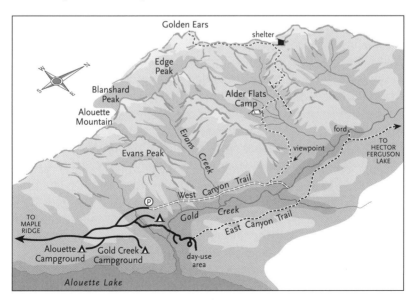

64 ALOUETTE MOUNTAIN

Round trip 22 km (14 mi)   Allow 9 hours
Elevation gain 1100 m (3610 ft)   High point 1366 m (4482 ft)
Average grade 10.0%

Best July to October   Maps 92G/08 Stave Lake;
                         B.C. Parks Golden Ears
                         Provincial Park
Driving distance from Vancouver 60 km (35 mi)

Mount Blanshard, viewed from the summit.

In the early years of this century, what is now the most popular part of Golden Ears Provincial Park—the Alouette Valley—was the scene of intense logging operations. Although those days are long gone, there is still evidence of their existence in the artifacts to be found along many of the trails, some of which also follow the old railroad grades. Such a trail is the one to Alouette Mountain. Although this trail is long, for the most part it has an easy grade and its woodland stretches give pleasant walking on sunny days. It is interesting to contrast the second-growth timber of the lower stretches with the original tree cover at higher elevations—the stands of mountain hemlock and yellow cedar near Lake Beautiful being of impressive dimensions and venerable age. From the top, Blanshard Peak and Edge Peak are prominent to the north and Mounts Judge Howay and Robie Reid to the northeast. Although Hikes 62, 63 and 64 are all in the southeast corner of Golden Ears Provincial Park, each trip has a different parking lot and trailhead.

Travelling east on Highway 7 (Lougheed Highway) through Maple Ridge, turn left onto 228 Street at the B.C. Parks sign for Golden Ears

Provincial Park. Then go right onto Dewdney Trunk Road. Go left again onto 232 Street, cross the South Alouette River, then travel right onto Fern Crescent to the entrance of the park. From here, drive 4.5 km (2.8 mi) turning off left at the park headquarters sign. Go left again where the road forks, and drive for just over 1.6 km (1.0 mi) to the signpost pointing to Incline Trail. Limited parking space is available at the trailhead; there is more at Mike Lake, about 300 m (1000 ft) along.

Incline Trail, so named because it follows the shortcut used to "skyline" logs down from the railroad grade above, goes north passing an interesting piece of drowned forest. It then rises steeply to a fire access road, successor to the old railway. At the road, go right for some distance, then take the signposted cut-off trail uphill through second-growth timber. This trail again intersects the road, stays briefly with it, then cuts off uphill once more, finally emerging at the road below the logged-off area that is a relic of Hurricane Freda, the great storm of 1962. Cross the road and continue through prime forest northward, passing a signed trail to Lake Beautiful on the left (it's pretty, but its main beauty lies in the majestic old cedars around it). Shortly thereafter, a connecting trail from the hitching rack on the fire access road joins from the right, suggesting a possible short variant on the return trip. Staying west of the ridge crest, the trail passes several picturesque little alpine meadows and ponds before emerging from the forest, the objective now visible ahead. Finally comes the summit cairn with its commemorative marker and its magnificent panorama.

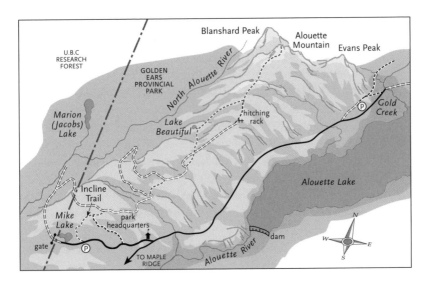

65 MOUNT CRICKMER

Round trip 20 km (12.4 mi)   Allow 8 hours
Elevation gain 1190 m (3900 ft)   High point 1357 m (4452 ft)
Average grade 11.9%

Best July to October   Map 92G/08 Stave Lake
Driving distance from Vancouver 70 km (40 mi)

Summit view looking west across Alouette Lake to Golden Ears. (IM)

This is a hike that takes you into the high country between Alouette and Stave Lakes. From the summit are fine views over Stave Lake and several smaller lakes north and east. To the west, those familiar peaks of the Golden Ears group look a little less familiar from this side: Mount Robie Reid dominates the northern skyline and to the east are the ranges that lie between you and the Chehalis Valley. From here, too, you may see how logging has cleared the ridges in every direction; this is a very different scene from that which the Rev. William Crickmer must have surveyed when he served as pastor at Langley and Yale between 1859 and 1862.

Travelling east on Highway 7 (Lougheed Highway) cross the Pitt River, pass Harris Road then turn left onto Dewdney Trunk Road. Stay on Dewdney Trunk for 23 km (14 mi) to just west of B.C. Hydro's Stave Falls Dam. Turn left onto Florence Lake Forest Service Road, which goes north along the west side of Stave Lake. Drive to the 7 km sign and turn left into a parking area before a gate with a sign for "Kearsley Road."

The present road winds uphill across a cutblock with views to Stave Lake and little Devils Lake to the west of it opening up almost immediately. Then it enters standing timber and quite soon meets its predecessor, the original road, coming up from the left. Here you turn right (look for the Mount Crickmer sign on a tree), gradually gaining height until, after less than 1 hour from the start, you go left at a fork and enter an extensive cutover area. Ten minutes later take a right fork. Further along, after a quarry and a creek, there is another fork at which you again go right. Another 15 minutes takes you around the end of a ridge to yet another fork where again you hold right, descending slightly to cross Kearsley Creek, a major stream in a spectacular box canyon. Now turn left, immediately beyond the bridge, on washed-out switchbacks. Cross then recross the washout. Stay with the road as it zigzags uphill and begins to veer right, around Mount Crickmer's southwest ridge. Keep right again at a fork on an elbow bend and watch for orange markers high on the left about 50 m (160 ft) farther on, taking you off the road and up the hillside. Now you follow the marking tapes carefully as you rise steeply through the lusty young growth on the logged-off section and into the trees on the ridge above as it approaches the mountain's main spine and levels off briefly in attractive subalpine country before the final ascent. The summit is a rocky knoll. To return you can retrace your ascent route.

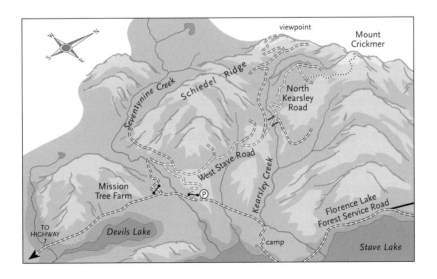

66
STATLU LAKE

to Statlu Lake	Round trip 5 km (3.1 mi)	Allow 2 hours
	Elevation gain 215 m (700 ft)	High point 580 m (1900 ft)
	Average grade 8.6%	
	Best May to November	
to upper lake	Round trip 8 km (5 mi)	Allow 6 hours
	Elevation gain 610 m (2000 ft)	High point 1020 m (3350 ft)
	Average grade 15.3%	
	Best July to October	

Maps 92G/08 Stave Lake; 92G/09 Stave River
Driving distance from Vancouver 130 km (80 mi)

The danger area on the trail.

Statlu Lake sits in a pocket valley surrounded by mountains that draw climbers like pins to a magnet. The upper lake nestles in a bowl beneath the faces of Mount Clarke, and Recourse and Viennese Peaks. This jewel of an area is accessible only after a 39 km (24 mi) drive over the Chehalis logging road system, dusty in dry weather and muddy in wet. To compound the difficulty, the last 5 km (3.1 mi) of the road has 194 water bars. These were constructed on the recommendation of the coroner after three fatal accidents at Statlu Falls. For those who accept these conditions, the reward is well worth the inconvenience. The statistics are from the trailhead. If you decide to walk the last 5 km (3.1 mi), add at least 2 hours to the times quoted.

Drive east on Highway 7 (Lougheed Highway) to Harrison Mills, 32 km (20 mi) beyond Mission, turn left onto Morris Valley Road and shortly go left again onto the gravel logging road. The Canfor logging office is on the right, about 600 m (0.4 mi) from the highway. Proceed northward, passing Elbow Lake and ignoring branch roads until at 15 km

(9.3 mi) you cross Statlu Creek and turn right, circling to gain height. Next keep left, where right leads to a forest recreation site, continuing along Chehalis Lake, first seen at about 25 km (15 mi). After crossing Skwellepil Creek at 32 km (20 mi) stay right. Go left at a fork just beyond the north end of the lake at 35 km (22 mi) then left again at the bridge over the Chehalis River. The next 5 km (3.1 mi) of road is steep, rough and questionably negotiable by 4WD vehicles. Just beyond two bridges in quick succession the trail starts up an old road on the left.

After 15 minutes on the old road a rough but well-marked trail ascends quickly, high above the young Chehalis River, to cross a tributary gully near the top of the waterfall. This is the accident scene: take care! A few minutes later you reach the east end of Statlu Lake, less than 0.5 hour from the start. Now the trail, bushy in places, follows the north side of the lake, crossing two large rock slides before it turns slightly uphill into a stretch of fine old forest and comes to a creek with a series of falls cascading down on the right. Here the trail forks: one branch continues left to the upper Chehalis; the right fork ascends east of the tributary creek on the Brotherhood Trail to reach an open bluff with splendid views over the lake to the Ratney mountains. Beyond the viewpoint the grade eases, but the bush closes in on the track, so you may have some route-finding to do on your way to the upper lake in its spectacular mountain bowl.

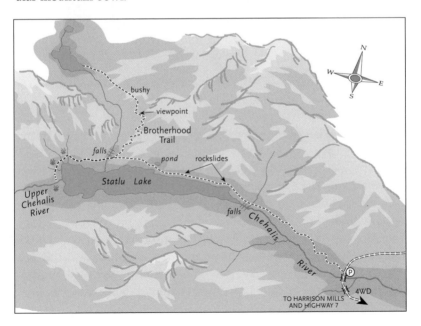

67 BEAR MOUNTAIN

Round trip 19 km (11.8 mi)	Allow 6 hours
Elevation gain 1010 m (3315 ft)	High point 1048 m (3440 ft)
Average grade 10.6%	

Best June to October	Map 92H/05 Harrison Lake
Driving distance from Vancouver 150 km (90 mi)	

View northwest to Harrison Lake and Echo Island. (JNS)

Bear Mountain lies to the east of Harrison Hot Springs at the south end of Harrison Lake. The ascent provides a day of not-too-strenuous exercise and some striking views of both Harrison Lake and Harrison River as you ascend. The bonus is the jump-out-and-hit-you-in-the-eye view from the top: you clear the trees and there's the winding Fraser River below with the Cheam Range ramping up behind. You can see the valley from Hope to Vancouver (if the smog is not too bad), and since all the straightforward Cheam Range hikes are from the other side, this is a view that you do not normally see. This summit is also used by paragliders who helicopter to the top, then attempt to land on the beach at Harrison Hot Springs.

Driving east on Highway 1, take Exit 135 for Highway 9 across the Rosedale–Agassiz bridge and follow the signs, through the town of Agassiz, to Harrison Hot Springs. In Harrison, one block before the lake, turn right onto Lillooet Avenue and follow it as it turns up the east side of the lake. Pass the arts centre, the marina and the Rivtow dock. At 5 km (3.1 mi), near the top of a hill, a rough road forks off right. Park here, clear of the gate. The road is signed Bear Mountain Forest Service Road.

Pass the gate and walk up the road, heading north. Shortly it switchbacks south and you encounter lots of debris from work by Kerr Addison Mines, which is apparently all abandoned. Stay with the travelled logging road. At the next switchback to the north there is a pretty little waterfall, a potable water source for the community below. After another two switchbacks, south then north, some talus slopes provide spectacular views of Harrison Lake directly below you and Harrison River flowing out of the lake. After the fourth south-turning switchback there is a fork in the road. Right takes you to the overgrown Bear Lake; left, your route, brings you to the top. About 45 minutes after the fork the road is totally overgrown and you take to the big trees on your left (finally, a real trail!). Only 25 minutes of trail separate you from the top, but it is a fine little trail through an open stand of balsam and hemlock weaving up and down and left and right. Suddenly you burst into the open, rewarded with the eye-popping views.

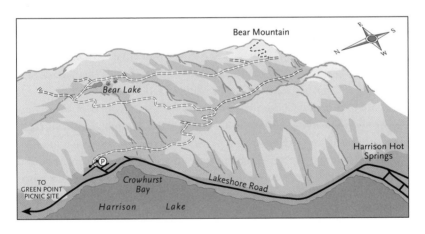

68 SUMAS MOUNTAIN

from west		
	Round trip 13.5 km (8.4 mi)	Allow 6.5 hours
	Elevation gain 715 m (2350 ft)	High point 885 m (2900 ft)
	Average grade 10.6%	
from east	Round trip 16 km (9.9 mi)	Allow 8 hours
	Elevation gain 870 m (2850 ft)	High point 885 m (2900 ft)
	Average grade 10.9%	
	Best May to November	Map 92G/01 Mission
	Driving distance from Vancouver 90 km (60 mi)	

Eastern view from the west end of Sumas Mountain to the Cheam Range in the distance.

All who have travelled Highway 1 east from Vancouver are aware of this little mountain just beyond Abbotsford. Although a 4WD road comes close to the top, the trails are well separated from it. The east and west trails are part of the Centennial Trail that makes its way over the shoulder of the mountain. Thus you may go to the summit and back from either trailhead or, with a two-car party, turn the outing into a crossover. Chadsey Lake and the top of the mountain are within Sumas Mountain Provincial Park. The lower west trail and part of the east trail are within Fraser Valley Regional Road District's Sumas Mountain Regional Park.

For the western approach, leave Highway 1 at Exit 95 (Whatcom Road) and follow North Parallel Road east to Sumas Mountain Road, on which you go north for 9 km (5.6 mi), the last 0.5 km (0.3 mi) on gravel. After a tight downhill right-hand bend, there is a long left-hand bend. In the middle, on the outside of this bend, the poorly marked trail takes off to the right. Park just below.

Follow the orange markers as the trail drops to a small creek and rises again. Next you descend again to cross Wades Creek, then climb out of the gully and gain altitude on a series of old logging roads, until just beyond the 2 km sign you cross a tributary creek filled with tumbled trees. Soon thereafter, on a relatively flat stretch, you make an abrupt change of direction: 90° and uphill once more. Now you rise through pleasant open forest to emerge briefly on a steep sidehill, with glimpses to the north. Then you head into another valley, encounter a fast-flowing stream complete with small waterfalls and very soon come within sight of Chadsey Lake. Make your way along its south shore to the east end where the trail starts to rise once more to the double summit: Main Peak, with its eye-filling sight of Mount Baker, and North Peak, with its splendid views of the Fraser Valley and the mountains to the north.

To hike the east end of the mountain, leave Highway 1 at Exit 104 (No. 3 Road). Drive east on the north frontage road and turn left on Quadling Road over the Sumas River and park by the dam. The trail starts opposite, beneath a rocky bluff.

At first you zigzag upward quite steeply, then head eastward until you have Vedder Canal almost below you before you start to swing back westward. Follow the trail/road through the clear-cut for 600 m (0.4 mi). There is then 200 m (650 ft) of trail through a strip of old-growth to another road. Follow this road for less than 2 km (1.2 mi) to where a trail takes off left, 300 m (1000 ft) through another cutblock to the standing timber. Now you start to gain some elevation. It is only 400 m (1300 ft) from here to Chadsey Lake. By going clockwise along the lakeshore, you intersect the trail along the south side and turn left for the top.

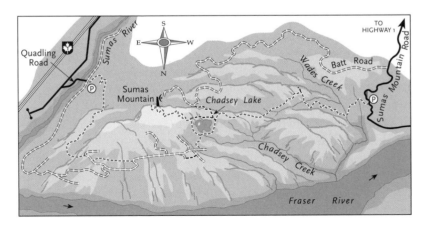

69 VEDDER MOUNTAIN

Round trip 11.5 km (7.1 mi)   Allow 6 hours
Elevation gain 575 m (1220 ft)   High point 945 m (3100 ft)
Average grade 10.0%

Best May to October   Map 92G/01 Mission
Driving distance from Vancouver 120 km (75 mi)

Cultus Lake and Vedder Mountain, seen from Mount Amadis.

Vedder Mountain is the southern border of the Fraser Valley between Abbotsford and Chilliwack. Its west end runs across the International Boundary, and to gain the valley of Cultus Lake you must cross the Chilliwack/Vedder River and switchback around Vedder Mountain's east end. There are a series of viewpoints as you traverse the ridge from east to west. Although none of them are panoramic, you get some views to the north, then some to the south. The final top requires a drop into a dark hollow before the last scramble to the summit, which offers views across Cultus Lake and Columbia Valley to International Ridge and Mount Amadis (Hike 71).

Travelling east on Highway 1, take Exit 119A (Sardis, Cultus Lake). Drive south through Sardis and Vedder Crossing to the bridge over the river, which is known as Chilliwack River upstream of the bridge, Vedder River downstream. Cross the bridge and, at the next traffic light, turn left. Just after the large wooden sign for Cultus Lake Provincial Park you go right on a wide gravel road, Parmenter Road. After 600 m (0.4 mi) go right again on Vedder Mountain Forest Service Road, then after another 600 m (0.4 mi) go left on its southeastern fork. Now stay with this road as it winds uphill for 3 km (1.9 mi) to the trailhead signpost. With a rugged 4WD you could turn uphill here and save about 15 minutes of walking, but the road is rough.

From the signpost, walk up this broken road and take the first left 200 m (650 ft) to a clearing. A user box on the right marks the new direction of the trail. For a time you are in pleasant forest heading fairly gently uphill and turning gradually from north to west, ignoring a track to the right just after the 2.5 km marker. Then shortly after the 3.5 km sign, a delightful viewpoint lies a few steps to the right, where you can look across the Fraser Valley to the distant peaks. Next, after another 500 m (0.3 mi) or so, comes a fine view to the east along the Chilliwack Valley with the peaks of the Cheam Range as a backdrop. If you are short of time or energy, this is a good destination. However, if you want to get to the real summit, continue west on the trail. You will find yourself dropping gradually to a little pond, well furnished with water lilies and surrounded by some marshy ground, before you start to regain height on your trek to the summit, meeting en route the old West Trail, now in poor condition, that comes up from low on the Yarrow side. There are some log ladders to ease your way over and along a steep rock. Then you pop out onto the summit. On top your reward is another view to the south, with the white summit of Mount Baker peeping over International Ridge.

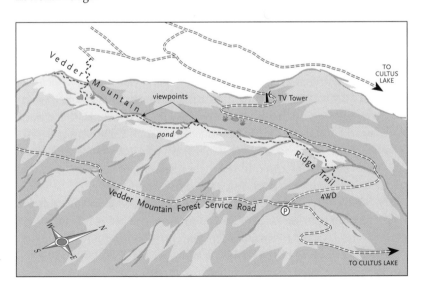

70 ELK–THURSTON

to Elk Mountain	Round trip 8 km (5 mi)	Allow 4 hours
	Elevation gain 800 m (2625 ft)	High point 1400 m (4595 ft)
	Average grade 20.0%	
to Mount Thurston	Round trip 15 km (9.3 mi)	Allow 7 hours
	Elevation gain 1030 m (3380 ft)	High point 1630 m (5350 ft)
	Average grade 13.5%	

Best July to October		Map 92H/04 Chilliwack
Driving distance from Vancouver 130 km (80 mi)		

This hike is probably the most popular trip, in the Chilliwack area, for local residents. It combines a mostly paved road, a wide well-maintained trail and beautiful meadows along the ridge from Elk Mountain to Mount Thurston. They are lovely at any time, but especially spectacular if the flowers are in bloom. If you have time for only a short hike, Elk alone is well worth your time. Locals often hike it in the evening after work. With the day at your disposal, amble along the ridge to Thurston. The views are to the south looking down on the valley of the Chilliwack River and across to Mount Baker, Tomyhoi Peak, the Border Peaks, Mount Slesse and Mount Rexford. However, the road approach is from the Fraser Valley. In fact, part of the interest of this outing is the deviousness of your approach to the parking spot, which involves an exercise in following rural roads. The route takes you through the well-established little community of Ryder Lake.

Travelling east on Highway 1, pass Chilliwack and turn south onto Prest Road (Exit 123). After 4 km (2.5 mi) turn left onto Bailey Road and shortly thereafter take the right fork onto Elk View Road, which immediately begins to rise. Stay with the main travelled road, which twists and winds, losing its hardtop just past Ryder Lake Fire Hall and Park. After nearly 10 km (6.2 mi) it becomes Chilliwack Bench Forest Service Road, and you park about 500 m (0.3 mi) beyond in a small gravel pit on the left. The start of the trail is on the east side of the pit. Note that water is lacking on the ridge, once the snow leaves.

The trail goes behind the quarry, turning from northwest to east as you rise. The rounded west ridge of Elk Mountain is reached in less than 2 km (1.2 mi) and a gain of 400 m (1300 ft). The Fraser Valley is now to your left (north); but because of the timber, it is not visible until 1.5 km (0.9 mi) later at 1240 m (4070 ft). Here you break out onto a rocky step with views to the north, west and south. From this spot it is back into the trees until you arrive at Elk Mountain's open flower meadows, which should be at their best in July and August, as should the wild strawberries. From here the summit of Mount Thurston is another 4 km (2.5 mi) along the ridge, but only 200 m (660 ft) higher; it is easy hiking although there are a few dips and hollows. On your way across the alpine meadows you have as much mountain and valley scenery as you can possibly desire. To return, retrace your ascent route. Stay on the trail for at least two reasons: these meadows are fragile and easily damaged, and there are a number of stub trails that don't lead to home.

The meadows, with Cultus Lake and Vedder Mountain behind.

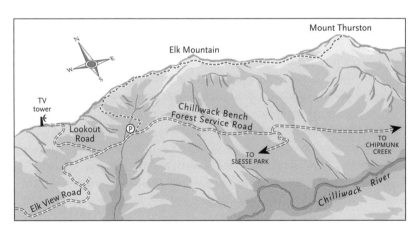

71 MOUNT AMADIS

Round trip 22 km (14 mi)   Allow 10 hours
Elevation gain 1445 m (4740 ft)   High point 1506 m (4940 ft)
Average grade 13.1%

Best July to October   Map 92H/04 Chilliwack
Driving distance from Vancouver 125 km (75 mi)

View north to the Fraser Valley and Mounts Robie Reid and Judge Howay on the skyline.

This trip, which is in the newly created International Ridge Provincial Park, takes you to the high point of the ridge, Mount Amadis. Here you are only 2 km (1.2 mi) from the International Boundary, hence the name for both the ridge and the park. As to Amadis: he was the hero of a medieval Spanish romance, not a hiker. This is an amazing ridge walk. The map contours do not do justice to the steepness of the north side of the ridge as it plunges down into Cultus Lake. The view to the northwest is out over Vedder Mountain and across the Fraser Valley to Golden Ears, Mounts Robie Reid and Judge Howay, and the Chehalis peaks. This hike is a full day since a small shale slide about 4 hours up the trail requires care and deadfall slows your progress along the easy-angle top of the ridge.

Travelling east on Highway 1, take Exit 119A (Sardis, Cultus Lake). Drive south through Sardis and Vedder Crossing to the bridge over the river, which is known as Chilliwack River upstream of the bridge, Vedder

River downstream. Cross the bridge and, at the next traffic light, turn left. Stay on Cultus Lake Road which becomes Columbia Valley Highway. As the road starts along the south shore of the lake turn left, just at the marina, onto Edmeston Road. About 200 m (650 ft) up this road, there is a gate on your right. Park here at an elevation of 60 m (200 ft).

Pass the gate and follow the old logging road. After 40 minutes go left at a fork, where the right-hand branch says "Horse Trail." The road winds uphill and after a switchback west (about 1.5 hours) take another left fork, so that you are now going east. Looking back over your left shoulder, you should see a sign saying "Park Boundary: no motorbikes." This is the border of Cultus Lake Provincial Park. You then cross a shale slide which has almost removed the road and a few minutes later, on your right, is the well-marked trail. You rise quickly on this route to emerge some 150 m (500 ft) above on a higher leg of the road. Now you go right for 80 m (260 ft) until the trail beckons you left once more, climbing steadily up the narrow ridge. At 1120 m (3675 ft) is a viewpoint, but hold your photographic urge; there is a far better viewpoint 5 minutes later. At last the strain eases as you skirt a minor summit on its east side and start to descend, leaving the screen of forest to see the ridge still stretching ahead and curving to the southwest. Finally, after dropping some 100 m (330 ft) to the saddle separating you from your goal, you begin an ascending traverse around the north side to the open slope southwest of the forested summit. Here are views, southward to Mounts Baker and Shuksan and westward to the Fraser River with its valley disappearing in the haze over its delta. To return, retrace your ascent route.

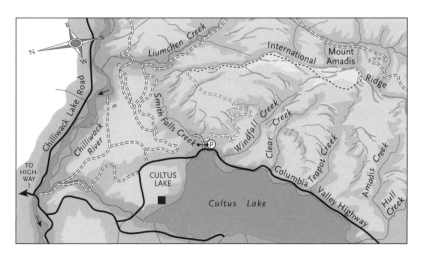

72 MOUNT MCGUIRE

from start of 4WD	Round trip 12 km (7.5 mi)	Allow 6 hours
	Elevation gain 959 m (3145 ft)	High point 2019 m (6625 ft)
	Average grade 15.9%	
from trailhead	Round trip 8 km (5 mi)	Allow 4 hours
	Elevation gain 659 m (2165 ft)	High point 2019 m (6625 ft)
	Average grade 15.7%	
	Best June to November	Map 92H/04 Chilliwack
	Driving distance from Vancouver 140 km (85 mi)	

Mount McGuire's south ridge, with the Border Peaks and Tomyhoi Peak behind.

Mount McGuire tends to be overshadowed by its more spectacular mountain neighbours: Tomyhoi Peak, the Border Peaks and Slesse Mountain. Yet it is a short ascent from the end of the logging roads, and the views from the top are stunning. The trade-off, as in much of today's access, is the industrial wasteland created by the very roads that you use to approach the mountains. From the top, the Chilliwack and Fraser Valleys seem to be right below your feet. The little lake in a bowl on Mount McGuire's north side probably has not seen more than a dozen visitors for all its closeness to the population centres. As you turn to descend, the sightline of Ten Mile Ridge running southeast draws your vision towards the Border Peaks. It is hard to turn back down into the valleys.

Travelling east on Highway 1, take Exit 119A (Sardis, Cultus Lake). Drive south through Sardis and Vedder Crossing to the bridge over the river, which is known as Chilliwack River upstream of the bridge, Vedder River downstream. Turn left and zero your odometer here. This is Chilliwack Lake Road. Drive east for 20 km (12.4 mi) and turn right just before the bridge over Slesse Creek. This is Slesse–Borden Creek Forest Service Road, which zigzags uphill heading southwest. At 25 km (15 mi) the road levels, heading west before turning south into the valley of Borden Creek. A bridge crosses the creek, to river-left, at 28 km (17 mi). Continue another 2 km (1.2 mi) to where the road begins to deteriorate. With a 4WD you might make another 2 km (1.2 mi), gaining 300 m (1000 ft), but the terrain is volatile and subject to annual change. Your route, Mount McGuire's southeast ridge, is visible here. The current 4WD parking and trailhead are at GR915310, at an elevation of 1360 m (4460 ft).

Take the left fork 100 m (325 ft) from the start. At 1200 m (0.7 mi), GR910313, again go left at a triple fork. On the north side of the landing is the start of the trail proper. There is 100 m (325 ft) of cutover ground before entering the trees; the trail is indicated by red metal markers. You are already into subalpine terrain, therefore the meadows begin to predominate, although less than 1 hour's travel gets you onto a sharp alpine ridge. Rocks have needless red paint splotches; you will have little desire to stray from the ridge crest. A short distance below the summit is an obvious cave entrance 30 m (100 ft) east of the trail. It is a 40 m (130 ft) vertical shaft and should not be entered without proper equipment and experience. The final 100 m (325 ft) to the top is a narrow ridge with substantial exposure. If you are unhappy with a vertical drop beneath your feet, you may not want to go that far. The views are grand from wherever you turn around.

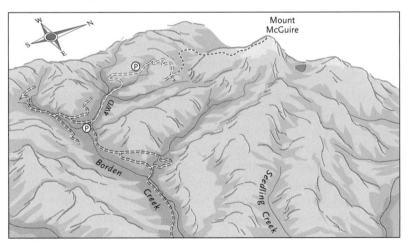

73 MOUNT MACFARLANE

to lower Pierce Lake	Round trip 16 km (9.9 mi)	Allow 7 hours
	Elevation gain 1040 m (3410 ft)	High point 1375 m (4510 ft)
	Average grade 13.0%	
to summit	Round trip 21 km (13 mi)	Allow 10 hours
	Elevation gain 1765 m (5785 ft)	High point 2100 m (6885 ft)
	Average grade 16.8%	
	Best July to September	Map 92H/04 Chilliwack
	Driving distance from Vancouver 135 km (80 mi)	

View of Mount Pierce (middle) and the Cheam Range (behind). (CM)

Mount MacFarlane is at the north end of the spectacularly rugged ridge running north from Slesse Mountain. As well as the view to Slesse and the Border Peaks, the top offers a side-on view of the complete Cheam Range: Cheam, Lady, Knight, Baby Munday, Stewart, The Still, Welch and Foley Peaks. You do not have to hike all the way to MacFarlane, however; the two Pierce Lakes, upper and lower, both make satisfying destinations. The trail is maintained by the Chilliwack Outdoor Club under the Federation of Mountain Clubs of British Columbia's Adopt-a-Trail Program and it has seen substantial work in the last few years. Much of that work has involved re-routing the trail around a major landslide.

Travelling east on Highway 1, take Exit 119A (Sardis, Cultus Lake). Drive south through Sardis and Vedder Crossing to the bridge over the river, which is known as Chilliwack River upstream of the bridge, Vedder River downstream. Turn left and zero your odometer here. This is Chilliwack Lake Road. Drive east, cross Slesse Creek and pass the Department of National Defence firing range on your right. After about 23 km (14 mi), on a long straight stretch of road, watch for a narrow track on the right. There should be a British Columbia Forest Service sign, "Pierce Creek Trail," at the entrance. Turn in here and drive 300 m (1000 ft) to the parking area.

On foot you start rising immediately, switchbacking twice, then heading southeast through young timber, but with no views until you zigzag to reach a boulder field above the landslide. Do not drop below the trail to view the slide: the ground is still unstable! Then the trail continues through a stretch of fine trees before dropping slightly to cross Pierce Creek at about 975 m (3200 ft). There is a steep climb above the creek crossing to the elevation of the lower lake. The steepness of the valley sides and the many wet meadows keep the trail above the lake, a dark jade-green jewel lying below on your right. The trail continues past the lake to the meadows in the southeast corner, close to the creek from the upper lake some 305 m (1000 ft) higher. Follow the trail east of the creek (river-right) up the steep valley headwall. From the upper lake, Mount MacFarlane lies southwest up a well-defined ridge, but there is only a sketchy trail. The safest route follows the ridge all the way from the lake to the summit. There are a couple of steep steps but, if the ground is icy, snowy or even just wet, the open slopes on the sides of the ridge can be treacherous. On top, looking northeast you see Mount Pierce, much diminished from here, its summit 140 m (460 ft) lower than yours but also attainable from the upper lake. On the return, as you retrace your ascent route, take care as you descend between the lakes. The terrain is steep and unforgiving!

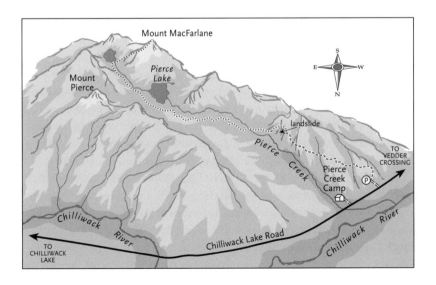

74 CHEAM PEAK

Round trip 9.5 km (5.9 mi)	Allow 4.5 hours
Elevation gain 665 m (2175 ft)	High point 2112 m (6929 ft)
Average grade 14.0%	

Best July to October	Map 92H/04 Chilliwack
Driving distance from Vancouver 150 km (90 mi)	

Summit view south along the Cheam Range to distant Welch Peak.

As the Lions are to Vancouver, so Cheam Peak is to the eastern Fraser Valley; it is dominant over Highway 1 between Chilliwack and Hope. Until recently the route to this eminence was the long slog from the valley floor at Popkum to gain the ridge some 2 hours southwest of the peak. That demanding hike was fully 30 km (19 mi), climbed 2080 m (6825 ft) in elevation and occupied all of a very long day. In the early years of the last century it was an annual pilgrimage made by whole families: one hundred people on the top was nothing unusual! Think on that as you drive to within 2 hours of the top of the world. Now just a short hike allows you to have the Fraser Valley spread out at your feet—with views to Vancouver if the smog is not too thick.

Travelling east on Highway 1, take Exit 119A (Sardis, Cultus Lake). Drive south through Sardis and Vedder Crossing to the bridge over the river, which is known as Chilliwack River upstream of the bridge, Vedder River downstream. Turn left and zero your odometer here. This is Chilliwack Lake Road. Drive about 28 km (17 mi), and just after crossing the Chilliwack River (river-left to river-right), turn left onto Chilliwack–

Foley Forest Service Road. Cross Foley Creek after 2 km (1.2 mi) and go left at the T-junction. After another 2 km (1.2 mi) you cross the Chipmunk Creek bridge. Just uphill from the bridge, go right and uphill onto Chipmunk Creek Forest Service Road. Stay on this logging road for almost 7 km (4.3 mi) before going right on a very steep and rough road for another 4 km (2.5 mi), if your vehicle can handle it. The parking area is before a barrier about 1 km (0.6 mi) from the end of the logging road.

Walk the logging road to the alpine meadows and think about how much more spectacular it would have been if this hillside had not been cut all the way to the meadows. Once on the trail proper, you continue to rise a little before dropping into the meadows around Spoon Lake. Then you start to ascend again in earnest via long zigzags, trending a little to the south at first, then pursuing a generally northward direction along the front of Lady Peak, Cheam Peak's massive neighbour to the southeast. Next, passing just below the saddle between the two mountains, you veer slightly west of north towards your goal, the rich meadows of the lower slopes giving way to bare, gravelly terrain with the occasional rocky outcrop. Finally, close to the peak, you join the long trail from the Fraser Valley and turn right for the summit. Although Lady Peak can also be ascended from the col between the two peaks, it is not as straightforward a hike as Cheam Peak. The trail is less obvious and more rocky; there is more potential for taking a fall. Why not enjoy the views from Cheam Peak instead?

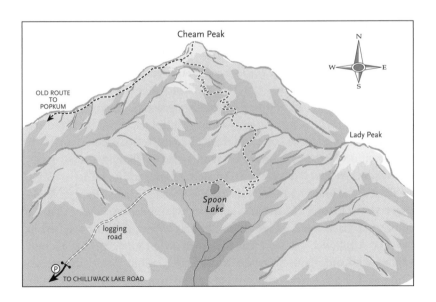

75 MOUNT LAUGHINGTON

Round trip 10 km (6.2 mi)	Allow 4.5 hours
Elevation gain 620 m (2030 ft)	High point 1800 m (5900 ft)
Average grade 12.4%	

Best June to November	Map 92H/04 Chilliwack
Driving distance from Vancouver 145 km (90 mi)	

Mount Cheam and Lady Peak, seen from the summit. (DM)

The attraction of Mount Laughington is primarily its location with regard to the Cheam Range. Where Hike 73, to Mount MacFarlane, gives you a full-on view of the range from Cheam to Foley Peaks, Mount Laughington gives you that same view but in super wide-angle. The peaks are just on the other side of Airplane Creek—almost close enough to touch. Airplane Creek is also the access route for ascents of Knight, Baby Munday and Stewart Peaks and The Still. The other attractive feature of Mount Laughington is the relative ease of ascent if Airplane Creek Road is driveable. The spectacular views, from the top, to the south are a bonus.

Travelling east on Highway 1, take Exit 119A (Sardis, Cultus Lake). Drive south through Sardis and Vedder Crossing to the bridge over the river, which is known as Chilliwack River upstream of the bridge, Vedder River downstream. Turn left and zero your odometer here. This is Chilliwack Lake Road. Drive about 28 km (17 mi), and just after crossing the Chilliwack River (river-left to river-right), turn left onto Chilliwack–Foley Forest Service Road. Cross Foley Creek after 2 km (1.2 mi) and go right at the T-junction, upstream on river-right. After another 2 km (1.2 mi) a bridge takes you back to river-left, and 300 m (1000 ft) after that Airplane Creek Road goes left, recrossing Foley Creek and going sharply uphill. The elevation here is 440 m (1445 ft). Follow this road for about 4 km (2.5 mi) to an elevation of 1160 m (3805 ft), GR007425. Park here, where the old overgrown road continues ahead and a newer road switchbacks right.

Walk up the old road for about 2 km (1.2 mi), following several switchbacks, until the road ends in the subalpine at 1520 m (4990 ft). From the end of the road, a taped route takes you through an old burned-over area, now covered with a lush growth of shrubs and small trees, to the end of the ridge proper, passing to the left of a bare knoll at about 1600 m (5250 ft). Your route beyond here, ill-defined in places at first, becomes more distinct as you proceed along the main ridge to the high point, enjoying the variety of plant life at your feet and the views of mighty summits all around.

An alternative to the above, which requires more 4WD but less 2FW (two-foot walking), is to continue on the road up Airplane Creek. Take the switchback right where the above route parked. The road continues for about another 4 km (2.5 mi) gaining another 240 m (790 ft). Half a kilometre (0.3 mi) before the road end, park around GR986445 and walk uphill to the southwest. There is no marked route! However, the top is only 1.5 km (0.9 mi) from you and 400 m (1310 ft) above. Other than its shortness, this route does not have a lot to recommend it.

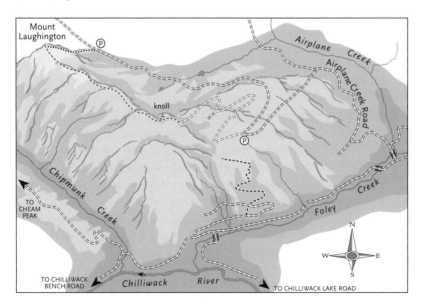

76 WILLIAMSON LAKE

on original trail	Round trip 13 km (8.1 mi)	Allow 7 hours
	Elevation gain 1175 m (3850 ft)	High point 1655 m (5430 ft)
	Average grade 18.1%	
from 4WD road	Round trip 6 km (3.7 mi)	Allow 3.5 hours
	Elevation gain 505 m (1655 ft)	High point 1655 m (5430 ft)
	Average grade 15.2%	

Best July to October   Map 92H/04 Chilliwack
Driving distance from Vancouver 145 km (90 mi)

View south across the lake to Mount Rexford and Slesse Mountain.

In a high cirque at the south end of the Cheam Range, with the majestic summits of Welch and Foley Peaks above, lies Williamson Lake, the site of a small British Columbia Mountaineering Club cabin until an avalanche swept it away. That fact will have more significance when you reach the lake and see the site. If there is much snow on the ground, reconsider your attempt to reach the lake. You have two options for access, but you should decide which approach you are going to use before you set out. The statistics are given above. The original trail starts, essentially, from the road west of Foley Lake. The newer approach requires a 4WD to reach the end of a high logging road that starts east of Foley Lake. The final section of trail to the lake is common to both routes.

Travelling east on Highway 1, take Exit 119A (Sardis, Cultus Lake). Drive south through Sardis and Vedder Crossing to the bridge over the river, which is known as Chilliwack River upstream of the bridge, Vedder River downstream. Turn left and zero your odometer here. This is

Chilliwack Lake Road. Drive about 28 km (17 mi), and just after crossing the Chilliwack River (river-left to river-right), turn left onto Chilliwack–Foley Forest Service Road. Cross Foley Creek after 2 km (1.2 mi) and go right at the T-junction, upstream on river-right. After another 2 km (1.2 mi) a bridge takes you back to river-left, and 300 m (1000 ft) after that Airplane Creek Road goes left. This is decision time.

For the original trail, drive across Foley Creek on Airplane Creek Road and park on the right about 100 m (325 ft) up the hill. This avoids the problem that used to exist: how to safely cross Foley Creek. From your parking spot, a spur road goes right, crosses Airplane Creek and ascends into a cutblock. Follow this decommissioned road to its end. A short piece of newer trail traverses east across the cutblock to meet the original trail on its fall-line ascent. This is a Paul Binkert trail, and Paul did not believe in switchbacks. Pick up the markers and start rising steeply, following a prominent spur of Welch Peak.

For the 4WD road, drive past Foley Lake over a bridge to river-right. Take the next left (uphill) fork, pass a gate and ascend steep switchbacks into the open bowl at 1160 m (3800 ft) below Williamson Lake. A rough trail crosses the creek and the logging slash to meet the original route.

The trail crests the ridge at 1440 m (4720 ft) and the angle eases. You then break into the alpine as you bear right and work your way across a steep sidehill, rising towards the high basin in which the lake is located. Don't feed the marmots! Don't spook the goats!

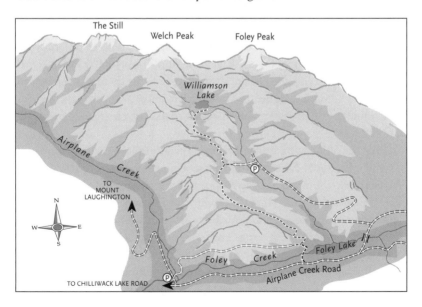

SLESSE MEMORIAL

Round trip 8 km (5 mi)   Allow 3 hours
Elevation gain 460 m (1500 ft)   High point 1100 m (3600 ft)
Average grade 11.5%

Best June to November   Map 92H/04 Chilliwack
Driving distance from Vancouver 150 km (90 mi)

In November 1956, a TransCanada Airlines flight from Vancouver to Calgary crashed into the south summit of Slesse Mountain. None of the sixty-two passengers and crew survived. This trail leads to a plaque erected in 1995, by relatives and friends of the deceased, when the area was finally designated a commemorative site. From the plaque is a view of the spectacular bowl below the northeast buttress of Slesse Mountain, with its wild rock walls and active pocket glaciers. The trail to the plaque was built, and is maintained, by the Valley Outdoor Association through the Federation of Mountain Clubs of British Columbia's Adopt-a-Trail Program.

Travelling east on Highway 1, take Exit 119A (Sardis, Cultus Lake). Drive south through Sardis and Vedder Crossing to the bridge over the river, which is known as Chilliwack River upstream of the bridge, Vedder River downstream. Turn left and zero your odometer here. This is Chilliwack Lake Road. Drive east for 31 km (19 mi) and, just after the Riverside Forest Service Recreation Site, turn right onto Chilliwack South Forest Service Road. Zero your odometer again here. You immediately cross over the Chilliwack River and at 400 m (1300 ft) turn right. This is Nesakwatch Creek Road. At 5.6 km (3.5 mi) there is a small road on your right with a signed post at its entrance. You can park here or drive another 200 m (650 ft) on this stub road. The elevation here is 640 m (2100 ft).

Since the old logging bridge has washed out, follow the flagging tapes to a log crossing of Nesakwatch Creek. This can be very difficult if icy. The trail follows an old logging road south. Twenty minutes up the trail, over a side creek, is a bridge built by the inmates at Ford Mountain Camp, one of the correctional facilities in the Chilliwack Valley. Other than occasional flagging tape, the trail is unmarked. However, the footbed is substantial and obvious. About 2 km (1.2 mi) from the start, the trail makes a switchback to the north. Twenty minutes later, a rock slide above and below the trail allows excellent views across the valley to

The memorial plaque and the northeast bowl
of Slesse Mountain behind.

the west sides of the Illusion Peaks and Mount Rexford. The trail to the
latter is Hike 78. Another 20 minutes brings you to a sign requesting that
you respect this commemorative site. As the trail curves around to the
left, you reach the plaque with its vista of Slesse Mountain's northeast
faces. The old road does continue south up the hillside, past the plaque,
but terminates shortly after another turn north.

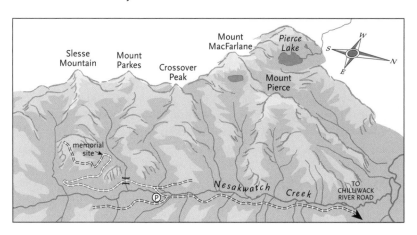

78 MOUNT REXFORD TRAIL

Round trip 6 km (3.7 mi) Allow 5 hours
Elevation gain 920 m (3020 ft) High point 1840 m (6040 ft)
Average grade 30.1%

Best June to November Map 92H/04 Chilliwack
Driving distance from Vancouver 155 km (95 mi)

The walls of South Illusion Peak overhead and Slesse Mountain on the skyline.

Like the Slesse Mountain Trail in the next valley to the west, this is a climbers' access route. It is another Paul Binkert trail, therefore it is steep and demanding. Recent small logging operations have been no friend to the trail, despite British Columbia Forest Service assurances to "put the trail back into its original condition" after the cut. So why bother? This trip takes you into a rocky, alpine, pocket wilderness. The route traverses under the west wall of South Illusion Peak. Behind you as you ascend is a profile of Slesse's northeast buttress: one of North America's fifty classic climbs. Your objective is the open rocky shoulder beneath Mount Rexford's west ridge: a boulder-strewn heather meadow with a gorgeous aspect. At most times there is no running water in this area.

Travelling east on Highway 1, take Exit 119A (Sardis, Cultus Lake). Drive south through Sardis and Vedder Crossing to the bridge over the river, which is known as Chilliwack River upstream of the bridge, Vedder

River downstream. Turn left and zero your odometer here. This is Chilliwack Lake Road. Drive east for 31 km (19 mi) and, just after the Riverside Forest Service Recreation Site, turn right onto Chilliwack South Forest Service Road. Zero your odometer again here. You immediately cross over the Chilliwack River and at 400 m (1300 ft) turn right. This is Nesakwatch Creek Road. At 5.6 km (3.5 mi) the Slesse Memorial Trail (Hike 77) starts. The next 2 km (1.2 mi) probably require 4WD. At 7.7 km (4.8 mi) there is a spur road to the left which can be driven for 100 m (325 ft). Park here.

Walk south up the road to a switchback turning north. About 150 m (500 ft) above the switchback look for flagging tape on the right taking you up the bank into the cut. This, the real trailhead, is at GR054324, elevation 920 m (3020 ft). The trail follows up a steep little ridge north of the unnamed creek that drains the bowl between the Illusion Peaks and Mount Rexford. Grunt your way upward until you break out of the trees underneath the big walls of South Illusion Peak. Traverse right, ascending, along the bottom of the wall. There has been a recent slide here, therefore until a footbed is dug into the slope it provides poor footing. When you break out of the subalpine timber you are faced by a rocky bowl, the marmots whistling protest at your presence. Practise your boulder-hopping skills as you make a right-ascending traverse towards the open shoulder beneath Mount Rexford's west ridge at 1840 m (6040 ft). It's a great place to throw your bivy sack on the heather and fall asleep staring at the stars.

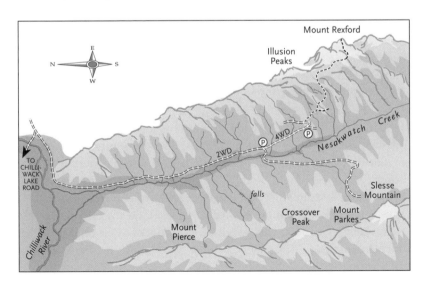

79 WILLIAMS RIDGE

Round trip 11 km (6.8 mi)   Allow 8 hours
Elevation gain 1435 m (4700 ft)   High point 1880 m (6170 ft)
Average grade 26.1%

Best July to October   Map 92H/04 Chilliwack
Driving distance from Vancouver 145 km (90 mi)

Williams Ridge and Peak, Chilliwack Lake (behind) and Mount Webb (right), viewed from Foley Peak.

The Grouse Grind? It's a walk in the park, a stroll, a dawdle! You want a steep trail? This is it! To practise for Williams Ridge, run over to the Skyride and do the Grind twice before breakfast. For the fit or for those who want to get fit, this trail is a pipe-opener as it rises from the floor of the Chilliwack River Valley to a knoll on the ridge 1400 m (4600 ft) above. If you have some technical skill and experience, keep going and climb the last 720 m (2360 ft) to the top: a fine Class 3 scramble, although not for the uninitiated! It would also add another 3 to 4 hours to your day. If you can reduce your pulse rate sufficiently to see some distance, the views from the ridge are grand.

Travelling east on Highway 1, take Exit 119A (Sardis, Cultus Lake). Drive south through Sardis and Vedder Crossing to the bridge over the river, which is known as Chilliwack River upstream of the bridge, Vedder River downstream. Turn left and zero your odometer here. This is Chilliwack Lake Road. Drive east for 34 km (21 mi). Pass the Centre

Creek corrections facility on your right and 500 m (0.3 mi) later is the trailhead on your left.

A number of old trails and logging roads start from the same point, so care is necessary at first in following the orange markers, especially at a point about 90 m (300 ft) into the bush, where these fork left from the logging road and into the trees. Now the trail begins to rise, zigzagging upward relentlessly with few opportunities to draw breath. Still later, just short of the ridge, an opening in the forest reveals a view up the Centre Creek Valley with the spires of Mount Rexford and the Illusion Peaks just opposite on the right. Then you come to a T-junction with the route from Mount Ford coming in from the west. You turn right and east, however, undulating along the ridge, still mainly in forest, though at a number of open bluffs you may enjoy spectacular views of mountains, valleys and glaciers to the south across the Chilliwack River. Finally you leave the trees behind and you see the symmetrical shape of Williams Peak ahead, a beacon urging you on over grass and rock to the saddle that gives climbers access to the peak. A rocky knoll is the end of the hiking trail; only as a member of a properly equipped party should you go farther on what is a moderately difficult scramble. From your vantage point on the knoll you have views of the Cheam Range across Foley Creek to the northwest, Chilliwack Lake with its mountain backdrop lies to the east and Mount Rexford dominates the southern horizon. As you descend, remember to make the left turn off the ridge at the T-junction for the "knee-knackering" descent to the valley.

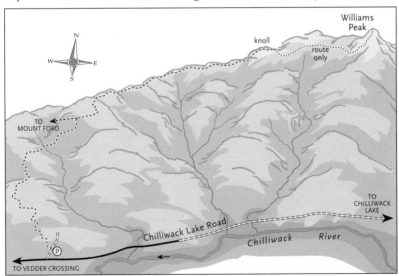

RADIUM LAKE

Round trip 12 km (7.5 mi)   Allow 6 hours
Elevation gain 910 m (2980 ft)   High point 1460 m (4800 ft)
Average grade 15.1%

Best July to October   Map 92H/03 Skagit River
Driving distance from Vancouver 150 km (90 mi)

View north to Williams and Porcupine Peaks.

This hike and the area around it have recently been included in the new Chilliwack Lake Provincial Park. It takes you into high wilderness country just north of the Canada–United States border and south of the Chilliwack River not far from where it exits Chilliwack Lake. The lake's immediate surroundings are parklike, and there is an old British Columbia Forest Service cabin at the lake. It is now, however, in very poor condition. A trail leads from Radium Lake to the col between Mount Webb and Macdonald Peak, and ascents of the peaks are usually done by this route. Note that B.C. Parks plans to move the trailhead to a new parking area at the head of Chilliwack Lake. When this change is implemented, some of the directions below will not apply.

Travelling east on Highway 1, take Exit 119A (Sardis, Cultus Lake). Drive south through Sardis and Vedder Crossing to the bridge over the river, which is known as Chilliwack River upstream of the bridge, Vedder River downstream. Turn left and zero your odometer here. This is

Chilliwack Lake Road. Drive east for 40 km (25 mi) and, depending on whether the gate is open or not, park on the roadside or in the park.

Take the footbridge over Post Creek, followed shortly by another over the Chilliwack River. On the far bank the route shares its track with the Centennial Trail for a short distance. Ascend in a series of switchbacks to where the Centennial Trail goes off to the west; you turn sharp left and continue south, following the line of an old logging road back towards Radium Creek. Next some steps take you up to the old road again, just above where it has been cut by a slide, and now you swing west a little, then back, to ascend high above the creek's west side, levelling off after the 1.5 km marker for a crossing to river-right on an impressive but bouncy suspension bridge. You are not finished with crossing either, for after climbing east away from the creek, you return to the river-left close by the remains of an old cabin, now sometimes used as a camping spot. Thereafter, following a short spell on that bank, you return to the river-right and stay on that side to the lake. As you rise and leave the shade of the trees you enter a slide area with luxuriant bush then descend slightly through it to cross a wet meadow assisted with planks and corduroy underfoot. Then you continue, always upward, until with one last steep pitch you reach the lake and the old cabin by its shore. To ascend to the Webb–Macdonald col, take a sharp left shortly after the cabin and follow the taped route; do not go to the end of the lake.

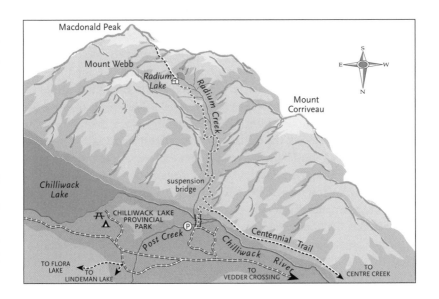

81 LINDEMAN AND GREENDROP LAKES

to Lindeman Lake	Round trip 5 km (3.1 mi)	Allow 3 hours
	Elevation gain 215 m (700 ft)	High point 825 m (2700 ft)
	Average grade 8.6%	
to Greendrop Lake	Round trip 13 km (8.1 mi)	Allow 6 hours
	Elevation gain 395 m (1300 ft)	High point 1010 m (3300 ft)
	Average grade 6.1%	
	Best June to October	Map 92H/03 Skagit River
	Driving distance from Vancouver 150 km (90 mi)	

The west shore of Lindeman Lake. (TH)

This hike and the area around it have recently been included in the new Chilliwack Lake Provincial Park. You follow a section of the Centennial Trail on its crossover from the Chilliwack Valley to the Skagit Valley, remaining close to the Post Creek valley bottom throughout and glimpsing some striking views of one-time glaciated valleys. Along the way you pass the two lakes, Lindeman and Green-drop. Best of all, the trail's relatively low level means that it remains open when higher trails are under snow. Note that B.C. Parks plans to move the trailhead to a new parking area at the head of Chilliwack Lake. When this change is implemented, the initial access described below will not apply.

Travelling east on Highway 1, take Exit 119A (Sardis, Cultus Lake). Drive south through Sardis and Vedder Crossing to the bridge over the river, which is known as Chilliwack River upstream of the bridge, Vedder River downstream. Turn left and zero your odometer here. This is Chilliwack Lake Road. Drive east for 40 km (25 mi), and just after crossing Post Creek, turn left and go 200 m (650 ft) to a small parking area. Hikes 81 and 82 both start from here.

Head off north, following the creek, first on the east then the west side, reaching the near end of Lindeman Lake after some 40 minutes. Here, with the steepest part of the trail behind you, you may pause to admire the picturesque scene with pinnacles and gargoyles rising high on the east side above the reflective waters of this beautiful lake. Thereafter, you make your way up and down along the lakeside via a rock slide, a forested stretch, then more rocks before the trail works its way around a steep bluff at the north end and drops to cross the creek. On this stretch between one lake and the other, you proceed across talus slopes and through forest alternately. Although views are limited beyond the valley itself, there are plenty of interesting plants on the forest floor and mosses and lichens clothing the rocks. Then, after recrossing to the creek's west bank and travelling quietly through pleasant, open forest, you reach a fork: right heads for the near end of Greendrop Lake; left, the Centennial Trail, goes left and on, eventually descending Hicks Creek to the Skagit Valley. If you want more exercise and a better view, take the Centennial Trail. The steep sides of the lake force the path to rise sharply some 215 m (700 ft) before crossing a creek that plunges precipitously to the lake. Here you may enjoy fine views of the lake and of the hanging valley opposite, in which lies Flora Lake. This spot makes a satisfying destination for a day hike, or you may continue to the wilderness recreation site at Greendrop Bluff above the far end of the lake for views back down the Post Creek Valley.

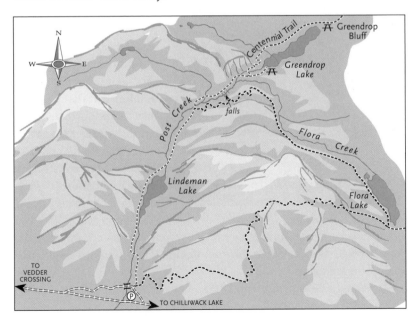

82 FLORA LAKE

to lake	Round trip 12 km (7.5 mi)	Allow 8 hours
	Elevation gain 1585 m (5200 ft)	High point 1770 m (5800 ft)
	Average grade 26.4%	
Flora–Lindeman Loop	Round trip 20 km (12.4 mi)	Allow 10 hours
	Elevation gain 1160 m (3800 ft)	High point 1770 m (5800 ft)
	Average grade 11.6%	

Best July to October   Map 92H/03 Skagit River
Driving distance from Vancouver 150 km (90 mi)

The shore of Flora Lake. (TH)

This hike and the area around it have recently been included in the new Chilliwack Lake Provincial Park. The trip to Flora Lake has long had a reputation as a wonderful outing, but not one done easily. It is for those prepared to hike over a 1770-m (5800-ft) pass with a drop of 395 m (1300 ft) on the other side to reach the lakeshore. Then there is the re-ascent to the pass and descent to the trailhead. If that is more than a comfortable day's outing, you may be content with the ridge which makes a very satisfactory destination. Another longer alternative is to keep going past Flora Lake, descend using a rough, sketchy route to meet the Lindeman–Greendrop Trail (Hike 81), then head down that to the trailhead.

Travelling east on Highway 1, take Exit 119A (Sardis, Cultus Lake). Drive south through Sardis and Vedder Crossing to the bridge over the river, which is known as Chilliwack River upstream of the bridge, Vedder River downstream. Turn left and zero your odometer here. This is Chilliwack Lake Road. Drive east for 40 km (25 mi), and just after crossing Post Creek, park on the roadside. Hikes 81 and 82 both start from here.

Pass the yellow gate and after 200m (650 ft) turn right up an old road, following orange markers, and go left at a crossroads. Now head east away from Post Creek, gaining height. As you rise your route swings back and forth and finally, when you emerge from the trees, you have no lack of views of the valley, the lake and its surrounding peaks. Then you cross an avalanche slope and the switchbacks become tighter as the trail steepens. Next you contour the ridge to reach the east side of a broad basin before you turn uphill again towards the pass. Once over the pass, the trail soon drops from open heather slopes into the heavy forest above Flora Lake. The best views are now behind you. To return by the Post Creek route, continue along the west side of Flora Lake, following tapes and cairns as they lead you through bush and one rock slide after another, until about 1 hour from the lake the route begins to approach Flora Creek. Do not cross the creek, stay on river-left! From a vantage point above Greendrop Lake, the trail switchbacks down to Post Creek, which you cross to go left on the main trail not far south of the lake and less than 2 hours from your vehicle.

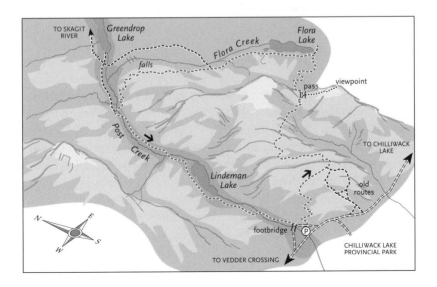

EATON LAKE

Round trip 8 km (5 mi)	Allow 5.5 hours
Elevation gain 915 m (3000 ft)	High point 1325 m (4340 ft)
Average grade 22.8%	
Best June to October	Maps 92H/03 Skagit River;
	92H/06 Hope
Driving distance from Vancouver 160 km (100 mi)	

View west across the lake. (IM)

Eaton Lake used to be known as Crescent Lake because of its shape. However, the name was officially changed to Eaton Lake to commemorate William Eaton, who was shot down over Germany in 1943 at age nineteen. The mountain in whose shadow the lake lies, Eaton Peak, is named for William's elder brother Doug, who was killed in Italy in 1944. Many of the topographic features in the upper Fraser Valley are named after people lost in World War II. As to the trip, it gives access to the high country on the Silverhope–Sumallo Divide. The route is a short, steep, but well laid-out trail that leads to the attractive lake in its rocky bowl. The lake may be the destination for a day trip but can also serve as a stop en route to the peaks above the valley. Note, however, that these peaks are steep; Eaton Peak South at 2105 m (6900 ft) requires some technical climbing.

Travelling east on Highway 1, take Exit 168, then just before the bridge over Silverhope Creek, go south onto Silver Skagit Road. Now you follow this road 16 km (9.9 mi) as it heads upstream, crossing and recrossing the creek. Stay left at the approach to Silver Lake Provincial Park and pass to the east of the lake. Then, a little past the 16 km sign (9.9 mi), turn left onto an old road signposted for the Eaton Creek Forest Recreation Site. This road soon deteriorates and narrows as new growth crowds in beyond the barrier at the trailhead, 200 m (650 ft) from the main thoroughfare.

Follow the old road until in 10 minutes it becomes a trail. You are then close to Eaton Creek. A series of short switchbacks lies above, still close to the creek as it plunges madly downhill. There is a fine little waterfall just before you cross on a high log bridge from river-right to river-left. Another waterfall is immediately above the bridge, so you have a fine view. Next you swing away to the south with glimpses of the mountains across the main valley as you turn to traverse back towards the main creek, close to which you cross a tributary with a wooden seat by its bridge. After that you zigzag upward on the divide between the two creeks, admiring the flowers and other plants that thrive on the shady floor of this tall forest. A short distance after the 3 km marker, the grade eases and you cross a much subdued main creek. This crossing is in need of repair and can be difficult. Ten minutes later you cross the creek again and stay on river-left until the lake. Here is an area of ancient rock slides with large moss-covered boulders strewn about that must be negotiated. You soon reach the crest, drop slightly to the log-jammed outlet and keep going to enjoy the sight of the lake and its mountain backdrop.

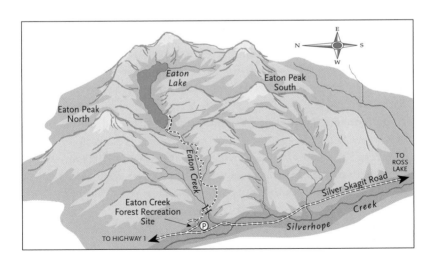

84 SKAGIT RIVER

One-way trip 14.5 km (9.0 mi)   Allow 6 hours
Elevation gain -105 m (-350 ft)   High point 625 m (2050 ft)
Average grade -0.7%

Best June to October   Map 92H/03 Skagit River
Driving distance from Vancouver 185 km (115 mi)

View south down the trail.

If you are fortunate, you will hit the brief mid-June flowering of rhododendrons on this trail. Even without that bonus, the trip from Silver Skagit Road at its 26 Mile Bridge, following the route of the historic Whatcom Trail upstream, to Highway 3 at the western end of Manning Provincial Park is a rewarding one, as is the corresponding downstream hike. For complete success, however, it does require a two-car shuttle. Otherwise you must cut your trip short, unless you are prepared for a 29 km (18 mi) march there and back. The trip is described here in the downstream direction, and is wholly within Skagit Valley Provincial Park.

For the downstream end of the trail: drive east on Highway 1, take Exit 168, then just before the bridge over Silverhope Creek, go south on Silver Skagit Road. Now you follow this road as it heads upstream, crossing and recrossing the creek. Stay left at the approach to Silver Lake Provincial Park and pass to the east of the lake. Then drive 43 km (27 mi), crossing the Skagit River and parking either on the road or in the day-use area.

To reach the upstream end of the trail: drive east on Highway 5 past Hope and fork right onto Highway 3. Drive another 26 km (16 mi) and turn right into Sumallo Grove. There is a parking lot with B.C. Parks information boards.

From Sumallo Grove, follow the trail south and cross the Skagit River on a bridge, to river-left, just upstream of the confluence with the

Sumallo River. The Silverdaisy Trail (Hike 97) starts here. Old mine buildings are visible to the left of your route. Although the ecological reserve is farther south, there are giant Douglas-firs along this stretch. A little more than 1 hour brings you to Delacey Camp, some flats beside the river that are covered in high water. South of Twentysix Mile Creek is the ecological reserve set aside for its magnificent cedars and Douglas-firs. Your trip through the reserve, as you wind your way amongst these forest giants, both standing and fallen, lasts for about 40 minutes. The trail travels up and down, sometimes beside the river, sometimes up on the hillside. The footbed is generally excellent and makes for easy walking. After crossing Twentyeight Mile Creek, an old section of trail close to the river may still be obvious; however, take the marked higher trail, which avoids a wet section close to the water. Before the trail finally flattens out, there is a view to the northwest of Silvertip Mountain and its little glacier. The last couple of kilometres to the road are initially on the flats through clusters of rhododendrons, lodgepole pine and small Douglas-fir; you may think that you have been transported to the interior of British Columbia. Turn right onto the Centennial Trail when you intersect it, 20 minutes from the end. There is a small elevation drop taking you back suddenly to wetter coastal vegetation. Then you pop out onto the road.

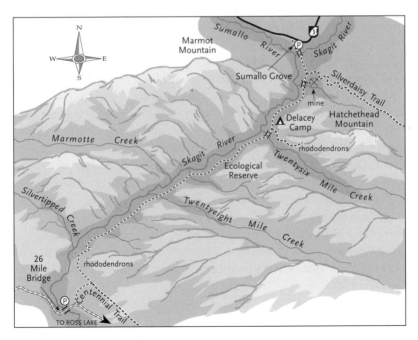

85 SKYLINE TRAIL
(West)

Round trip 22 km (14 mi)   Allow 9 hours
Elevation gain 1370 m (4500 ft)   High point 1860 m (6100 ft)
Average grade 12.5%

Best July to October   Maps 92H/02 Manning Park;
    92H/03 Skagit River
Driving distance from Vancouver 205 km (125 mi)

View southwest across Ross Lake to the Picket Range.

The complete Skyline Trail links Skagit Valley Provincial Park with Manning Provincial Park. However, the complete hike is a long day; then there is the time required for a vehicle shuttle. The trail is therefore described in two parts. Below is the west end of the trail; Hike 103 is the east end. It is a grand hike from either end. The west end allows views across the lower Skagit Valley and Ross Lake to the boundary country from Mount Challenger, past Devil's Tongue, all the way up to Silvertip Mountain. This is a B.C. Parks trail, so the grades are mild and the tread is wide.

Travelling east on Highway 1, turn off on Exit 168, then just before the bridge over Silverhope Creek, go south on Silver Skagit Road. Now you follow this road as it heads upstream, crossing and recrossing the creek. Stay left at the approach to Silver Lake Provincial Park and pass to the east of the lake. Then, a little past 54 km (33 mi), park on the left at the information board. This is the trailhead.

Once on foot, you head east in open forest across the level floor of the valley, in a zone transitional between the coastal vegetation and the drier

Interior. After several minutes of pleasant walking, you are joined by the Centennial Trail from the northwest and subsequently the two trails become one as you begin to rise, crossing the first of the creeks that you must negotiate. Once on its south side, you follow it for a short time before your route veers off right and you traverse the first of two raised benches indicative of one-time lake levels. Next you find yourself heading into the valley of a second creek, with a series of switchbacks to greet you once you emerge, turning from south to east in the process. All this time you have been rising steadily through tall forest with only two spots to provide viewpoints to the outside world. Now, however, the trees thin out as you approach the subalpine meadows, which are glorious in late July and August. Finally you traverse the last ridge before the headwaters of Mowich Creek, into which the trail drops were you to follow it farther. At around 11 km (6.8 mi) from the start, this spot makes a suitable destination for a day hike. You are in true alpine country with vistas galore. The most spectacular of the peaks is undoubtedly Hozomeen Mountain—heading south towards which there is a trail. Hozomeen is also the visual link between the east and west ends of the Skyline Trail. Nepopekum Mountain to the north has a vague trail if you wish to hike in that direction. To the east, only 1.5 km (0.9 mi) away, is Lone Goat Mountain, the western terminus of Hike 103.

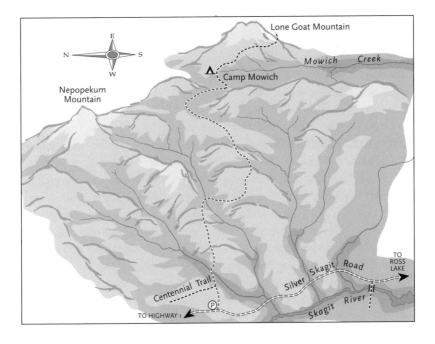

86 STEIN VALLEY

to teepee camp	Round trip 17 km (10.6 mi)	Allow 7 hours
	Elevation gain 230 m (755 ft)	High point 425 m (1400 ft)
	Average grade 2.7%	
to cable crossing	Round trip 26 km (16 mi)	Allow 10 hours
	Elevation gain 355 m (1160 ft)	High point 550 m (1800 ft)
	Average grade 2.7%	

Best March to November	Map 92I/05 Stein River
Driving distance from Vancouver 265 km (165 mi)	

The return downstream on the trail. (CM)

The Stein Valley is an intact watershed, one of the very few left in British Columbia. It is a river of climatic transition: the west end is coastal forest, the east end is Interior forest. With its preservation, you can be assured of experiencing a valley in its natural albeit dynamic state. Two approaches to the Stein River watershed, by Blowdown Creek (Hike 12) and Lizzie Creek (Hike 13), have already been described in this book. This trip is the obvious route, going upstream from the Stein River's confluence with the Fraser River a short distance north of Lytton. It involves an interesting crossing of the Fraser on a cable ferry.

Drive Highway 1 past Hope, through the Fraser Canyon, then take Highway 12 through Lytton. Cross the Thompson River just above the Thompson–Fraser confluence, then go left at the ferry sign some 800 m

(0.5 mi) beyond. The ferry itself runs on call from early morning to 10 pm. Once on the west bank, turn right and, ignoring one road going left quite soon and the Earlscourt Farm turnoff, also on the left, travel almost 5 km (3.1 mi) to a road signposted for the Stein Heritage Trail. Go left to parking near the trailhead, 1 km (0.6 mi) from the main West Side Road.

From the bench the trail descends to the river flats, crosses Stryen Creek and meanders through an open ponderosa pine and Douglas-fir forest typical of the dry Interior. The rush of the turbulent Stein River on your right is always in your ears. This trail is easy for the most part, staying fairly level except where you rise over canyon walls and talus slopes. For a day trip you may make your destination the teepee camp, situated on a large river flat. This is also an attractive and popular spot for camping, although there are many such sites along the way. Continuing upstream, you will find yourself rising to bench level and over a small hill with fine views of the river below before these are lost in a stretch of cedar forest. Next you reach Earl's Cabin and then the creek commemorating the same man, a prospector from the early years of the century. Nearing the river again the trail negotiates some bluffs near the water's edge, and on these rock walls you may be able to discern some pictographs, which are well worth coming to see. And now, not far ahead, just below the site of the infamous cable crossing is the new suspension bridge over the main river. A long day's hike takes you to this spot, a possible overnight stopping place also if you are backpacking. In fact, with time at your disposal, you may make this the first stop of a seven- or eight-day return trip to Stein Lake.

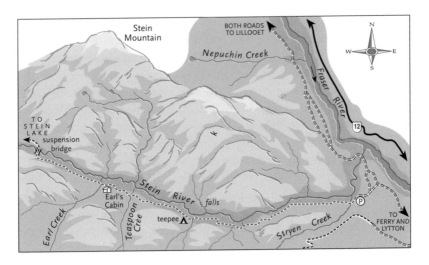

87 GATE MOUNTAIN

Round trip 16 km (9.9 mi)	Allow 7 hours
Elevation gain 1175 m (3850 ft)	High point 1450 m (4760 ft)
Average grade 14.7%	

Best June to October	Maps 92H/11 Spuzzum;
	92H/14 Boston Bar
Driving distance from Vancouver 200 km (125 mi)	

Summit view south down the Fraser River.

Also known as the 1858 Trail, this trip is a pleasant hike in its own regard; however, another attraction is its historical significance. Like Hike 88, this one uses an old pack trail, established at the time of the gold rush to the Fraser River and the Cariboo. In view of its steepness, one can only feel sorry for the mules that carried loads over the ridge between the Fraser and the Anderson River to the east, while admiring the determination of the people who refused to be stopped by the natural difficulties associated with the bluffs above Hell's Gate. The view that greets you is panoramic: the Fraser Canyon stretches north and south, the Anderson River system lies spread out to the east and southeast; in the distance to the south stand Hope Mountain and Isolillock Peak, and Mount Urquhart rises in the southwest. Due to its panoramic aspect, this was a B.C. Forest Service lookout. However, now a multitude of antennae and associated helicopter-transported debris litter the summit. You might be happier with the view from the knoll above The Notch.

Drive north on Highway 1 through the Fraser Canyon, past Alexandra Lodge and through Alexandra Tunnel. About 5 km (3.1 mi) past the lodge, as you ascend a long hill, there is a pull-off on the left (west) side of the highway. There should be a wooden trail sign at the top of the bank on the right (east) side of the road. If you come to the Cooper's Corner Rest Area, you have gone too far.

The route itself, adorned with tape and orange markers, ascends steeply for the first 600 m (2000 ft) or so in a series of switchbacks, making an early start advisable to avoid the heat of the day. As you climb, the grade eases a little before you meet the Bluffs Trail (the connecting link with the 1848 Trail) that joins from the right. After the trail goes left and rises a little more, the markers lead you slightly to the right into a bushy draw before veering left (north) again on a very faint trail through open forest. Next you meet the old access road for the abandoned lookout, and here, at present, the orange markers end. Stay with the road to its end, enjoying wildflowers and strawberries in season, then turn left and rise steeply up the ridge, the trail now marked here and there with tapes. Follow the trail up the ridge to a minor summit, The Notch, at almost 1220 m (4000 ft). This is a possible destination if you think that another 90 minutes is beyond you, especially as the trail has become overgrown with a few windfalls and the summit is an industrial wasteland. If you do advance from here, you pass one or two minor summits on your left as you remain generally on the east side of the ridge, then, after one last draw, you find yourself on the rocky summit.

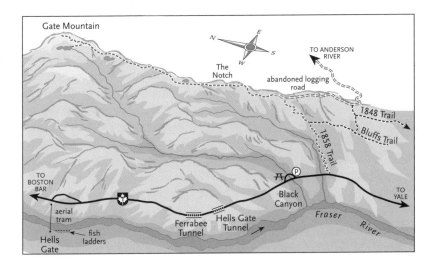

88 FIRST BRIGADE TRAIL

Round trip 13 km (8.1 mi)   Allow 5.5 hours
Elevation gain 780 m (2560 ft)   High point 920 m (3020 ft)
Average grade 12.0%

Best June to October   Maps 92H/11 Spuzzum;
92H/14 Boston Bar
Driving distance from Vancouver 205 km (125 mi)

View up the Fraser River to Black Canyon.

This trip and Hike 87 are inextricably tied together, both of them woven into the history of the Fraser and Cariboo gold rushes and a link with British Columbia's colourful past. In 1848 A.C. Anderson of the Hudson's Bay Company set out to establish a fur-trading route to the north and east overland from Yale. Therefore this walk is a must; not only is it attractive scenically, it also allows the hiker to retrace one of the earliest pioneer routes to the Interior.

Drive north on Highway 1 through the Fraser Canyon to Alexandra Lodge, the one-time 14-Mile House, now a heritage building. The old trail started here. However, today it begins some 300 m (1000 ft) north, midway up a long hill. Parking is available on the same side of the highway about 150 m (475 ft) beyond the trailhead.

The trail begins by a small stream and, joined very soon by the original route from the lodge, climbs in a series of zigzags in open timber, heading east. You pass above an old rock slide before reaching a high, open bluff with views of the peaks along the canyon's west side. From here the trail continues in open timber along the bluff before swinging right to ascend a parallel ridge leading to a fork with a metal plaque: straight ahead leads "To Lakes and Anderson River"; the rough, taped route left is the "Bluffs Trail used by miners to Boston Bar and Lytton, 1858." Forging ahead you rise steeply again to the high point of the day, then undulate along the ridge past little lakes. Near one of these lakes was the conjectured site of Lake House, the first stopping place for the brigades. Farther north from here you leave the Brigade Trail, veer left to come out on a high bluff overlooking the canyon and meet the Bluffs Trail coming from the south. Your return follows the latter trail south as it winds first through large, sparse trees on a broad ridge that narrows to a bluffy spine coated with small lodgepole pine. It then passes a final outcrop that provides the last fine viewpoint over the river and the Black Canyon Rapids. Beyond this point the route becomes more obscure as it passes through a thicket of young hemlock before curving left around a small lake to reach the fork and the main trail back to Alexandra Lodge.

If you have a two-car party, make this trip a crossover by parking the second vehicle at the start of the 1858 Trail: Gate Mountain (Hike 87), which would then be your descent route. From the junction of the main trail with the Bluffs Trail, instead of turning south as described above, you would turn north to meet the Gate Mountain Trail and descend to the highway on it.

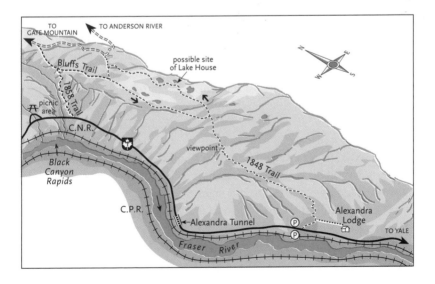

89 MOUNT LINCOLN

Round trip 5 km (3.1 mi)	Allow 3 hours
Elevation gain 580 m (1900 ft)	High point 655 m (2150 ft)
Average grade 23.2%	

Best April to October	Map 92H/11 Spuzzum
Driving distance from Vancouver 170 km (105 mi)	

View north over the Fraser River to the peak.

Just east and north of the village of Yale is a dome of rock pierced by Highway 1; this is Mount Lincoln. Although steep, it does have a rough track up it, several exposed sections being fitted with standing ropes to give you confidence. At many places on the trail and from the summit you have fine views over the little town and along the Fraser Canyon with its road and two railway tracks, one on either side of the river. If you dislike Mount Lincoln's steep, rocky terrain or if you want another short hike to fill your day, the Spirit Caves Trail to the south of the village is also described.

Drive east on Highway 1 through Hope then through Yale. About 500 m (0.3 mi) beyond the traffic light in Yale pull off on the right-hand side of the highway where the old main road branched right and crossed the CPR tracks. On the roadside ahead is a yellow sign saying "Avalanche Danger: Do not stop for 4 km."

Cross the highway and walk east to a large boulder on the left just beyond the point where the highway crosses Mary Ann Creek.

Immediately to the left of this boulder a faint trail leads off uphill over the rock, soon encountering the first of the forty-seven switchbacks that ascend steadily, sometimes on scree, sometimes on grass or moss. After about 35 minutes you reach some steep rock and the first rope, and another 30 minutes brings you to the second. Shortly after, a third rope provides the confidence to negotiate an exposed bare rock face. After that you have time to look around and admire the varieties of mosses and low shrubs at your feet. Then comes your final scramble to the summit with the remains of a television relay station for the town below. Your route, in fact, was used for servicing the station, as you are fairly close to the old cable all the way. On the top, besides admiring the view, you may indulge in a little retrospective fantasy—calling up scenes from the time when Yale was a busy river port, the head of Fraser River navigation and the transfer point for supplies to the Cariboo goldfields during the stirring days of 1859.

For the Spirit Caves Trail, drive back 2 km (1.2 mi) to the trailhead, which is 25 m (80 ft) south of Whisky Fill Road and 20 m (65 ft) north of a large sign saying "Welcome to Historic Yale." Park on the shoulder.

This hike has much in common with the one on Mount Lincoln: it offers superb views over Yale and the Fraser Canyon, has almost the same elevation gain and duration but lacks the exposed rock scrambles, angling as it does up the face of the slope in long, slow zigzags for just over an hour to reach its one magnificent viewpoint. Beyond that a pleasant little loop in the forest leads up to the crest of the ridge, passing en route a rockpile with its shallow caves, before circling back to the viewpoint.

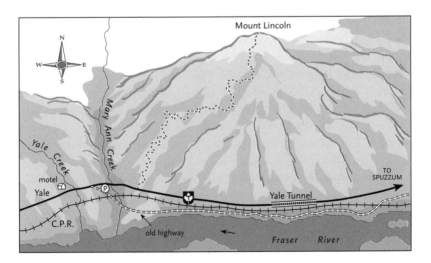

90 STOYOMA MOUNTAIN

Round trip 12 km (7.5 mi)   Allow 5 hours
Elevation gain 670 m (2200 ft)   High point 2282 m (7486 ft)
Average grade 11.2%

Best July to October   Maps 92H/14 Boston Bar;
92I/03 Prospect Creek
Driving distance from Vancouver 325 km (200 mi)

Cabin Lake, seen from the old burn on the north slope of the mountain.

As you drive north on the Coquihalla Highway towards Merritt, there is an obvious high rounded double summit off to the west: this is Stoyoma Mountain, the highest peak between the Fraser Canyon and the Coquihalla. It is an area of high meadows and lakes with a resident goat population. The route starts from just above Cabin Lake, a beautiful pocket of water with a finger of land on which stood an old log cabin. As you ascend Stoyoma, the conspicuous double peak to the west is the rarely visited Mount Hewitt Bostock. To the south are the striking summits of the Coquihalla–Anderson River area.

Drive east on Highway 1 past Hope onto Highway 5, the Coquihalla Highway. Pay your dues and drive to Merritt. At the traffic lights in Merritt, turn west onto Highway 8 towards Spences Bridge. Drive 18 km (11.2 mi), past Sunshine Creek Road West, to turn left down onto Petit Creek Road and cross the Nicola River. In less than 1 km (0.6 mi) make a left turn—you are still on Petit Creek Road—to travel south for the next 35 km (22 mi). It is a good 2WD road most of the way. At 10 km (6.2 mi) a sign informs you that this road is called Prospect Creek Forest Service Road, and at 24 km (15 mi) you cross Prospect Creek. The road climbs steeply out of the creek to level off around 31 km (19 mi). Cross a one-lane bridge and 1 km (0.6 mi) later, at around 35 km (22 mi), go right at a fork. About 800 m (0.5 mi) up this road, a spur cuts back to the right. The road deteriorates from here and becomes 4WD. With a rugged vehicle you may wish to drive to Cabin Lake, another 3.5 km (2.2 mi); however, the walking route starts on the high ground before the descent to the lake. Turnaround and parking spots are hard to come by.

From wherever you park on the road, the double summit should be obvious to the west, above the growing plantation. The southern peak is the higher. Follow the road, as it oscillates up and down, to its high point at 1860 m (6100 ft). When the hillside above you is open meadow and you can see the silver snags of an old burn, turn uphill off the road. Cabin Lake, although not visible where you left the road, will be seen below you almost immediately as you ascend. The scrubby spruce and pine divide gorgeous meadows of heather, lupines and phlox. There is a vague trail, west around a little pond, following some cairns but always on the ridge crest. From the top, being on the highest point around, you can see forever.

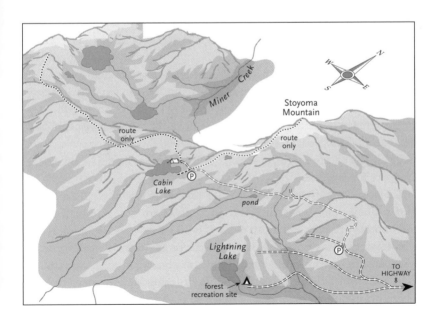

91 MOUNT THYNNE

Round trip 10.5 km (6.5 mi)   Allow 5 hours
Elevation gain 305 m (1000 ft)   High point 2028 m (6655 ft)
Average grade 5.5%

Best July to October   Maps 92H/10 Tulameen;
                                   92H/15 Aspen Grove
Driving distance from Vancouver 285 km (175 mi)

View north over the summit meadows.

This is one of those unusual trips where, although it is possible to drive all the way to a summit cluttered with antennae, it is still worth hiking there. The value stems from two things. Firstly the road ascends on the north slope, therefore snow lies late, the snow patches stopping vehicles for much of the year. Second, the summit is wide and rolling, and you do not have to be far off the road to forget that it is there. So, if you time it just right, you can catch the summit meadows in full flower before the 4WD hordes arrive. Even after, drive your outdoor-loving grandmother up here; she'll adore it! One final bonus: the old B.C. Forest Service lookout still has the fire-sighting device installed. You can sit in the tower and play fire-watcher.

Drive east on Highway 1 past Hope onto Highway 5, the Coquihalla Highway. Pay your dues and drive another 33 km (20 mi) north of the toll booth, to Coldwater Road (Exit 256). As you were dropping elevation towards this exit, your route towards Brookmere was visible, heading south, on the hillside to your right. Nearly 200 m (650 ft) from the exit is a T-junction at which you go right; there is a snowmobile sign saying "Thynne Mtn. 8 km." After 4 km (2.5 mi) the road becomes gravel and after 11 km (6.8 mi) you enter Brookmere, a fine little town that was once an important stop on the Kettle Valley Railway. As you exit the town, and just prior to recrossing the tracks, you come to a fork. Where the left-hand option is Coalmont Road, go right onto Thynne Mountain Road. The kilometre markers start from this junction. Gain height and at 2 km (1.2 mi) stay left where Brook Creek Road goes right. At 7 km (4.3 mi) go right where Lower McPhail Road goes left. At 10 km (6.2 mi), go left onto Upper McPhail Road. Road conditions from here will dictate your parking spot. After a long right-hand swing, around 16 km (9.9 mi) is the Merritt Snowmobile Clubhouse on the right at an elevation of 1740 m (5700 ft). There is lots of parking here; the road ahead deteriorates even more.

Follow the road uphill from wherever you park. It is possible to follow the road all the way to the top, past the north summit with more antennae, into the hollow and lake, then up to the main (south) summit with its fire lookout and antenna towers. At almost any point you can leave the road, to either east or west, to wander through the meadows. It is subalpine country, so there are bands of timber separating the open areas. With the north summit behind you the views are concentrated to the south, from an east to west horizon. The dominant summit is Coquihalla Mountain and the middle ground in that direction is Mount Henning (Hike 92). Off to the west are the Coquihalla–Anderson River peaks: Yak, Alpaca and Zupjok. To the southeast is Snass Mountain.

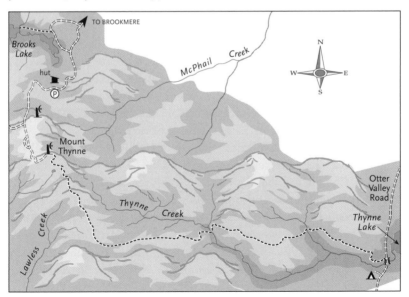

MOUNT HENNING

Round trip 8 km (5 mi)	Allow 3.5 hours
Elevation gain 550 m (1805 ft)	High point 1645 m (5400 ft)
Average grade 13.8%	

Best July to October	Maps 92H/10 Tulameen;
	92H/11 Spuzzum
Driving distance from Vancouver 225 km (140 mi)	

Mount Henning (middle) and Coquihalla Mountain (behind), seen from Mount Thynne.

This hike takes you into a pleasant high-country area east of the Coquihalla Highway. It is north of the toll booth, so to get your money's worth you might want to do another hike in this area. There is an alpine route north from Mount Henning to Thynne Mountain (Hike 91) although the traverse is not described in this guide. It may also serve as a prelude to other hikes in the Merritt, Kamloops or Okanagan areas. The hike as described here makes a loop up one old track to alpine country, then down another mining road to your starting point.

Drive east on Highway 1 past Hope onto Highway 5, the Coquihalla Highway. Pay your dues and drive another 4 km (2.5 mi) north of the toll booth, to Coquihalla Lakes (Exit 228). At the intersection just off the exit, turn right, then left onto Tulameen Forest Service Road. You cross a cattle grid and turn left onto a narrow dirt road which immediately forks, so you go left again, which takes you to the pipeline right-of-way. Turn left onto the right-of-way and, 100 m (325 ft) along, turn right onto a track into the trees. There is a sign on a tree saying "Mt. Henning; Merritt Forest District." Barely 200 m (650 ft) farther is a fork; turn left and park before the creek.

Cross the creek on the dirt road and follow the switchbacks upward. There are some minor viewpoints as you ascend. After the switchbacks, the trail levels off and contours the side of the mountain. Then comes a fork. Take the worn and rutted left-hand track to the meadows of the northwestern spur. Beyond the last tire marks an intermittent faint trail starts off southeast, indicating an approach across subalpine terrain to the open ridge of which Mount Henning is the highest bump. On the crest, the views of distant peaks and valleys all around and the meadows underfoot make it hard to resist the urge to wander on and on. There is no trail on the ridge but its openness makes one unnecessary. When you decide to descend, you can backtrack to the fork or take the line of least resistance downhill; but watch your direction! The road traverses the hillside below, coming from the right fork at which you earlier went left. The old grass-covered mine road continues straight ahead into the pass to a dilapidated shack, all that is left of the one-time Independence Mine Camp. There is also a newer snowmobile cabin. To complete the circuit from here, first take the track to the right (south), then almost immediately go right again, working west around the head of the valley to descend on its south side, reaching your vehicle by the other fork than the one on which you set out. This route is less scenic than the ascent, lying as it does mainly among trees, but it does give a shady return on a hot day.

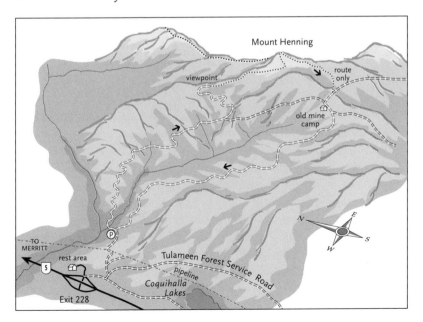

ZOA PEAK

Round trip 11 km (6.8 mi)   Allow 6 hours
Elevation gain 635 m (2090 ft)   High point 1875 m (6150 ft)
Average grade 11.5%

Best July to October   Map 92H/11 Spuzzum
Driving distance from Vancouver 200 km (125 mi)

The north face of Yak Peak, viewed from the col between Zoa Peak's two summits.

Of the hikes in the high divide area of Highway 5, this one is, for now at least, one of the most appealing. Not only is the bush light but the grade is generally gentle, although you do have to lose some height to get from one prong of the double summit to the other. The picturesque name of the peak owes its origins to a British Columbia mountaineer who named the mountains of this area after animals indigenous to the alpine regions of central Asia. Zoa is a member of the yak family.

Drive east on Highway 1 past Hope onto Highway 5, the Coquihalla Highway. Take the Falls Lake exit (Exit 221), which is 3 km (1.9 mi) south of the toll booth, and follow the narrow road 1 km (0.6 mi) to the Falls Lake parking area and trailhead.

Ignore the trail to Falls Lake. Cross the creek from the parking area and go north up the old Coldwater road a short distance, to where the remains of an old 4WD road to Falls Lake go left. Take this road to the pipeline right-of-way which is less than 5 minutes above. Turn right and head north along the right-of-way, rising fairly painlessly for approximately 30 minutes. Look for a cairn on the right-of-way and red flagging tape up the cutbank to your left. If you somehow pass this point, you will meet a narrow access road coming in from the right. Turn around. The trail goes into the trees 80 m (260 ft) back down the pipeline. As soon as you climb the cutbank and enter the trees, the footbed is obvious. There are no markers other than occasional flagging tape. Less than 1 hour up the trail, around 1585 m (5200 ft), is an open rocky area covered in phlox and stonecrop, with a fine view of Coquihalla Mountain to the south. The trail can be faint and intermittent in places, but you are rising on the rounded east ridge of Zoa Peak. The further you rise the more obvious the ridge becomes. However, the tapes are few and far between high on the ridge. Therefore, pay attention to your surroundings and direction. Trees thin out as you ascend, and you travel in pleasant, subalpine country to the first summit at just over 1850 m (6000 ft), with a good view to the south for your efforts. To complete the picture you must lose 54 m (175 ft), and regain it, to reach the second summit, a large, relatively flat area with trees, meadows and excellent views to the west and north from separate view spots between the tree patches. The starkness of the nearby animal-named peaks is particularly impressive, with their bare walls and massive grey slabs of rock.

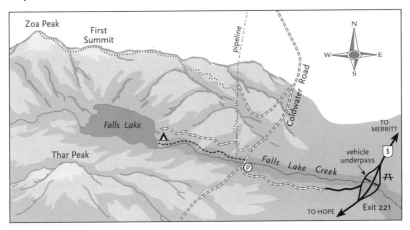

94 NEEDLE PEAK

Round trip 13 km (8.1 mi)   Allow 7 hours
Elevation gain 855 m (2900 ft)   High point 2105 m (6900 ft)
Average grade 13.2%

Best July to September   Map 92H/11 Spuzzum
Driving distance from Vancouver 195 km (120 mi)

Needle Peak, seen southwest from Thar Peak.

As you reach the high point of the Coquihalla Highway, the eye tends to be drawn to the rock wall of Yak Peak to the north of the road. This unfortunately distracts you from looking to the south where Needle Peak rises on the divide between Boston Bar Creek and the Coquihalla River. Needle Peak is a fine-looking rocky summit that is popular as both a summer and a winter destination. One of its attractions as a backcountry ski trip is the safety of the well-defined west ridge, which turns to become a well-defined north-running ridge towards the highway. This is also the summer route.

Drive east on Highway 1 past Hope onto Highway 5, the Coquihalla Highway. Take the Zopkios Ridge Lookout exit (Exit 217), which is 9 km (5.6 mi) south of the toll booth. Before the highways works yard, turn right onto the pipeline right-of-way. Drive 100 m (325 ft) and park just before the creek.

As soon as you cross the creek, turn left into the trees.

Look for flagging, then markers left and uphill on a well-trodden route through tall trees at first, then a thicket of smaller trees, which in turn gives way to mixed forest and meadow. Then you reach a cairn; the grade eases and you are soon striding along in fine subalpine surroundings, becoming purely alpine as you progress. From here the hike is sheer pleasure as you make your way up and down over granite slabs and heathery meadows, with views of Needle Peak and its precipitous face ahead and the mountains with the Himalayan animal names to your rear, a foretaste of the view on the return trip. Finally, at about 1850 m (6000 ft), the ridge you have been following southward merges with another from the west. Here you change direction towards the peak, which is easier to climb than its name suggests although it does require some expertise near the top. Finding the right gully, of two leading to the summit, is a problem—both ascending and descending—so perhaps you may want to rest on your laurels once you reach the base. If, however, you decide to press on to the end, do take time to search out the easier, albeit the less obvious, route on the right and to note its position for your return.

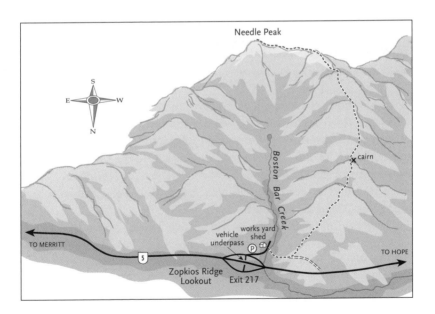

95 HOPE MOUNTAIN

Round trip 10 km (6.2 mi)   Allow 5 hours
Elevation gain 800 m (2625 ft)   High point 1837 m (6026 ft)
Average grade 16.0%

Best July to September   Map 92H/06 Hope
Driving distance from Vancouver 160 km (100 mi)

Summit view north to Hope and the Fraser River.

Hope Mountain is due south of the town of Hope, and from the top the streets of town seem only a stone's throw away. There are also fine views up the Fraser River to Yale (Hike 89 being obvious, albeit dwarfed by your altitude) and down-river to Chilliwack. To the south is an interesting view of Silver Lake and the north end of the Silver–Skagit Valley. From the parking area two trails also lead to Wells Peak, although they are not described in this guide.

Drive east on Highway 5 past Hope. Take Exit 177 onto Highway 3. Less than 2 km (1.2 mi) later, with Nicolum River Provincial Park across the highway on your left, turn right. There is a large sign saying "Mount Hope Trail System...." Zero your odometer here. The road turns back west paralleling the highway, and the pavement ends in less than 1 km (0.6 mi). At 2.5 km (1.6 mi) take the left, uphill fork and continue to 4 km (2.5 mi), where a short hill with a loose surface will stop 2WD vehicles. Four Mile Creek, into the headwaters of which you are driving, has a new concrete bridge to river-right at 5.5 km (3.4 mi). A sign at the junction at 8.5 km (5.3 mi) tells you to continue straight ahead. It is 500 m (0.3 mi) to a large landing and the trailhead.

The trail drops west into the plantation and the head of Four Mile Creek. It would be a muddy route without all the logs and planks that have been laid down. Uphill on the west side of the valley you pick up an old logging road and follow it to a junction where one of the Wells Peak trails turns south as you turn right and head north towards Hope Mountain. Just 50 m (160 ft) farther along is a large orange diamond where you leave the road. Turn uphill on a couple of switchbacks and, in 15 minutes, crest a narrow ridge: the divide between Four Mile Creek and Alexander Creek. Descend 60 m (200 ft) to pick up another old road and follow it around the head of Alexander Creek. Where the trail leaves the road and makes for the south ridge of Hope Mountain, a brown sign points left and uphill. To gain the ridge at 1430 m (4700 ft) is only 20 minutes from here. The trail turns right (north) and follows the ridge crest where it can. When the ridge is too steep the trail traverses to the west side, allowing some grand views across to Silver and Isolillock Peaks. In small boulder fields the trail switchbacks but there is flagging tape of many varieties to follow. The final rise to the top, after a short drop to a saddle, looks much steeper than it is. The summit has, other than the views, two pleasant heather-ringed ponds.

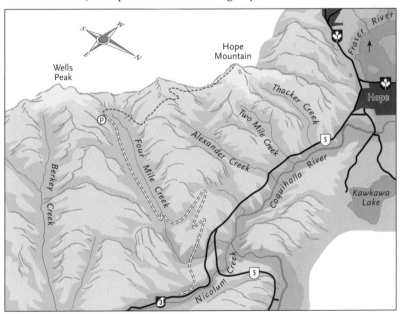

96 MOUNT OUTRAM

Round trip 18 km (11.2 mi)   Allow 9 hours
Elevation gain 1800 m (5900 ft)   High point 2440 m (8000 ft)
Average grade 20.0%

Best July to September   Maps 92H/06 Hope; B.C.
                                Parks Manning Provincial
                                Park
Driving distance from Vancouver 170 km (105 mi)

Silvertip Mountain (right) and Redoubt Peak (far right), viewed from near the top. (CM)

Although this hike starts inside Manning Provincial Park, the mountain itself, and 90 per cent of the hike, is outside the park. It is educational to look at the shape of the park boundaries and investigate why the strange little panhandle exists. There is another historical aspect to this trip since some of the route is along Engineers Road, which was built around 1860 as a route to the Interior. The mountain itself provides a fine hike into high open country with panoramic views from the top, since Mount Outram is the highest point in the area. The peak is also close to the eastern perimeter of the Cascade Mountains, therefore the view to the northeast is of a much gentler landscape than the view to the west and south.

Drive east on Highway 5 past Hope. Take Exit 177 onto Highway 3, which you follow for 18 km (11.2 mi) to the West Gate of Manning Provincial Park. Here, on your left, is a parking lot, its entrance adorned with a large carved marmot.

The start of the trail is also used for the short Engineers Loop Trail.

Therefore, a couple of switchbacks above the parking lot where the Loop Trail turns west, you turn right and travel east on Engineers Road initially across a talus slope. Then the road descends slightly before you leave it to go left onto the trail signposted for Mount Outram, your route lying in deep forest. At first the trail heads east to avoid steep, rocky slopes and gains height in a series of tight zigzags. It then swings back west and north across a relatively level section before switchbacking again and heading west in a long ascending traverse towards Seventeen Mile Creek, alongside which it zigzags a few more times, the trees now sparser and smaller. Finally, at about 1500 m (4900 ft), the trail drops slightly to cross the creek and begin its ascent on the far side, the forest soon yielding to subalpine meadow as you swing to and fro up the ridge, your route deep in flowers of rainbow hues. Then just beyond the 7.5 km marker you work around the rocky ridge to an eminence above a tiny lake nestled in the basin below on your right. So far the going has been excellent, on a well-graded trail that makes hiking easy, but from now on the slope steepens and the last 300 m (1000 ft) of your hike become a rocky scramble as you follow the paint splashes marking the route to the summit with its large cairn. Silvertip Mountain is a standout peak to the south. To return you can retrace your ascent route, being especially careful if visibility is limited—these open ridges are somewhat featureless, so follow the markers.

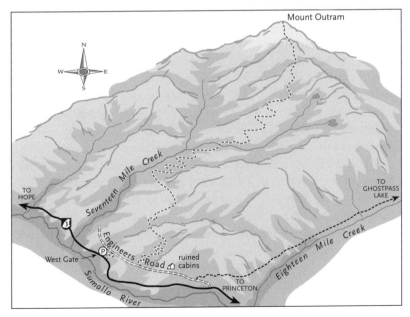

SILVERDAISY MOUNTAIN

Round trip 20 km (12.4 mi) Allow 9 hours
Elevation gain 1440 m (4725 ft) High point 2051 m (6725 ft)
Average grade 14.4%

Best July to September Maps 92H/02 Manning Park;
92H/03 Skagit River
Driving distance from Vancouver 185 km (115 mi)

The open southeast ridge to the top. (JS)

Two routes lead to this picturesque mountain area, which is in a little pocket of non-park land between Skagit Valley and Manning Provincial Parks. One route takes a mine road and the other a trail restored and maintained by dedicated volunteers. The second of these, although longer, is the more attractive as well as being more interesting historically. It uses the old wagon road to the one-time aerial tram that was installed to remove mineral wealth from Silverdaisy Mountain.

To access the trail, drive east on Highway 5 past Hope. Take Exit 177 onto Highway 3, which you follow for 26 km (16 mi) to turn right into Sumallo Grove. There is a parking lot with B.C. Parks information boards. This is also the starting point for Hike 84.

Follow the trail south and cross the Skagit River on a bridge, to river-left, just upstream of the confluence with the Sumallo River. Then continue south for about 15 minutes to where the Silverdaisy Trail forks left from the main Skagit River Trail with which, so far, it has been sharing the route. Taking this left fork you start zigzagging upward, with seven switchbacks before you get clear of the main valley and swing east, high above the north side of Silverdaisy Creek. The next section is somewhat steeper with one or two rock slides, from the first of which is a good view down the Skagit Valley. After this you veer away from the creek, level slightly, then zigzag upward again to join an old 4WD road coming in from the east, which brings you onto the cut made by the tramway from the old Invermay Mine. Next, as bush begins to crowd your route, you see above you on the left the spoil from a former operation just before you emerge on another old road leading down to some collapsed mine buildings a little below; but you go left and up, then right, staying with this road as it rises steadily along the side of the mountain to a pass over which it continues to the one-time A.M. Mine. You, however, turn left at the saddle, following the route up the crest of the ridge towards the double summit. The top provides a panorama of mountain scenery: from nearby Hatchethead Mountain southwest along the ridge from the col, to the breathtaking sight of Hozomeen Mountain farther away in the south and the high country of the Cascade Divide.

You may, of course, make a crossover using the access road to the A.M. Mine. To do so, leave one vehicle by the entrance to the mine road, which goes off right (south) at the sign for Cayuse Flats, some 9 km (5.6 mi) east of the Sumallo Grove turnoff. When you return from the summit to the pass, follow the road downhill on the opposite side of the mountain from your ascent.

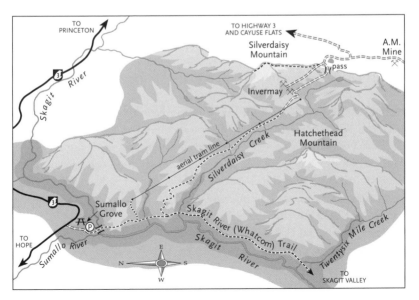

98 PUNCH BOWL

Round trip 30 km (19 mi)	Allow 10 hours
Elevation gain 1020 m (3350 ft)	High point 1784 m (5850 ft)
Average grade 6.8%	
Best July to September	Maps 92H/03 Skagit River; 92H/06 Hope; 92H/07 Princeton
Driving distance from Vancouver 185 km (115 mi)	

View of Dry Lake on the way down the Dewdney Trail.

This is a trip into British Columbia's colourful past. The hike follows the Dewdney Trail, a horse trail, to Snass Forks; branches off onto the hiker-only Whatcom Trail, which takes you up the east fork of Snass Creek and over Punch Bowl Pass; drops down to the Punch Bowl (the head-waters of the Tulameen River) to Paradise Meadows; reconnects there with the Whatcom Trail, on which you descend the north fork of Snass Creek to your start. The counter-clockwise loop gives you your elevation gain early in the day, with the long gradual descent on the return. It is a long day trip so, if you decide not to make it an overnighter, you have to keep moving. There are camping spots on the meadow just beyond the pass or at the north end of the Punch Bowl. Although the trip starts in Manning Provincial Park, 95 per cent of it is outside the park boundaries in the Cascade Recreation Area.

Drive east on Highway 5 past Hope. Take Exit 177 onto Highway 3, which you follow for 32 km (20 mi) to the Cascade Recreation Area.

After passing Rhododendron Flats, move into the left lane to be ready for your turn a little beyond the bridge over Snass Creek. Drive the short distance into the parking area with its Dewdney Trail historic marker.

Walk north from the parking area and almost immediately cross Snass Creek to river-right. About 35 minutes should take you to Snass Forks, where you drop off the Dewdney Trail to cross the west fork of the creek. There should be a bridge. You are now on the Whatcom Trail up the creek's east fork. After a short level section, the trail switchbacks up the toe of a ridge to gain sufficient elevation above the narrow creek bottom. The trail then sidehills on river-right high above the creek. As you gain elevation the terrain opens up—there is substantial avalanche danger here. Cross the creek 245 m (800 ft) below Punch Bowl Pass and follow little timbered ridges until just below the pass it becomes alpine terrain. From the pass, drop 135 m (450 ft) to the lake; less than 3 km (1.9 mi) takes you to Paradise Meadows with its outhouse and information board. Turn left here down the valley of the north fork, which is dry for much of its length, so much rock having been deposited on its floor that the stream flows underground for much of the year. There is even a genuine dry lake. This valley too, in its upper reaches, has high avalanche risk. Just before Dry Lake it has a lost-valley look since an ancient rock slide has erected a 30 m (100 ft) barrier across the route. The slide has since grown some fine large trees. From Dry Lake back to the parking lot is about another 1.5 hours of straightforward hiking.

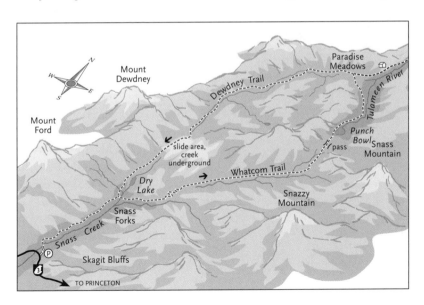

99
HOPE PASS
AND NICOMEN LAKE

Round trip 50 km (31 mi)   Allow 2 days
Elevation gain 1035 m (3400 ft)   High point 1824 m (5980 ft)
Average grade 4.1%

Best July to September   Maps 92H/02 Manning Park;
                                  92H/07 Princeton
Driving distance from Vancouver 190 km (120 mi)

View south across Nicomen Lake to Nicomen Ridge.

Part of this trip is in Manning Provincial Park, the rest in the Cascade Recreation Area. It is a delightful area with historical connections. The trail dates back to its building by Royal Engineers in the early 1860s, and it remained a major packhorse road between Hope and Princeton until Highway 3 was completed in 1949. The trip is described as a clockwise loop, which leads up the Skaist River 8 km (5 mi) to the Grainger Creek junction, continues up the Skaist to Hope Pass, runs south across the plateau to Nicomen Lake, descends Grainger Creek back to the Skaist River at the junction and then heads back to the highway. The Skaist River section is also a horse trail.

Drive east on Highway 5 past Hope. Take Exit 177 onto Highway 3, which you follow for 35 km (22 mi) to park on the right-hand side of the highway at Cayuse Flats, a short distance west of the bridge over the Skaist River.

The trail starts on the north side of the highway and runs upstream to cross the river, then jogs back to travel upstream on river-left on the original trail, now a worn road. At 8 km (5 mi) comes a fork where the hiking trail to Nicomen Lake via Grainger Creek goes off right, while your trail crosses the creek and continues up the main valley. Some time later you cross the Skaist River itself, and from here on you stay on river-right as you gradually swing east and climb high, the trail rising by way of two zigzags—features that early travellers recorded. Leave the Hope Pass Trail at Marmot City, with its park sign and map, in the first open area you come to on top before you reach the pass. Now start the cross-country hike to Nicomen Lake, some 9 km (5.6 mi) to the south. Pick up the trail, which, blazed with orange paint and some markers, heads more or less due south along the divide to Nicomen Lake, travelling through beautiful park-like surroundings. Be cautious where the trail has become braided because of its use by animals, especially at Twin Lakes, where a necessary right-hand turn could be missed. Finally you reach the lake with its wilderness campsite lying below a striking rock ridge. From here you go west on the hiking trail, which brings you down the Grainger Creek Valley. You stay high in the forest on the south side of its impressive canyon, crossing two tributaries and eventually descending by switchbacks to the Skaist–Grainger junction. From here it's only 8 km (5 mi) back to Cayuse Flats.

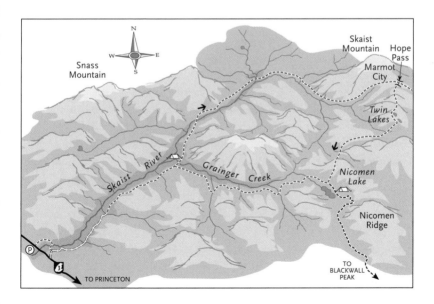

100 THREE BROTHERS MOUNTAIN

to First Brother Mountain	Round trip 21 km (13 mi)	Allow 7 hours
	Elevation gain 320 m (1050 ft)	High point 2273 m (7453 ft)
	Average grade 3.0%	
	Best July to September	Map 92H/02 Manning Park
	Driving distance from Vancouver 230 km (140 mi)	

The summit of First Brother Mountain. (MM)

Three Brothers Mountain is a triple summit with the three sub-peaks being unofficially named First, Second and Third Brother Mountains. Fourth Brother Mountain is separate from, and some distance north of, the other three. The open alpine meadows over which you travel provide the most popular hiking country in Manning Provincial Park because of their easy accessibility and their flowers, which are abundant from about mid-July through August. With this in mind, you might wish to camp near the park headquarters so that you have the advantage of an early start to avoid the crowds, or you may prefer to shoulder your backpack and spend some days enjoying the alpine wonderland from one of the campsites in the high country. By continuing on the Heather Trail, past Fourth Brother Mountain, it is possible to link with Hike 99 at Nicomen Lake.

Drive east on Highway 5 past Hope. Take Exit 177 onto Highway 3, which you follow for 67 km (42 mi) to Manning Park Lodge. On the north side of the highway, opposite the lodge, turn uphill and drive for 15 km (9.3 mi) to the Blackwall Peak parking lot at the end of the road. The elevation here is 1980 m (6500 ft).

From here, several nature trails lead more or less north across the meadows, where, in season, a park naturalist is often on hand to lead nature walks and answer questions. Follow Heather Trail for access to the Brothers; it gets its name from the abundance of that shrub around, although it is by no means the only plant you will see in these luxuriant meadows. After you have passed Buckhorn Camp at 5 km (3.1 mi), the trail rises through an old burn and meanders across rolling country, skirting the west side of Big Buck Mountain. The Brothers are now close at hand and it is perhaps fitting that the first is Big Brother, the highest. To reach the summit is easy; simply head upward east from the trail until you have only the sky above, meadows and valleys below and views all around. From the top, its two slightly junior companions are near, but the ascent of the first may be sufficient for a day trip. If you are backpacking, however, you may continue north on Heather Trail to Kicking Horse Camp at 14 km (8.7 mi) with camping platforms, an outhouse and a creek for water. This is a good striking point for the other brothers. From here you may return by the same route.

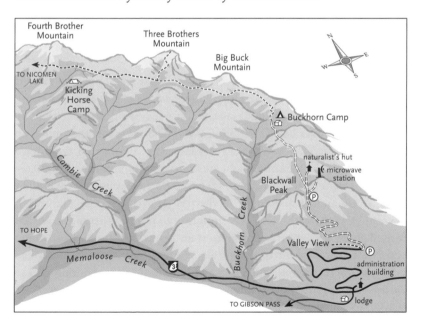

101 LIGHTNING LAKES

Round trip 24 km (15 mi) Allow 8 hours
Elevation gain 30 m (160 ft) High point 1250 m (4100 ft)
Average grade 0.3%

Best May to October Map 92H/02 Manning Park
Driving distance from Vancouver 220 km (135 mi)

The north shore of Thunder Lake.

Although Lightning Lake and its neighbour, Flash Lake, are well known even to casual visitors to Manning Provincial Park, you may penetrate farther into their valley and leave the crowds behind on the way to Strike and Thunder Lakes, the other two bodies of water that make up the chain. Whatever your choice, you are assured of an easy walk with little elevation change through an area of contrasts, from the forest surrounding the first lakes to the arid, scree-covered slopes above Thunder Lake. You may give a thought to the past as well, for these improved park trails you tread today were originally created by trappers in the early days of the century. There are trails along both sides of Lightning and Flash Lakes, permitting a choice of routes. However, as described here, the trip takes the south shore of both Lightning and Flash Lakes before crossing to follow the north shores of Strike and Thunder. Note that on the outward leg of the trip you are dropping elevation so that as you return it is all uphill, albeit very gradual. Take that into account in scheduling your time.

Drive east on Highway 5 past Hope. Take Exit 177 onto Highway 3, which you follow for 67 km (42 mi) to Manning Park Lodge. Turn right onto Gibson Pass Road and drive 3 km (1.9 mi) to the Lightning Lakes day-use area.

Cross the dam at the eastern end of Lightning Lake, and passing Frosty Mountain Trail, which diverges left, proceed west and then south passing, but not crossing, the Rainbow Bridge at the Lightning Lake Narrows. To access the south side of Flash Lake, it is necessary to cross then recross the creek between the lakes. From the far end of Flash Lake, cross the creek to the north side which you now follow to trail's end. On the hillside above Strike Lake are the remains of an old burn, still all silver snags. There is a campsite at the west end of Strike Lake. Somewhat removed from the others and a little lower in the valley is Thunder Lake, some 3 km (1.9 mi) beyond. Here the enclosing slopes are steep and bare, making this a place to be avoided in winter and spring due to its avalanche hazard. The shore of Thunder Lake shows the evidence of highly variable water level, with a line of logs well up the bank. The trail terminates partway down the lake; it does not go all the way to the end. On your return the north-side trails on Strike Lake and Lightning Lake could be followed back to the parking lot. Note that there are Lone Duck and Spruce Bays to circumnavigate, so the trail around the north shore of Lightning Lake is farther than it looks. If your spirits are flagging, you could cross the Rainbow Bridge to the south shore for a shorter return trip.

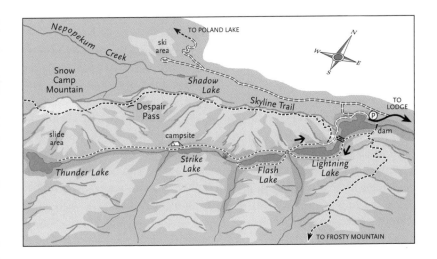

102 FROSTY MOUNTAIN

Round trip 28 km (17.4 mi)   Allow 8 hours
Elevation gain 1150 m (3770 ft)   High point 2410 m (7900 ft)
Average grade 10.5%

Best July to October   Map 92H/02 Manning Park
Driving distance from Vancouver 220 km (135 mi)

The east summit, with the Windy Joe junction on the knoll at the left.

Frosty Mountain, with its crenellated rocky ridge, is the highest summit in Manning Provincial Park. The views, as might be expected, are panoramic, and the high open country over which you travel en route has a truly amazing stand of alpine larch, some of which are currently British Columbia's oldest living trees. The final plus is the well-graded park trail. What's the downside to all this? You do not actually get to the summit: you ascend the east peak, since the main peak is a loose, steep climb. Timing is also a problem: you should do this trip in October when the larches are at their golden best, but before the snow flies. As described here this loop ascends the west side from Lightning Lake and descends on the east side to meet the Pacific Crest Trail (PCT), then Windy Joe Trail. If you can arrange a second car at the PCT/Beaver Pond parking lot it saves the 4 km (2.5 mi) walk alongside the road back to Lightning Lake.

Drive east past Hope, taking Exit 177 to stay on Highway 3 which you follow for 67 km (42 mi) to Manning Park Lodge. Turn right onto Gibson Pass Road and drive 3 km (1.9 mi) to the Lightning Lakes day-use area.

The Pacific Crest Trail/Beaver Pond parking area is on the south side of Highway 3 just east of Gibson Pass Road.

Head for the lake's eastern end and cross the dam to its south side. Here the Frosty Mountain Trail rises to the left, in a series of switchbacks on the north flank of the mountain, for nearly 7 km (4.3 mi) before levelling off slightly in the vicinity of Frosty Creek Camp. Not long thereafter you pass through a stretch of larch forest, which is beautiful when fall turns it to gold. The trail then heads up over country that becomes progressively more open, with large broken rocks for you to negotiate even before you reach the end of the final ridge and the fork where the trail from Windy Joe Mountain joins from the left. From here you scramble up the next 100 m (330 ft) to the east peak. The ridges and mountains of Manning Provincial Park lie before you on three sides and, on the fourth, the peaks of Hozomeen Mountain in the North Cascades across the border. Now descend to the east on the Windy Joe side on a trail that descends more gently but for that reason is longer than the Lightning Lake route. There is open alpine terrain with splendid views to north and east for over an hour, then the trail enters the trees and winds along in heavy forest all the way to the Similkameen River, joining en route first the PCT then the Windy Joe Trail. Without a car at the PCT lot, an additional walk of about 4 km (2.5 mi) along the Similkameen and Little Muddy Trails would complete the circuit entirely on foot.

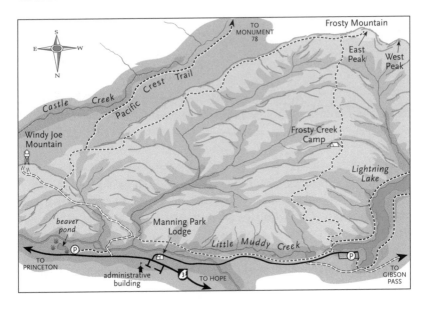

103 SKYLINE TRAIL
(East)

to Lone Goat Mountain

Round trip 20 km (12.4 mi)

Elevation gain 665 m (2175 ft)

Average grade 6.7%

Allow 7 hours

High point 2005 m (6575 ft)

Best July to October

Maps 92H/02 Manning Park;
B.C. Parks Manning
Provincial Park

Driving distance from Vancouver 225 km (140 mi)

View southwest to the twin summits of Hozomeen Mountain. (MM)

The complete Skyline Trail links Skagit Valley Provincial Park with Manning Provincial Park. However, the complete hike is a long, long day; then there is the time required for a vehicle shuttle. The trail is therefore described, in this guide, in two parts. Below is the east end of the trail; Hike 85 is the west end of the trail. It is a grand hike from either end. The trip described here starts at Strawberry Flats, ascends the Skyline I Trail, drops to Despair Pass, ascends Snow Camp Mountain and ends at the top of Lone Goat Mountain. This may sound tough, but remember that this is a B.C. Parks trail, therefore the grades are mild, there are lots of switchbacks and the tread is wide.

Drive east on Highway 5 past Hope. Take Exit 177 onto Highway 3, which you follow for 67 km (42 mi) to Manning Park Lodge. Turn right onto Gibson Pass Road and drive 8 km (5 mi) to the Strawberry Flats parking area.

Set off westward, downstream on Nepopekum Creek, before branching left (south) and heading for the ridge while the Three Falls Trail continues straight ahead. The first 4 km (2.5 mi) is a big wide track. At the 5 km sign there are views of your objectives, Snow Camp and Lone Goat Mountains, as well as views of Red and Hozomeen Mountains. On the ridge just before the 6 km sign is the junction with the Skyline I Trail from Spruce Bay. Turn right and follow the switchbacks down to Despair Pass at 1700 m (5600 ft). The trail is narrower from here and, in places, growing in with heather and blueberries but it is still a substantial footbed and easy to follow. Regaining height to Snow Camp Mountain, the trail traverses its south side, but it is a short and worthwhile diversion to the open summit at 1980 m (6497 ft). Then back on the trail you descend slightly into the saddle between Snow Camp and Lone Goat, where there is a track at 90° to your route that seems to indicate a regular wildlife corridor. You pass the 10 km sign on the southeast slopes of Lone Goat. The trail continues along the south side of Lone Goat Mountain, since it is making for the Skagit Valley. Therefore pick the line of least resistance and turn uphill to the summit at 2005 m (6575 ft), your high point for the day. To return, retrace your ascent route.

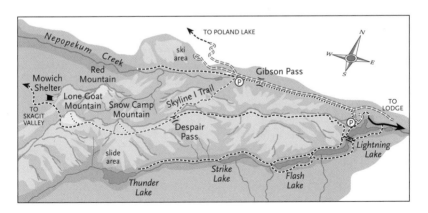

HIKING TIMES

HIKES SORTED BY TIME REQUIRED (hours)

Time	#	Hike name
2.0	66	Statlu Lake (to Statlu Lake)
3.0	18	Brandywine Meadows
3.0	89	Mount Lincoln
3.0	81	Lindeman and Greendrop Lakes (to Lindeman Lake)
3.0	27	Sigurd Creek (to Crooked Falls)
3.0	77	Slesse Memorial
3.5	92	Mount Henning
3.5	13	Lizzie–Stein Divide (to cabin)
3.5	33	Stawamus Chief (to Centre Peak)
3.5	76	Williamson Lake (from 4WD road)
4.0	70	Elk–Thurston (to Elk Mountain)
4.0	72	Mount McGuire (from trailhead)
4.0	3	Salal Creek (to west fork)
4.5	11	Cerise Creek
4.5	74	Cheam Peak
4.5	50	Goat Mountain
4.5	75	Mount Laughington
4.5	33	Stawamus Chief (to North Peak)
5.0	21	Black Tusk (from Taylor Meadows)
5.0	12	Blowdown Pass (to pass)
5.0	31	Boise Trail (from road end)
5.0	26	Bug Lake (to second viewpoint)
5.0	37	Deeks Bluffs Circuit
5.0	57	Dilly-Dally Peak (to Croker Lookout)
5.0	25	Elaho Canyon
5.0	51	Lower Grouse Mountain
5.0	29	High Falls Creek
5.0	95	Hope Mountain
5.0	47	Howe Sound Crest Trail South (to St. Marks Summit)
5.0	41	Leading Peak
5.0	22	Panorama Ridge (from Taylor Meadows)
5.0	78	Mount Rexford Trail
5.0	54	Mount Seymour
5.0	27	Sigurd Creek (to second viewpoint)
5.0	90	Stoyoma Mountain
5.0	49	Mount Strachan
5.0	91	Mount Thynne
5.0	28	Tricouni Meadows (to Cypress Lake)
5.5	56	Diez Vistas
5.5	83	Eaton Lake
5.5	88	First Brigade Trail

Time	#	Hike name
6.0	43	Mount Artaban
6.0	67	Bear Mountain
6.0	60	Dennett Lake
6.0	1	Mount Hallowell (from washout)
6.0	9	Joffre Lakes
6.0	42	Mount Liddell (to Gambier Lake)
6.0	81	Lindeman and Greendrop Lakes (to Greendrop Lake)
6.0	59	Lindsay Lake
6.0	24	Mamquam Lake (to Opal Cone)
6.0	10	Marriott Meadows (from trailhead)
6.0	72	Mount McGuire (from start of 4WD)
6.0	34	Petgill Lake (to lake)
6.0	7	Phelix Creek (from road end)
6.0	30	Pinecone Lake (from road end)
6.0	80	Radium Lake
6.0	16	Rainbow Lake
6.0	84	Skagit River
6.0	66	Statlu Lake (to upper lake)
6.0	45	Sunset Trail
6.0	69	Vedder Mountain
6.0	93	Zoa Peak
6.5	23	Elfin Lakes
6.5	20	Garibaldi Lake
6.5	68	Sumas Mountain (from west)
7.0	40	Binkert (Lions) Trail
7.0	46	Black Mountain
7.0	12	Blowdown Pass (to Gott Peak)
7.0	19	Brew Lake
7.0	70	Elk–Thurston (to Mount Thurston)
7.0	44	Mount Gardner
7.0	87	Gate Mountain
7.0	39	Mount Harvey
7.0	48	Hollyburn Mountain
7.0	47	Howe Sound Crest Trail South (to Unnecessary Mountain)
7.0	4	Hundred Lakes Plateau
7.0	13	Lizzie–Stein Divide (to Heart Lake)
7.0	73	Mount MacFarlane (to lower Pierce Lake)
7.0	10	Marriott Meadows (from start of 4WD)
7.0	94	Needle Peak
7.0	103	Skyline Trail East
7.0	2	Mount Steele (to cabin)
7.0	86	Stein Valley (to teepee camp)
7.0	100	Three Brothers Mountain
7.0	28	Tricouni Meadows (to Tricouni Peak)
7.0	76	Williamson Lake (to original trail)
7.5	63	Golden Ears (to Panorama Ridge)
7.5	1	Mount Hallowell (from start of 4WD)
7.5	14	Wedgemount Lake
8.0	31	Boise Trail (from start of 4WD)
8.0	38	Brunswick Mountain

Time	#	Hike name
8.0	65	Mount Crickmer
8.0	58	Eagle Peak
8.0	82	Flora Lake (to lake)
8.0	102	Frosty Mountain
8.0	52	Hanes Valley
8.0	6	Haylmore–Melvin Divide
8.0	42	Mount Liddell (to summit)
8.0	101	Lightning Lakes
8.0	2	Mount Steele (to summit)
8.0	68	Sumas Mountain (from east)
8.0	61	Widgeon Lake
8.0	79	Williams Ridge
8.5	17	Helm Lake
9.0	64	Alouette Mountain
9.0	55	Mount Elsay
9.0	24	Mamquam Lake (to lake)
9.0	96	Mount Outram
9.0	7	Phelix Creek (from start of 4WD)
9.0	30	Pinecone Lake (from start of 4WD)
9.0	8	Place Glacier
9.0	97	Silverdaisy Mountain
9.0	85	Skyline Trail West
10.0	71	Mount Amadis
10.0	21	Black Tusk (from parking lot)
10.0	35	Deeks Peak
10.0	57	Dilly-Dally Peak (to summit)
10.0	82	Flora Lake (to Flora–Lindeman Loop)
10.0	36	Howe Sound Crest Trail (North)
10.0	73	Mount MacFarlane (to summit)
10.0	22	Panorama Ridge (from parking lot)
10.0	34	Petgill Lake (Goat Ridge)
10.0	98	Punch Bowl
10.0	15	Russet Lake
10.0	86	Stein Valley (to cable crossing)
10.0	5	Tenquille Lake
10.5	53	Coliseum Mountain
11.0	63	Golden Ears (to summit)
11.0	62	Hector Ferguson Lake
12.0	32	Mount Roderick
12.0	3	Salal Creek (to Athelney Pass)
48.0	99	Hope Pass and Nicomen Lake

DRIVING DISTANCES

HIKES SORTED BY DRIVING DISTANCE FROM VANCOUVER (km)

Distance	#	Name	Distance	#	Name
10	51	Lower Grouse Mountain	100	1	Mount Hallowell
15	53	Coliseum Mountain	100	30	Pinecone Lake
15	50	Goat Mountain	105	29	High Falls Creek
15	52	Hanes Valley	105	27	Sigurd Creek
20	48	Hollyburn Mountain	110	21	Black Tusk
25	43	Mount Artaban	110	19	Brew Lake
25	46	Black Mountain	110	20	Garibaldi Lake
25	55	Mount Elsay	110	22	Panorama Ridge
25	44	Mount Gardner	120	18	Brandywine Meadows
25	41	Leading Peak	120	28	Tricouni Meadows
25	42	Mount Liddell	120	69	Vedder Mountain
25	54	Mount Seymour	125	71	Mount Amadis
30	47	Howe Sound Crest Trail (South)	125	17	Helm Lake
			125	15	Russet Lake
30	49	Mount Strachan	130	70	Elk–Thurston
30	45	Sunset Trail	130	16	Rainbow Lake
35	56	Diez Vistas	130	66	Statlu Lake
35	57	Dilly-Dally Peak	135	73	Mount MacFarlane
35	58	Eagle Peak	140	72	Mount McGuire
35	59	Lindsay Lake	145	75	Mount Laughington
40	40	Binkert (Lions) Trail	145	14	Wedgemount Lake
40	38	Brunswick Mountain	145	79	Williams Ridge
40	37	Deeks Bluffs Circuit	145	76	Williamson Lake
40	60	Dennett Lake	150	67	Bear Mountain
40	39	Mount Harvey	150	74	Cheam Peak
50	35	Deeks Peak	150	82	Flora Lake
50	36	Howe Sound Crest Trail (North)	150	81	Lindeman and Greendrop Lakes
55	61	Widgeon Lake	150	80	Radium Lake
60	64	Alouette Mountain	150	77	Slesse Memorial
60	63	Golden Ears	155	78	Mount Rexford Trail
60	62	Hector Ferguson Lake	160	26	Bug Lake
60	34	Petgill Lake	160	83	Eaton Lake
65	32	Mount Roderick	160	95	Hope Mountain
65	33	Stawamus Chief	170	25	Elaho Canyon
70	65	Mount Crickmer	170	89	Mount Lincoln
85	23	Elfin Lakes	170	96	Mount Outram
85	24	Mamquam Lake	185	98	Punch Bowl
8	52	Mount Steele	185	97	Silverdaisy Mountain
90	68	Sumas Mountain	185	84	Skagit River
100	31	Boise Trail	185	5	Tenquille Lake

Distance	#	Name
190	99	Hope Pass an Nicomen Lake
190	9	Joffre Lakes
190	8	Place Glacier
195	10	Marriott Meadows
195	94	Needle Peak
200	87	Gate Mountain
200	13	Lizzie–Stein Divide
200	93	Zoa Peak
205	88	First Brigade Trail
205	85	Skyline Trail (West)
210	11	Cerise Creek
215	6	Haylmore–Melvin Divide

Distance	#	Name
215	7	Phelix Creek
220	12	Blowdown Pass
220	102	Frosty Mountain
220	101	Lightning Lakes
225	92	Mount Henning
225	103	Skyline Trail (East)
230	100	Three Brothers Mountain
235	3	Salal Creek
245	4	Hundred Lakes Plateau
265	86	Stein Valley
285	91	Mount Thynne
325	90	Stoyoma Mountain

HIGH POINTS

HIKES SORTED BY ELEVATION OF HIGH POINT (m)

Elevation	#	Hike name
425	86	Stein Valley (to teepee camp)
440	57	Dilly-Dally Peak (to Croker Lookout)
480	37	Deeks Bluffs Circuit
490	27	Sigurd Creek (to Crooked Falls)
520	42	Mount Liddell (to Gambier Lake)
550	86	Stein Valley (to cable crossing)
580	66	Statlu Lake (to Shatlu Lake)
607	56	Diez Vistas
609	43	Mount Artaban
625	84	Skagit River
640	25	Elaho Canyon
652	33	Stawamus Chief (to Centre Peak)
655	89	Mount Lincoln
665	33	Stawamus Chief (to North Peak)
715	29	High Falls Creek
719	44	Mount Gardner
755	41	Leading Peak
760	62	Hector Ferguson Lake
760	34	Petgill Lake (to lake)
770	61	Widgeon Lake
825	81	Lindeman and Greendrop Lakes (to Lindeman Lake)
885	27	Sigurd Creek (to second viewpoint)
885	68	Sumas Mountain
903	42	Mount Liddell (to summit)
920	88	First Brigade Trail
945	69	Vedder Mountain
960	60	Dennett Lake
1010	81	Lindeman and Greendrop Lakes (to Greendrop Lake)
1020	66	Statlu Lake (to upper lake)
1045	45	Sunset Trail
1048	67	Bear Mountain
1100	77	Slesse Memorial
1125	51	Lower Grouse Mountain
1160	59	Lindsay Lake
1180	3	Salal Creek (to west fork)
1200	63	Golden Ears (to Panorama Ridge)
1217	46	Black Mountain
1220	36	Howe Sound Crest Trail North
1250	26	Bug Lake
1250	57	Dilly-Dally Peak (to summit)
1250	101	Lightning Lakes
1250	1	Mount Hallowell

Elevation	#	Hike name
1280	58	Eagle Peak
1300	52	Hanes Valley
1325	83	Eaton Lake
1325	48	Hollyburn Mountain
1355	47	Howe Sound Crest Trail South (to St. Marks Summit)
1357	65	Mount Crickmer
1366	64	Alouette Mountain
1375	73	Mount MacFarlane (to lower Pierce Lake)
1400	70	Elk–Thurston (to Elk Mountain)
1401	50	Goat Mountain
1420	19	Brew Lake
1422	55	Mount Elsay
1446	53	Coliseum Mountain
1450	87	Gate Mountain
1454	49	Mount Strachan
1455	54	Mount Seymour
1460	80	Radium Lake
1465	16	Rainbow Lake
1475	32	Mount Roderick
1495	28	Tricouni Meadows (to Cypress Lake)
1500	18	Brandywine Meadows
1500	20	Garibaldi Lake
1500	2	Mount Steele (to cabin)
1506	71	Mount Amadis
1525	40	Binkert (Lions) Trail
1525	47	Howe Sound Crest Trail South (to Unnecessary Mountain)
1525	24	Mamquam Lake (to lake)
1565	23	Elfin Lakes
1585	31	Boise Trail
1585	9	Joffre Lakes
1600	13	Lizzie–Stein Divide (to cabin)
1630	70	Elk–Thurston (to Mount Thurston)
1645	92	Mount Henning
1645	2	Mount Steele (to summit)
1655	76	Williamson Lake
1675	35	Deeks Peak
1680	11	Cerise Creek
1690	4	Hundred Lakes Plateau
1705	39	Mount Harvey
1706	63	Golden Ears (to summit)
1710	7	Phelix Creek
1710	5	Tenquille Lake
1740	17	Helm Lake
1740	24	Mamquam Lake (to Opal Cone)
1740	10	Marriott Meadows
1750	34	Petgill Lake (to Goat Ridge)
1770	82	Flora Lake
1784	98	Punch Bowl
1785	38	Brunswick Mountain
1800	75	Mount Laughington
1824	99	Hope Pass and Nicomen Lake

Elevation	#	Hike name
1830	8	Place Glacier
1830	3	Salal Creek (to Athelney Pass)
1837	95	Hope Mountain
1840	78	Mount Rexford Trail
1860	85	Skyline Trail (West)
1875	93	Zoa Peak
1880	79	Williams Ridge
1920	13	Lizzie–Stein Divide (to Heart Lake)
1920	14	Wedgemount Lake
1950	15	Russet Lake
1980	30	Pinecone Lake
2005	103	Skyline Trail (East)
2019	72	Mount McGuire
2028	91	Mount Thynne
2051	97	Silverdaisy Mountain
2100	73	Mount MacFarlane (to summit)
2100	28	Tricouni Meadows (to Tricouni Peak)
2105	94	Needle Peak
2105	22	Panorama Ridge
2112	74	Cheam Peak
2195	12	Blowdown Pass (to pass)
2260	6	Haylmore–Melvin Divide
2273	100	Three Brothers Mountain
2282	90	Stoyoma Mountain
2315	21	Black Tusk
2410	102	Frosty Mountain
2440	96	Mount Outram
2530	12	Blowdown Pass (to Gott Peak)

ELEVATION GAINS

HIKES SORTED BY ELEVATION GAIN (m)

Gain	#	Hike name
–105	84	Skagit River
30	101	Lightning Lakes
90	25	Elaho Canyon
150	3	Salal Creek (to west fork)
215	81	Lindeman and Greendrop Lakes (to Lindeman Lake)
215	66	Statlu Lake (to Statlu Lake)
230	86	Stein Valley (to teepee camp)
275	11	Cerise Creek
275	50	Goat Mountain
305	91	Mount Thynne
305	28	Tricouni Meadows (to Cypress Lake)
310	10	Marriott Meadows (from trailhead)
315	57	Dilly-Dally Peak (to Croker Lookout)
320	13	Lizzie–Stein Divide (to cabin)
320	100	Three Brothers Mountain
355	86	Stein Valley (to cable crossing)
365	9	Joffre Lakes
365	24	Mamquam Lake (to Opal Cone)
395	31	Boise Trail (to from road end)
395	81	Lindeman and Greendrop Lakes (to Greendrop Lake)
400	37	Deeks Bluffs Circuit
400	10	Marriott Meadows (from start of 4WD)
425	27	Sigurd Creek (to Crooked Falls)
430	7	Phelix Creek (from road end)
440	47	Howe Sound Crest Trail South (to St. Marks Summit)
455	56	Diez Vistas
455	54	Mount Seymour
460	77	Slesse Memorial
505	76	Williamson Lake (from 4WD road)
520	42	Mount Liddell (to Gambier Lake)
538	49	Mount Strachan
545	2	Mount Steele (to cabin)
550	18	Brandywine Meadows
550	92	Mount Henning
575	69	Vedder Mountain
580	12	Blowdown Pass (to pass)
580	89	Mount Lincoln
590	33	Stawamus Chief (to Centre Peak)
605	33	Stawamus Chief (to North Peak)
609	43	Mount Artaban
610	47	Howe Sound Crest Trail South (to Unnecessary Mountain)
610	24	Mamquam Lake (to lake)

Gain	#	Hike name
610	22	Panorama Ridge (from Taylor Meadows)
610	66	Statlu Lake (to upper lake)
620	23	Elfin Lakes
620	75	Mount Laughington
635	62	Hector Ferguson Lake
635	93	Zoa Peak
640	29	High Falls Creek
640	13	Lizzie–Stein Divide (to Heart Lake)
640	34	Petgill Lake (to lake)
659	72	Mount McGuire (from trailhead)
665	74	Cheam Peak
665	103	Skyline Trail (East)
670	30	Pinecone Lake (from road end)
670	90	Stoyoma Mountain
685	51	Lower Grouse Mountain
690	2	Mount Steele (to summit)
715	68	Sumas Mountain (from west)
719	44	Mount Gardner
745	4	Hundred Lakes Plateau
755	41	Leading Peak
760	1	Mount Hallowell (from washout)
770	61	Widgeon Lake
780	88	First Brigade Trail
800	70	Elk–Thurston (to Elk Mountain)
800	95	Hope Mountain
800	3	Salal Creek (to Athelney Pass)
820	21	Black Tusk (from Taylor Meadows)
825	31	Boise Trail (from start of 4WD)
825	16	Rainbow Lake
825	27	Sigurd Creek (to second viewpoint)
850	26	Bug Lake
855	94	Needle Peak
860	60	Dennett Lake
870	68	Sumas Mountain (from east)
895	48	Hollyburn Mountain
903	42	Mount Liddell (to summit)
910	80	Radium Lake
915	12	Blowdown Pass (to Gott Peak)
915	83	Eaton Lake
915	17	Helm Lake
915	28	Tricouni Meadows (to Tricouni Peak)
920	20	Garibaldi Lake
920	78	Mount Rexford Trail
959	72	Mount McGuire (from start of 4WD)
975	45	Sunset Trail
1010	67	Bear Mountain
1010	1	Mount Hallowell (from start of 4WD)
1010	7	Phelix Creek (from start of 4WD)
1020	19	Brew Lake
1020	59	Lindsay Lake
1020	98	Punch Bowl

Gain	#	Hike name
1030	70	Elk–Thurston (to Mount Thurston)
1035	99	Hope Pass and Nicomen Lake
1040	63	Golden Ears (to Panorama Ridge)
1040	6	Haylmore–Melvin Divide
1040	73	Mount MacFarlane (to lower Pierce Lake)
1050	55	Mount Elsay
1100	64	Alouette Mountain
1100	52	Hanes Valley
1120	57	Dilly-Dally Peak (to summit)
1140	46	Black Mountain
1150	58	Eagle Peak
1150	102	Frosty Mountain
1160	82	Flora Lake (to Flora–Lindeman Loop)
1160	14	Wedgemount Lake
1175	87	Gate Mountain
1175	76	Williamson Lake (to original trail)
1190	65	Mount Crickmer
1190	36	Howe Sound Crest Trail (North)
1220	30	Pinecone Lake (from start of 4WD)
1250	15	Russet Lake
1265	53	Coliseum Mountain
1280	40	Binkert (Lions) Trail
1310	8	Place Glacier
1370	85	Skyline Trail (West)
1435	79	Williams Ridge
1440	97	Silverdaisy Mountain
1445	71	Mount Amadis
1460	5	Tenquille Lake
1465	39	Mount Harvey
1475	32	Mount Roderick
1500	63	Golden Ears (to summit)
1520	22	Panorama Ridge (from parking lot)
1550	38	Brunswick Mountain
1585	82	Flora Lake (to lake)
1615	35	Deeks Peak
1630	34	Petgill Lake (to Goat Ridge)
1740	21	Black Tusk (from parking lot)
1765	73	Mount MacFarlane (to summit)
1800	96	Mount Outram

ROUND-TRIP DISTANCES

HIKES SORTED BY ROUND-TRIP DISTANCE (km)

Distance	#	Hike name
5.0	89	Mount Lincoln
5.0	81	Lindeman and Greendrop Lakes (to Lindeman Lake)
5.0	66	Statlu Lake (to Statlu Lake)
6.0	18	Brandywine Meadows
6.0	26	Bug Lake
6.0	13	Lizzie–Stein Divide (to cabin)
6.0	78	Mount Rexford Trail
6.0	27	Sigurd Creek (to Crooked Falls)
6.0	76	Williamson Lake (from 4WD road)
7.5	12	Blowdown Pass (to pass)
8.0	83	Eaton Lake
8.0	70	Elk–Thurston (to Elk Mountain)
8.0	50	Goat Mountain
8.0	92	Mount Henning
8.0	72	Mount McGuire (from trailhead)
8.0	77	Slesse Memorial
8.0	66	Statlu Lake (to upper lake)
9.0	11	Cerise Creek
9.0	54	Mount Seymour
9.0	27	Sigurd Creek (to second viewpoint)
9.0	33	Stawamus Chief (to Centre Peak)
9.5	74	Cheam Peak
9.5	45	Sunset Trail
10.0	43	Mount Artaban
10.0	37	Deeks Bluffs Circuit
10.0	60	Dennett Lake
10.0	51	Lower Grouse Mountain
10.0	95	Hope Mountain
10.0	4	Hundred Lakes Plateau
10.0	75	Mount Laughington
10.0	41	Leading Peak
10.0	10	Marriott Meadows (from trailhead)
10.0	7	Phelix Creek (from road end)
10.0	30	Pinecone Lake (from road end)
10.0	3	Salal Creek (west fork)
10.0	49	Mount Strachan
10.5	12	Blowdown Pass (to Gott Peak)
10.5	91	Mount Thynne
11.0	21	Black Tusk (from Taylor Meadows)
11.0	47	Howe Sound Crest Trail South (to St. Marks Summit)
11.0	9	Joffre Lakes
11.0	33	Stawamus Chief (to North Peak)

Distance	#	Hike name
11.0	79	Williams Ridge
11.0	93	Zoa Peak
11.5	34	Petgill Lake (to lake)
11.5	69	Vedder Mountain
12.0	31	Boise Trail (from road end)
12.0	82	Flora Lake (to lake)
12.0	29	High Falls Creek
12.0	13	Lizzie–Stein Divide (to Heart Lake)
12.0	72	Mount McGuire (from start of 4WD)
12.0	80	Radium Lake
12.0	90	Stoyoma Mountain
12.5	39	Mount Harvey
13.0	19	Brew Lake
13.0	56	Diez Vistas
13.0	25	Elaho Canyon
13.0	88	First Brigade Trail
13.0	1	Mount Hallowell (from washout)
13.0	81	Lindeman and Greendrop Lakes (to Greendrop Lake)
13.0	24	Mamquam Lake (to Opal Cone)
13.0	94	Needle Peak
13.0	76	Williamson Lake (to original trail)
13.5	68	Sumas Mountain (from west)
14.0	10	Marriott Meadows (from start of 4WD)
14.0	28	Tricouni Meadows (to Cypress Lake)
14.0	28	Tricouni Meadows (to Tricouni Peak)
14.0	14	Wedgemount Lake
14.5	38	Brunswick Mountain
14.5	84	Skagit River
15.0	40	Binkert (Lions) Trail
15.0	70	Elk–Thurston (to Mount Thurston)
15.0	42	Mount Liddell (to Gambier Lake)
15.0	59	Lindsay Lake
15.0	22	Panorama Ridge (from Taylor Meadows)
16.0	46	Black Mountain
16.0	35	Deeks Peak
16.0	55	Mount Elsay
16.0	87	Gate Mountain
16.0	73	Mount MacFarlane (to lower Pierce Lake)
16.0	16	Rainbow Lake
16.0	68	Sumas Mountain (from east)
17.0	57	Dilly-Dally Peak (to Croker Lookout)
17.0	44	Mount Gardner
17.0	1	Mount Hallowell (from start of 4WD)
17.0	2	Mount Steele (to cabin)
17.0	86	Stein Valley (to teepee camp)
18.0	52	Hanes Valley
18.0	47	Howe Sound Crest Trail South (to Unnecessary Mountain)
18.0	96	Mount Outram
18.0	30	Pinecone Lake (from start of 4WD)
18.0	2	Mount Steele (to summit)

Distance	#	Hike name
18.5	58	Eagle Peak
18.5	20	Garibaldi Lake
18.5	61	Widgeon Lake
19.0	67	Bear Mountain
19.5	34	Petgill Lake (to Goat Ridge)
20.0	31	Boise Trail (from start of 4WD)
20.0	65	Mount Crickmer
20.0	82	Flora Lake (to Flora–Lindeman Loop)
20.0	63	Golden Ears (to Panorama Ridge)
20.0	6	Haylmore–Melvin Divide
20.0	17	Helm Lake
20.0	48	Hollyburn Mountain
20.0	36	Howe Sound Crest Trail (North)
20.0	7	Phelix Creek (from start of 4WD)
20.0	97	Silverdaisy Mountain
20.0	103	Skyline Trail East
21.0	73	Mount MacFarlane (to summit)
21.0	8	Place Glacier
21.0	100	Three Brothers Mountain
22.0	64	Alouette Mountain
22.0	71	Mount Amadis
22.0	23	Elfin Lakes
22.0	42	Mount Liddell (to summit)
22.0	24	Mamquam Lake (to lake)
22.0	85	Skyline Trail West
23.5	57	Dilly-Dally Peak (to summit)
24.0	102	Frosty Mountain
24.0	63	Golden Ears (to summit)
24.0	101	Lightning Lakes
24.5	53	Coliseum Mountain
26.0	32	Mount Roderick
26.0	86	Stein Valley (to cable crossing)
26.0	5	Tenquille Lake
27.0	15	Russet Lake
28.0	62	Hector Ferguson Lake
29.0	21	Black Tusk (from parking lot)
30.0	22	Panorama Ridge (from parking lot)
30.0	98	Punch Bowl
30.0	3	Salal Creek (to Athelney Pass)
50.0	99	Hope Pass and Nicomen Lake

* one-way distance

AVERAGE GRADES

HIKES SORTED BY AVERAGE GRADE (%)

Grade	#	Hike name
−0.7	84	Skagit River
0.3	101	Lightning Lakes
1.4	25	Elaho Canyon
2.7	86	Stein Valley (to cable crossing)
2.7	86	Stein Valley (to teepee camp)
3.0	3	Salal Creek (to west fork)
3.0	100	Three Brothers Mountain
3.7	57	Dilly-Dally Peak (to Croker Lookout)
4.1	99	Hope Pass and Nicomen Lake
4.4	28	Tricouni Meadows (to Cypress Lake)
4.5	62	Hector Ferguson Lake
5.3	3	Salal Creek (to Athelney Pass)
5.5	24	Mamquam Lake (to lake)
5.5	91	Mount Thynne
5.6	23	Elfin Lakes
5.6	24	Mamquam Lake (to Opal Cone)
5.7	10	Marriott Meadows (to from start of 4WD)
6.0	2	Mount Steele (to cabin)
6.1	11	Cerise Creek
6.1	81	Lindeman and Greendrop Lakes (to Greendrop Lake)
6.2	10	Marriott Meadows (from trailhead)
6.6	31	Boise Trail (from road end)
6.7	9	Joffre Lakes
5.5	103	Skyline Trail East
6.8	47	Howe Sound Crest Trail South (to Unnecessary Mountain)
6.8	98	Punch Bowl
6.9	50	Goat Mountain
6.9	42	Mount Liddell (to Gambier Lake)
7.0	56	Diez Vistas
7.3	2	Mount Steele (to summit)
8.0	47	Howe Sound Crest Trail South (to St. Marks Summit)
8.1	22	Panorama Ridge (from Taylor Meadows)
8.3	31	Boise Trail (from start of 4WD)
8.3	61	Widgeon Lake
8.5	44	Mount Gardner
8.6	81	Lindeman and Greendrop Lakes (to Lindeman Lake)
8.6	7	Phelix Creek (from road end)
8.6	66	Statlu Lake (to Statlu Lake)
9.0	48	Hollyburn Mountain
9.2	17	Helm Lake
9.3	15	Russet Lake
9.5	57	Dilly-Dally Peak (to summit)

Grade	#	Hike name
9.6	37	Deeks Bluffs Circuit
9.9	20	Garibaldi Lake
10.0	64	Alouette Mountain
10.0	69	Vedder Mountain
10.1	22	Panorama Ridge (from parking lot)
10.1	7	Phelix Creek (from start of 4WD)
10.1	54	Mount Seymour
10.3	53	Coliseum Mountain
10.3	16	Rainbow Lake
10.4	63	Golden Ears (to Panorama Ridge)
10.4	6	Haylmore–Melvin Divide
10.5	102	Frosty Mountain
10.6	67	Bear Mountain
10.6	68	Sumas Mountain (from west)
10.7	29	High Falls Creek
10.7	13	Lizzie–Stein Divide (to cabin)
10.7	13	Lizzie–Stein Divide (to Heart Lake)
10.8	49	Mount Strachan
10.9	68	Sumas Mountain (from east)
11.0	33	Stawamus Chief (to North Peak)
11.1	34	Petgill Lake (to lake)
11.2	90	Stoyoma Mountain
11.2	5	Tenquille Lake
11.5	77	Slesse Memorial
11.5	93	Zoa Peak
11.6	82	Flora Lake (to Flora–Lindeman Loop)
11.7	1	Mount Hallowell (from washout)
11.9	65	Mount Crickmer
11.9	1	Mount Hallowell (from start of 4WD)
11.9	36	Howe Sound Crest Trail North
12.0	88	First Brigade Trail
12.2	43	Mount Artaban
12.2	52	Hanes Valley
12.4	58	Eagle Peak
12.4	75	Mount Laughington
12.5	63	Golden Ears (to summit)
12.5	8	Place Glacier
12.5	85	Skyline Trail West
12.9	42	Mount Liddell (to summit)
13.0	73	Mount MacFarlane (to lower Pierce Lake)
13.1	71	Mount Amadis
13.1	55	Mount Elsay
13.1	33	Stawamus Chief (to Centre Peak)
13.1	28	Tricouni Meadows (to Tricouni Peak)
13.2	94	Needle Peak
13.4	21	Black Tusk (from parking lot)
13.4	30	Pinecone Lake (from road end)
13.5	70	Elk–Thurston (to Mount Thurston)
13.5	30	Pinecone Lake (from start of 4WD)
13.6	59	Lindsay Lake

Grade	#	Hike name
13.7	51	Lower Grouse Mountain
13.8	92	Mount Henning
14.0	74	Cheam Peak
14.1	27	Sigurd Creek (to Crooked Falls)
14.2	46	Black Mountain
14.4	97	Silverdaisy Mountain
14.7	87	Gate Mountain
14.7	32	Mount Roderick
14.9	21	Black Tusk (from Taylor Meadows)
14.9	4	Hundred Lakes Plateau
15.1	41	Leading Peak
15.1	80	Radium Lake
15.2	76	Williamson Lake (from 4WD road)
15.3	66	Statlu Lake (to upper lake)
15.5	12	Blowdown Pass (to pass)
15.7	19	Brew Lake
15.7	72	Mount McGuire (from trailhead)
15.9	72	Mount McGuire (from start of 4WD)
16.0	95	Hope Mountain
16.6	14	Wedgemount Lake
16.7	34	Petgill Lake (to Goat Ridge)
16.8	73	Mount MacFarlane (to summit)
17.1	40	Binkert (Lions) Trail
17.2	60	Dennett Lake
17.4	12	Blowdown Pass (to Gott Peak)
18.1	76	Williamson Lake (to original trail)
18.3	18	Brandywine Meadows
18.3	27	Sigurd Creek (to second viewpoint)
20.0	70	Elk–Thurston (to Elk Mountain)
20.0	96	Mount Outram
20.2	35	Deeks Peak
20.5	45	Sunset Trail
21.4	38	Brunswick Mountain
22.8	83	Eaton Lake
23.2	89	Mount Lincoln
23.4	39	Mount Harvey
26.1	79	Williams Ridge
26.4	82	Flora Lake (to lake)
28.3	26	Bug Lake
30.1	78	Mount Rexford Trail

MAPS and SOURCES

To get the big picture, you need topographic maps at a scale of 1:250,000. For this hiking guide, you need:

92G Vancouver
92H Hope
92I Ashcroft
92J Pemberton

For more detailed information, you need 1:50,000 scale topographic maps. The following list covers all the hikes in this book:

92G/01 Mission	*92G/06 North Vancouver*
92G/07 Port Coquitlam	*92G/08 Stave Lake*
92G/09 Stave River	*92G/10 Pitt River*
92G/11 Squamish	*92G/12 Sechelt Inlet*
92G/14 Cheakamus River	*92G/15 Mamquam Mountain*
92H/02 Manning Park	*92H/03 Skagit River*
92H/04 Chilliwack	*92H/05 Harrison Lake*
92H/06 Hope	*92H/07 Princeton*
92H/10 Tulameen	*92H/11 Spuzzum*
92H/14 Boston Bar	*92H/15 Aspen Grove*
92I/03 Prospect Creek	*92I/05 Stein River*
92J/01 Stein Lake	*92J/02 Whistler*
92J/03 Brandywine Falls	*92J/04 Princess Louisa Inlet*
92J/05 Clendenning Creek	*92J/07 Pemberton*
92J/08 Duffey Lake	*92J/09 Shalalth*
92J/10 Birkenhead Lake	*92J/11 North Creek*
92J/12 Mount Dalgleish	*92J/14 Dickson Range*

Paper copies of these maps are available from:

Geological Survey of Canada
605 Robson Street
Vancouver BC V6B 5J3
(604) 666-0271

The Geological Survey of Canada also sells the 1:50,000 maps on CD-ROM produced by:

Spectrum Digital Imaging
Site 692, C30, RR#6
Courtenay BC V9N 8H9

Many land surveyors in local communities also stock topographic maps of local areas and can order others. Check your local yellow pages under "Surveyors—Land."

International Travel Maps & Books
530 West Broadway
Vancouver BC V5Z 1E9
(604) 879-3621

sell the same topographic maps that are available from the Geological Survey of Canada. They also publish a series of recreation maps. Currently available maps which are relevant to this hiking guide are:

> *Garibaldi Region (1:100,000)*
> *North Shore Hiking Trails (1:50,000)*
> *Whistler & Region (1:50,000)*

The **B.C. Ministry of Environment, Lands and Parks** produces provincial park maps at various scales, which show trails, campgrounds and other facilities within the parks. To cover this hiking guide, you should obtain, at no charge:

Cultus Lake Provincial Park	*Golden Ears Provincial Park*
Cypress Provincial Park	*Manning Provincial Park*
Garibaldi Provincial Park	*Mount Seymour Provincial Park*
The Howe Sound Crest Trail	

Check the blue pages in your phone book for the Parks office nearest you.

The **B.C. Ministry of Forests** produces maps, usually at a scale of 1:250,000, which show the recreation facilities within the Forest District. To cover this hiking guide, you should obtain:

> *Chilliwack Forest District*
> *Lillooet Recreation Sites*
> *Merritt Forest District*
> *Squamish Forest District*
> *Sunshine Coast Forest District*

Until recently, they were free. Now however they are being sold by:

Canadian Cartographics
57B Clipper Street
Coquitlam BC V3K 6X2
1-877-524-3337

BIBLIOGRAPHY

Adam, Paul. *Whistler and Region Outdoors*. West Vancouver: Tricouni Press, 1993. ISBN 0969760108

Baldwin, John. *Exploring the Coast Mountains on Skis*, 2nd ed. Vancouver: John Baldwin, 1994. ISBN 0969155018

Copeland, Kathy and Craig. *Don't Waste Your Time in the B.C. Coast Mountains*. Riondel: Voice in the Wilderness Press, 1997. ISBN 0969801637

Fairley, Bruce. *A Guide to Climbing and Hiking in Southwestern British Columbia*, West Vancouver: Gordon Soules Book Publishers, 1986. ISBN 0919574998

Hanna, Dawn. *Best Hikes and Walks of Southwestern British Columbia*. Vancouver: Lone Pine Publishing, 1997. ISBN 1551050951

Kahn, Charles. *Hiking the Gulf Islands*. Victoria: Orca Book Publishers, 1995. ISBN 1551430347

Shewchuk, Murphy. *Coquihalla Country*. Merritt: Sonotek Publishing, 1998. ISBN 0929069102

Stedham, Glen. *Bush Basics: A Commonsense Guide to Backwoods Adventure*. Victoria: Orca Book Publishers, 1997. ISBN 1551430983

Stoltmann, Randy. *Hiking Guide to the Big Trees of Southwestern British Columbia*, 2nd ed. Vancouver: Western Canada Wilderness Committee, 1991. ISBN 1895123062

Sunshine Coast Forest District. *Trails of Powell River*. Powell River: Sunshine Coast Forest District, 1994.

Sunshine Coast Forest District. *Trails of the Lower Sunshine Coast*. Powell River: Sunshine Coast Forest District, 1995.

White, Gordon. *Stein Valley Wilderness Guidebook*. Vancouver: Sanhill, 1996. ISBN 0969461801

WEB SITES

The most useful site for local mountain access and conditions:
    http://www.bivouac.com
Federation of Mountain Clubs of British Columbia:
    http://www.mountainclubs.bc.ca
British Columbia Mountaineering Club:
    http://www.bcmc.ca
Alpine Club of Canada (Vancouver Section):
    http://members.axion.net/~vkc/acc/
Alpine Club of Canada (Whistler Section):
    http://sites.netscape.net/accwhistler/
Links to information on topographic maps:
    http://maps.NRCan.gc.ca/maps101/links.html
Vancouver Public Library collection of trail and park maps:
    http://www.vpl.vancouver.bc.ca/branches/LibrarySquare/his/trails.htm
British Columbia Geographical Names:
    http://www.gdbc.gov.bc.ca/bcnames/
Outdoor Recreation Council of British Columbia:
    http://www.orcbc.ca/
Canadian Avalanche Association:
    http://www.avalanche.ca/
British Columbia Forest Service Recreation:
    http://www.for.gov.bc.ca/hfp/rec/rec.htm
Elaho Trail Society:
    http://www.interchange.ubc.ca/gezav/elahotrail.html
British Columbia Provincial Parks:
    http://www.env.gov.bc.ca:80/bcparks/
Fraser Valley Regional District Parks:
    http://www.fvrd.bc.ca/Regional_Parks/regional_parks.htm
Greater Vancouver Regional District Parks:
    http://www.gvrd.bc.ca/services/parks/index.html
Western Canada Wilderness Committee:
    http://www.wildernesscommittee.org/
Vancouver bus information:
    http://www.translink.bc.ca/

INDEX